Prove It On Me

Prove It On Me

*New Negroes, Sex, and Popular
Culture in the 1920s*

Erin D. Chapman

OXFORD
UNIVERSITY PRESS

OXFORD
UNIVERSITY PRESS

Oxford University Press, Inc., publishes works that further
Oxford University's objective of excellence
in research, scholarship, and education.

Oxford   New York
Auckland   Cape Town   Dar es Salaam   Hong Kong   Karachi
Kuala Lumpur   Madrid   Melbourne   Mexico City   Nairobi
New Delhi   Shanghai   Taipei   Toronto

With offices in
Argentina   Austria   Brazil   Chile   Czech Republic France   Greece
Guatemala   Hungary   Italy   Japan   Poland   Portugal   Singapore
South Korea   Switzerland   Thailand   Turkey   Ukraine   Vietnam

Published by Oxford University Press, Inc.
198 Madison Avenue, New York, New York 10016

www.oup.com

Oxford is a registered trademark of Oxford University Press

Library of Congress Cataloging-in-Publication Data
Chapman, Erin D.
Prove it on me : new Negroes, sex, and popular culture in the 1920s / Erin D. Chapman.
p.   cm.
Includes bibliographical references and index.
ISBN 978-0-19-975831-9 (hardcover : alk. paper) — ISBN 978-0-19-975832-6 (pbk. : alk. paper) 1. African American
women in popular culture—History—20th century. 2. African American women—Intellectual life—20th century. 3.
African American women— Social conditions—20th century. 4. Popular culture—United States—History—20th
century. 5. United States—Race relations—History—20th century. 6. Harlem Renaissance. I. Title.
E185.86.C433 2011
305.48´896073—dc23   2011021277

1 3 5 7 9 8 6 4 2

Printed in the United States of America
on acid-free paper

CONTENTS

LIST OF FIGURES

‹∿›

ACKNOWLEDGMENTS

In writing *Prove It On Me*, I have benefited from the great wealth of scholarly mentorship, personal support, and financial assistance I have received throughout my education and work at multiple institutions. At George Washington University, new colleagues and mentors William Becker, Nemata Blyden, Linda Levy Peck, Eric Arnesen, and Jenna Weisman Joselit have offered much-needed advice about the review and publication processes at crucial moments. I thank the dean's office of the Columbian College of Arts and Sciences and the History Department at George Washington University for allowing me a leave during my first year of employment which was absolutely necessary for the completion of the manuscript.

I spent that leave year supported by a Ford Foundation Diversity Postdoctoral Fellowship at Princeton University's Center for African American Studies under Tera Hunter's mentorship. Ever since Tera agreed to chair the panel I organized for the 2005 Berkshire Conference on the History of Women, she has been a valued mentor offering advice and support on everything from navigating the job market to replying to readers' reports. She read various versions and pieces of this book throughout its evolution, and it is much better for her keen eye and hard questions. Tera is one of a group of women scholars across the academy, including Ula Taylor, Nan Woodruff, Nancy Bercaw, Sue Grayzel, Sharon Holland, Estelle Freedman, Michelle Scott, and Jennifer Baszile, whose mentorship has sustained me and facilitated my growth as a scholar. Each offered a word of advice and a warm personal interest in my success at crucial moments, and I thank them for these significant gifts.

The three years I spent at the University of Mississippi enriched my understanding of race politics and my scholarship in innumerable ways. For the historian, Mississippi's social matrix of race, class, nostalgia, repression, and modern aspiration presents a particularly fascinating enigma. Colleagues and friends in the History and African American Studies departments joined me in puzzling over it. Nancy Bercaw, Angela Hornsby-Gutting, Ethel Young-Minor, and Sue Grayzel provided reassurance and advice that first year as I learned to lecture while also maintaining my research and writing. I particularly thank Sue for organizing a women's writing group among history department faculty that proved so helpful in reading chapter drafts, book proposal drafts, and other materials along the way to publication. I thank Sue also for her faith that *Prove It On Me* would indeed be published and for her steadfast belief in the efficacy of cultural history. I must also thank Dean Glenn Hopkins and Chairs Joseph Ward of the History Department and Charles K. Ross of the African American Studies Department for their support of this project. Dean Hopkins provided me with two College of Liberal Arts Summer Research Grants that allowed me to devote the summer months to additional research and revision of this book. Chairs Joe Ward and Chuck Ross granted me course releases, provided limited enrollments, funded conference and research trips, and provided salaries for teaching and research assistants over the years. Thanks are also due to teaching and research assistant Telisha Dionne Bailey, whose hard work and dedication facilitated my revision process.

Prove It On Me initially emerged in the seminars I took as a graduate student in history and African American studies at Yale University. As the project evolved to the dissertation stage, it benefited from the stimulating interdisciplinary community of established and student scholars of race, gender, and ethnicity across the programs in African American studies, American studies, and history. My dissertation committee, Matthew Frye Jacobson, Hazel V. Carby, and Jonathan Scott Holloway, formed an ideal trio, challenging and pushing my work from distinct but complementary scholarly directions. Their support has been invaluable, and I continue to appreciate their friendship and advice. As one of my examiners, Paul Gilroy challenged my limited, Americanist views through his vast and varied knowledge of the history and politics of the Atlantic world. My work on race in the United States is richer for his perspective. While she was still at Yale, Nancy Cott directed one of my first independent research projects on the way to *Prove It On Me* and later included me in the Mellon Dissertation Seminar in Gender History she conducted at Harvard University in the summer of 2002. Robin Hayes, Besenia Rodriguez, Joshua Guild, Mary Barr, and Aisha Bastiaans formed a dissertation group useful to the early stages of the book.

My early work on *Prove It On Me* was also sustained by communities of scholars beyond Yale. Stéphanie Larrieux at Brown University organized the initial meeting of the Ivy League Women of Color Dissertation Collective, which became a vital space of scholarly and personal sustenance for my development as a scholar of race, gender, and black women's history. Since I was an undergraduate at Stanford University, the Mellon Mays University Fellows program, the gift that keeps on giving, has provided me funding, crucial sources of career advice, early experiences in conference presentations, and a diverse, far-flung, multigenerational community of scholars. So great is the MMUF network that I cannot list here all the mentors, colleagues, and friends it has granted me, but I duly thank them all. Clayborne Carson and Estelle Freedman were my MMUF mentors at Stanford, guiding my earliest scholarly endeavors in race and gender history. I hope they are sufficiently proud of the scholar I have become to "take credit for" my work, as Clay once joked.

Over the years of its evolution, *Prove It On Me* has been supported by numerous foundations and programs. The Ford Foundation Diversity Fellowship program funded my scholarship at both the pre- and post-doctoral stages. The Yale University Sterling Prize Fellowship supported me while I undertook course work in the first years of my graduate program. The Mellon Foundation and the Social Science Research Council provided money for research travel and materials. A Graduate Student Fellowship at the Beinecke Rare Book and Manuscript Library allowed for a summer's immersion in its James Weldon Johnson Collection. The American Association of University Women Educational Foundation supplied an American Dissertation Fellowship that supported my first year of sustained writing.

I spent the final year of dissertation work as an Africana Research Center Pre-Doctoral Fellow in History at Pennsylvania State University. There I met and was generously mentored by a number of smart and engaging historians. Nan Woodruff demanded that I break my writing hibernation to attend her fun and delicious dinner parties. Lori Ginzberg took me out to lunch and discussed the ins and outs of the professoriate and its gender politics. Anthony Kaye took time out of his busy schedule to read and offer great advice on the first chapter of this book. I thank all of them for their friendship and counsel. I must also thank the Center for Ethnic Studies and the Arts at the University of Iowa for sponsoring me as a Junior Fellow at its Junior Faculty Publication Workshop on Women of Color in Popular Culture.

My work as a scholar, writer, and teacher has been made easier by the dedication and invaluable knowledge of departmental staff. Geneva Melvin and Janet Giarratano in the Department of African American Studies at Yale and Michael Weeks and Evelyn Williams in the History Department at GWU have facilitated this book by helping me navigate institutional bureaucracies and providing the rare professionalism so necessary to the success of the academy. I heartily thank them.

Friendships made and kept long before, within, and beyond the academy have shaped me and my vision, carried me through the hard times and helped me enjoy the good times and thus made my ongoing work both possible and (mostly) enjoyable. Talesha Reynolds, Zakiyyah Langford, Claudia Aranda, Kimberly Juanita Brown, Brandi Hughes, Françoise Hamlin,

Marcia Chatelain, Melissa Stuckey, Muna Meky, Nancy Bercaw, Nicole Biggers, and Tasha Curry-Corcoran all know the value of being girls together, at any age. I thank them all for their sisterhood and for knowing (or learning) not to ask when I would finally be done with this book.

I must also thank my family for their support over the years and especially for providing me the best education possible, which has immeasurably enriched my life and granted me the tools to undertake this challenging, fulfilling work of reading, thinking, and writing for a living.

Fellow scholars and interlocutors Kimberly Juanita Brown and Jesse James Scott must have special gratitude for the depth and value of their friendship. In particular, I thank Jesse for his readership, absurd sense of humor, and constant inquiry, which have pushed, inspired, entertained, and sustained me as I finished this book. I am so glad our friendship has endured beyond the boundaries of the Magnolia State. Through grad school, post-docs, first jobs, and annual ASA conferences, Kimberly has remained the best of friends, believing in me and my work, critiquing drafts, slicing and dicing with her sardonic wit, and sustaining my feminism. Both have provided me an ear for rants, solace in low moments, challenging scholarly (and not so scholarly) conversation, and laughter, laughter, laughter—the stuff of health and sanity. I am ever grateful.

Prove It On Me

Introduction

Race and Sex in the Wake of the Great Migration

> They said I do it, ain't nobody caught me
> Sure got to prove it on me.

These are the words of Gertrude "Ma" Rainey, renowned blueswoman of the New Negro era.[1] Rainey's is a blues of defiance, challenging mainstream mores of decorum, gender, sexuality, and racial solidarity.[2] Her song dares the listener's condemnation, invites and then dismisses disapproval, and in doing so evinces a modern individuality and commitment to self-determination. The blueswoman both admits and denies any culpability—the lyrics of her song relate that she engages in gender-bending acts subversive to the moral, racial, patriarchal, and social status quo, but the chorus refrain challenges the listener to "prove it on" her. The burden is on society to prove the singer has broken the law or caused injury or damage—indeed, that she has done anything wrong at all. She knows she is not completely free, but she acts independently anyway. She refuses to care what they think; she does what she likes. In the face of social and moral condemnation, this New Negro woman determined to shape her own identity and fate.

All over the country, in rural hamlets and the sprawling cities, for white as well as black people, the New Negro era was lived to the rhythm of ragtime, jazz, and classic blues. The women performers, like Ma Rainey, who first recorded the blues, made "race records" one of the first commodities that were created by African Americans and then sold back to black consumers through white-owned and white-operated recording companies and national distribution networks. Recorded blues and the blueswomen who performed them are some of the most powerful markers of the changes in race, culture, and economy taking place in the period. The blues song "Prove It On Me" is thus emblematic of its era in multiple ways. Expressed in the most nationally popular, most racialized musical genre of the period are both the New Negroes' driving quest for self-determination and African American women's precarious position within the modernizing sexual mores and racial politics of the early twentieth century. In her famous blues, Rainey both expresses the myriad new choices of modernity and suggests the puzzling, debilitating, demoralizing, or even violent individual and social upheavals associated with so much sudden change.

Rainey insists on her right to enjoy, as sociologist E. Franklin Frazier lamented, the era's "larger freedom of women," which seemed so capable of destroying, or at least revolutionizing, the vaunted American family and patriarchal authority that ostensibly provided stability and social control.[3] Despite this larger freedom, however, the question remained whether women, especially African American women, really had any more social, political, or economic power than they had had before. In the New Negro era, the spectacle of women's freedom and sensual abandon—exemplified by Ma Rainey's image and the lyrics of her famous song—overshadowed the ongoing political suppression and exclusion of most black women's voices. Instead of representing liberation, the prevalence of such spectacles indicated society's use of black women's bodies, images, and subjectivities to "prove"—establish, test, assert, flout—the countless quandaries in gender roles, sexuality, and morality presented by the modern era and its new race politics.

An array of economic, social, and cultural transformations in the United States and the wider world converged in the early twentieth century to create the space for the emergence of Rainey's defiant blues. In the mid-1910s, the First World War raged in Europe, and U.S. industry sought to supply its allies with much-needed troops and materials, while the nation closed its borders to the multitudes who continued to seek entry. The United States had established imperial sovereignty over the Philippines, Cuba, Puerto Rico, and Haiti and had begun to exert a paternalistic economic and political authority over much of the Americas. The boll weevil ravaged Southern cotton crops, and D. W. Griffith's film *The Birth of a Nation* played to packed audiences throughout the nation, granting dominant cultural approval for the lynchings that continued unabated. A new generation of the Ku Klux Klan (KKK), motivated by the social shifts transforming sex, race, and the relationships between them, arose and spread from the rural Midwest with murderous, repressive intent.[4] Amid all this, African Americans went on the move.

By the thousands they migrated from rural hamlets and scattered farms to the burgeoning cities of the industrial North, Midwest, and revitalizing New South, making a flood out of the trickles and streams of migration that the freedmen and the Reconstruction generation had initiated.[5] Black men and women abandoned the hard life of the rural South in order to escape the most violent expressions of white supremacy, for the chance to make their way in the booming wartime economy, and to remake themselves in the city. Newspapers such as the *Chicago Defender* and the *New York Age* reflected the class-based, racial, and sexual anxieties and sociocultural turbulence churned up by the mass movement of thousands of black people, many of them young and single.

At the same time, African American men returned from the trenches of World War I determined to make democracy and black "manhood" a reality in the United States. The migrants and returning soldiers clashed with white workers and city leaders resolved to reaffirm white supremacist "Americanism" and to hold the line of the racial status quo. Lynchings and murderous urban race riots increased. The outbreak of riots in twenty-five cities across the nation in the summer of 1919 caused James Weldon Johnson to label it the "Red Summer."[6] Meanwhile, the "white slavery" scare heightened sexual and racial tensions and motivated strenuous progressive efforts to eliminate prostitution, liquor-consumption, and other vices, which only succeeded in pushing these illicit activities into under-policed, growing black urban areas.[7]

African American migrants nevertheless made homes for themselves in congested, inadequate sections of the city. Urban black populations increased exponentially, even doubled, in cities across the nation. By 1930, 240,000 filled the Chicago South Side and 327,000 crowded into the deteriorating housing in Harlem, a growth of 115 percent since 1920.[8] Smaller cities saw their share as well. Places like Milwaukee, Detroit, Pittsburgh, Omaha, Nebraska, Atlanta, Dallas, and St. Louis, Missouri were also sites of African American urbanization and the growth of New Negro popular culture and politics.[9] Although African Americans remained a small percentage of the total populations of most cities, the "*event* of the sudden surge in their numbers," made obvious by African Americans' distinctive phenotypical characteristics, was the significant element of this period.[10] This great migration, as it came to be known, and the social turmoil it unleashed began the reconstitution of the cultural and political discourses shaping racial knowledge and power in the United States.[11]

African American populations in urban centers multiplied so rapidly that black people became culturally and politically visible in unprecedented ways. These new city dwellers formed a new urban market willing and able to consume leisure and luxury products, and they engaged in mass political activism for the first time. In these and other ways, they made themselves noticeable to the popular culture industry, itself in the midst of modern transformations. African Americans' new conspicuousness made race popularly relevant on a national scale. While the burgeoning entertainment industries were quick to capitalize on this new consumer group and source of entertainment commodities, African Americans themselves utilized new technologies such as film and publishing to articulate evolving expressions of racial identity and advancement politics. To a greater extent than ever before, African Americans participated in the production, distribution, and purchase of their own popular representations. As a result, the production and reproduction of the meaning of race itself, its use as a symbol for popular understandings of character or value, and its relevance to African Americans' ideas of who they were and how they fit into society all became more complex.

In this new day, someone like New Negro writer Marita Bonner could question the efficacy of a long-standing political and cultural maxim such as racial solidarity, while an entrepreneur such as Madam C. J. Walker could manipulate solidarity to encourage the race-serving consumption of her beauty products and thereby increase her sales. These processes of transformation in the meanings and uses of race incorporated the perspectives, productions, and expressions of the New Negroes, and yet they were still formed and disseminated through the powerful arbiters of white supremacist understandings and capitalist exploitation. Neither race nor white supremacy was eliminated, nullified, or superseded in the interwar era, but both did change. What is more, the New Negroes initiated and helped direct much of that change. In the New Negro era, to an unprecedented degree, African Americans themselves participated in the formation of the racial and sexual discourses forming their world.

PRIMITIVISM AND GENDER IN THE NEW NEGRO ERA

First through the audacious act of transporting their bodies and lives across the country and then through the production of films, the recording of music, the publication of scholarship, the consumption of these and other products, and the formulation of mass politics, African Americans consciously re-created themselves and the racial discourses that shaped their society. Along the way, the aspiring race leaders among them attempted also to guide their fellows' transformations for a total reconstruction of African American identity and solidarity in the modern era. Although African Americans had used the term "New Negro" periodically at least since the publication of Booker T. Washington's *A New Negro for a New*

Century in 1900, the younger generation's appropriation of it after the onset of the great migration connoted a new militancy in their determination to receive respect for their humanity, defend constitutional rights and privileges, and participate fully in U.S. society. These New Negro political ideas extended across class lines and permeated the modern art and performance of the New Negro Renaissance of the late 1910s through the 1930s.

The New Negroes sought to accomplish self-transformation and social change not only through the didactic speeches and publications their predecessors in the Reconstruction generation had used but more significantly through their participation as producers, consumers, and commodities in the interracial arena of social communication and negotiation that was the sex-race marketplace. This was both an actual marketplace offering tangible goods for sale and a discursive space formed through and around the arresting images, teasing language, and fantastic territory of modern, popular cultural productions. In the sex-race marketplace, both the tangible goods and the intangible ideas that gave the goods meaning—the ideas, fantasies, thrills, hopes, judgments that were sold along with the goods—were steeped in racialized and sexualized language and significance.

The new visibility of black bodies and the modernist fascination with the natural and the primitive, which were often associated with ideas about black people, along with black political engagement and mass consumption, helped to create the sex-race marketplace. Within the marketplace, ideas about African Americans and their changing ideas about themselves collided with both nostalgic and progressive notions to reformulate U.S. racial politics and sensibility. According to the logic of the marketplace's sex-race discourse, blueswoman Bessie Smith was both a glamorous modern diva portrayed in a bejeweled crown befitting the "Empress of the Blues" and a performer of down-home, gritty, salacious music that was sold through cartoonish images displaying stereotypes of black sexual deviance and the manipulation of white and black nostalgia for simpler, plantation days.

As Bessie Smith's twinned popular image shows, even as the New Negroes' "newness" was celebrated and displayed on screen in popular films and in print through fiction, advertisement, and photography, recorded on race records, and disseminated through other media, they nevertheless epitomized primitivism. In interwar popular culture, primitivism was an effort to recover man's earliest days and the uninhibited expression of his most basic needs and habits. This recovery was accomplished through the consumption of the artistry and performances of dark bodies that were supposedly closer to their earthy desires and impulses. Primitivism worked as an antidote to the debilitating and alienating effects of life in the impersonal, overly civilized, harsh, modern city. Through dominant interwar popular culture, white people used dark bodies, consumption of their art, and participation in their amusements as a means of safely accessing the primitive within themselves without compromising their whiteness, respectability, and privilege. Hence the popularity of venues such as Harlem's Cotton Club where New Negro musicians such as Duke Ellington performed jazz and New Negro women dancers kicked up their legs for the benefit of white onlookers in a segregated audience.[12] In such segregated venues featuring black performers, white supremacy was reinforced as the white audience members consumed black art while distinguishing themselves from blackness through the segregated distance between performers and consumers. And yet the New Negro performers were no less talented, skilled, or modern in their performances for the use to which their subjectivities were put. Indeed, some New Negroes, too, utilized primitivism in their art to emphasize their uniqueness or as a foil to highlight their modernism.[13]

Through discursive moves like primitivism, white supremacy, while still reigning in the Jim Crow laws enforcing segregation and racial hierarchy in the South as well as in the de facto customs of the North, also came to function more insidiously, disguising itself in the dazzle and temptation of the films and recordings, advertisements, and performances produced by the popular culture industry, maintaining the racial status quo through illusion, cooptation, and commodification.

Thus it was that, while African Americans were consuming, they were also being consumed by others, especially white people, and they also consumed themselves. Within the cynical and self-consciously uninhibited mood of the 1910s and 1920s, African Americans and their culture became prominent and popular as entertainment and iconography. African American bodies and representations came to serve as icons of the era's fascination with lack of restraint and exotic temptation in various forms. African American consumption increased as their spending power rose, and companies' efforts to tap the black consumer market resulted in advertisement campaigns extolling the benefits of race records, cosmetics, and other entertaining luxuries. Blues culture, with its raucous music, suggestive lyrics, and even more suggestive dances, captivated America's urban populations.[14] This book investigates the political, cultural, and personal implications of the sex-race marketplace with its modern investment in black bodies and racialized images, particularly those of black women.

The widespread cultural investment in black women's subjectivities had particular implications for intra-racial New Negro discourses, especially as race intersected with sexuality, gender, and class in the period. This book also studies those implications. Born in the 1880s, 1890s, and early 1900s to parents who had come of age in the midst of Reconstruction's rising hopes and eventual bitter disappointment, the New Negro generation of black artists, educators, migrants, workers, social reformers, journalists, performers, and aspirants sought to free themselves once and for all from the stigma of slavery and the strictures of servile behavior. The New Negroes expected U.S. society to live up to its creed of equality, and they endeavored, in a variety of ways, to claim and demonstrate their equal humanity.[15] Thus, African American culture and politics in the New Negro era were shaped by the concerted, multifaceted effort the New Negroes mounted to achieve self-determination in political, cultural, and economic terms.

Through their art and activism and their commitment to self-determination, the New Negroes helped to construct modern racial discourses. Overall, New Negroes meant to assert themselves as agents and subjects—no longer mere objects—in these new racial discourses; they meant to affect the hegemonic understanding of racial character and racial politics. In the New Negro era, they succeeded in talking back to white supremacy and undertook the long, ultimately incomplete process of ensuring African American humanity would be fully understood, represented, and accepted in U.S. society, politics, and culture. In their aspirations, the New Negroes did not necessarily break radically from their parents' generation. They built on the inroads made by older volunteer activists, novelists, publishers, and performers like Ida B. Wells, Mary Church Terrell, Charles Chestnutt, Pauline Hopkins, T. Thomas Fortune, Anna Julia Cooper, Booker T. Washington, W. E. B. Du Bois, and Bert Williams. Indeed, many of these people—Du Bois is a prime example—still worked assiduously in the trenches of racial advancement and took up the identity and rhetoric of the New Negroes, using and shaping it as their own.

The self-determinative efforts of the Reconstruction generation had been constrained by many factors, including their broad dispersal across rural farmland, hamlets and small towns; the successful interference of white people, both well-meaning liberals and concerted white supremacists, who endeavored to decide African Americans' best social roles and fates for them; and the swift and humiliating imposition of "separate but equal" segregation, which many of the Reconstruction generation had failed to see coming.[16] Their efforts were hampered, too, by the deeply class-biased, ultimately self-defeating strategy of racial uplift they developed to combat white supremacy. Through this strategy, they sought to uplift their fellow members of the race to the successful emulation of dominant, gendered ideals of education, decorum, and gentility.[17] The creation of undeniably genteel *and* black ladies and gentlemen, the Reconstruction generation had hoped, would prove the race's capability and readiness for full citizenship. In migrating out of the vulnerable isolation of the Jim Crow rural South; massing in the nation's cities, which were increasingly important as centers of commerce and culture; and recognizing the necessity of promoting meaningful cooperation with white allies without permitting such relationships to become sycophantic or exploitative, the New Negroes sought to move beyond many of their parents' roadblocks. In many ways, too, they broadened and complicated the Reconstruction generation's racial outlook and idea of liberation. Certainly, the New Negroes' methods and tone signaled the novelty, militancy, and diversity of their perspectives and praxes of racial advancement.

Although modern African Americans determined to shape their own destinies, both in personal and political terms, and to take leading roles in the newly configured discursive debate over black humanity and worth, there was little agreement about the best means of accomplishing these aspirations. Thus, New Negroes were divided into two major camps. There were those who sought to modernize and professionalize established ideologies of racial advancement, solidarity, and uplift through a New Negro progressivism articulated by committed would-be racial leaders like Charles S. Johnson, E. Franklin Frazier, Elise Johnson McDougald, James Weldon Johnson, Jessie Fauset, and Oscar Micheaux. Others including Langston Hughes, Ethel Waters, Nella Larsen, Claude McKay, and Bessie Smith questioned, if not the very idea of racial solidarity itself, then at least the *obligation* of racial allegiance and respectability, and instead touted a radical individualism and independence from all but the most personal allegiances to "art" or "self" or some other self-generated ideal.

These divergent priorities resulted in, for example, differing perspectives on the significance and potential benefits of New Negro art. On the one hand, critics and editors W. E. B. Du Bois and Alain Locke called for the creation of art that could be used as an explicit tool of racial advancement by demonstrating African American accomplishments and representing the best of the race. They used their publications, *The Crisis* and *The New Negro*, as forums to display literature and images they considered commensurate with this goal. On the other hand, critic and generally sardonic social commentator George Schuyler sneered at what he called the "negro-art hokum" and denounced the racist primitivism he found in it. He adamantly denied that any specific cultural or racial artistic tendencies could or should be attributed to African Americans and thus rejected the usefulness of art as a means of demonstrating anything about the race. Meanwhile, writer Langston Hughes insisted that true New Negro artists celebrate "the low-down folks, the so-called common element" in all their gritty glory regardless of white sponsorship and predilections or any agendas for racial advancement.[18] Yet the ideals of self-determination and freedom, variously defined, infused the whole generation, from the migrants who threw off the yoke of rural sharecropping and endeavored to shape their own lives in

Southern and Northern cities, to the race men advocating equal opportunity, to the artists blazing a conflicted trail of individual self-expression.

Even as they sought freedom and to assert themselves through the sex-race marketplace, however, the New Negroes also developed a largely intra-racial discourse of struggle over gender ideals, sexual morality, and sexual politics encompassed by the label race motherhood. As the New Negroes emphasized economic concerns, created and joined labor unions and other working-class organizations, and developed class awareness, they accentuated the manhood rights of the black male worker as a tenet of racial advancement.[19] A masculinist impulse infused their political rhetoric and cultural expression. Male-dominated organizations set the agenda for racial advancement, revising the earlier woman-centered vision of uplift for the benefit of a man-centered conception of racial equality. Organizations such as the National Urban League and the National Association for the Advancement of Colored People overtook and professionalized many of the volunteer social and civic services black women had provided through the National Association of Colored Women and a multitude of local organizations. Several new organizations, including the Universal Negro Improvement Association, the Brotherhood of Sleeping Car Porters, the Communist Party USA, and the National Urban League, focused on the economic concerns of newly industrialized black male workers and the dignity and perspectives of black male "heads of household."

The volunteer activists and racial spokespeople of the Reconstruction generation had been excluded from late Victorian U.S. society by a white supremacy based on social Darwinist notions of civilization, and they had consequently focused on proving their ability to assimilate dominant ideals of gentility and gendered decorum—their ability to be "civilized." They had thus exalted the African American mother as the necessary creator and focal point of the ideal African American home that would demonstrate black worthiness and readiness for civic inclusion.[20] This strategy for racial advancement came to its full fruition in the Victorian black feminist uplift ideology of the National Association of Colored Women (NACW), which was founded in 1896. NACW uplift ideology assumed bourgeois homes to be both women's rightful sphere of influence and the basis for their civic activism outside the home. This ideology further assumed the creation of such bourgeois homes to be integral to the formation of respectable ladyhood and pure motherhood. This ideology considered black people's achievement of such ideal homes a preeminent indication of racial advancement through the demonstration of their "civilization." As first NACW president Mary Church Terrell emphasized, black ladies' creation and maintenance of "homes, more homes, better homes, purer homes" was a central tenet of the organization's goals, especially in the volunteer activities of the local clubs constituting the national association.[21]

NACW ideology was also black feminist in that it emphasized black women's specific stake in the struggle against racial oppression and defied and decried sexism, including that expressed by black men, whenever it emerged. For example, clubwomen fought for equal access to educational opportunities in the black colleges that were founded during Reconstruction, advocated women's suffrage, and endeavored to gain black male ministers' approval and recognition of women's prayer circles and church organizations, which were early sites for women's self-determination through independent biblical interpretation and church-based activism.[22] Paradoxically, the clubwomen's feminism advocated patriarchal family structures. They expected black men to materially support, rhetorically protect, and physically defend their homes and female relatives. Yet the clubwomen also expected equal partnership in the public arena and the struggle against oppression, and they did not see these expectations as incompatible. They used their status as symbols for the race's best achievements, its "civilization," and its fitness for civic equality as a platform for concerted racial leadership. Within the Reconstruction generation's class-biased efforts to uplift their fellow African Americans and prove the race's worthiness, African American women had cobbled a space for a woman-centered discourse of racial politics and amelioration.

By and large, the New Negroes did not seek to prove their worthiness through the demonstration of gentility, civilization, and the creation of ideal bourgeois homes run by ladies. As the black male worker took center stage in concepts of representative blackness, the racial advancement movement began to merge with the labor movement, and there emerged a new predominant vision of racial liberation achieved through insistence on a law-and-order ideology of equal access to rights and opportunities for all citizens. Thus, the race ceased to need or revere images of pure black ladyhood as standard-bearers for African American humanity, "civilization," and fitness for civic inclusion. Her symbolic importance as a pure mother waned and ceased to act as a source of intra-racial political capital for the New Negro woman's participation in the formation of racial advancement discourses.

Yet, the African American home and the black mother who served as its emotional and moral center remained significant in the New Negro era. The interwar period witnessed the emergence of the social scientific analysis blaming the supposed absence of "organized"—a word often used by E. Franklin Frazier—patriarchal, respectable families among African Americans for their ongoing oppression. African American women, especially mothers, went from representing the potential agency of racial advancement as exalted, pure mothers to serving as the pitiful, amoral objects of narratives of black familial backwardness. Progressive efforts to reconfigure, regulate, and reform black gender anomalies and familial pathology focused on the black mother's transformation according to masculinist priorities for racial advancement and the promotion of patriarchal ideals of black manhood.[23]

Amidst rising black masculinism and into the void left where the Reconstruction generation's lady-paragon had been, the race mother emerged. This new discourse of ideal black womanhood and intra-racial gender politics took the form of race motherhood, in part, out of a need for stability in the face of all the change the New Negroes were witnessing and fomenting. Access to reliable birth control increased, and the automobile became a means for young, unmarried couples to escape their communities' mores and share private moments. The sex-race marketplace sold images of glamorous, sexy vamps and divas as icons of modern femininity. Young, single black migrants began showing up by the thousands, crowding city street corners and public venues. The Nineteenth Amendment seemed to grant women equal access to political engagement and the social prerogatives that came with it. Some feared society was tearing apart at the seams. Long reliant on conservative, patriarchal gender codes to make their humanity manifest in the face of life-threatening oppression, African Americans in particular were generally deeply suspicious of anti-patriarchal social change and politics. In the minds of many, as race and gender were transforming, sexual mores shifting, and morality seemingly falling by the wayside, the meaning of black womanhood needed to remain stable, a pillar against which the race could test its novel successes and a supportive foundation for racial transformations. Race motherhood discourse made New Negro women into such pillars and foundations.[24]

The Reconstruction generation had declared women the race's vanguard. As the black woman was judged, so the race would be judged; "when and where" the black woman entered, the whole race entered with her, to paraphrase Anna Julia Cooper. These had been black women's self-generated subjectivities and platforms for empowerment to a Victorian black feminism, albeit one that was steeped in class assumptions and reliant, ultimately, on patriarchy. For the New Negro generation, however, as the "larger freedom of women" became a possibility and the whole of society began to move beyond idolization of the Victorian lady and her "civilizing influence" as the barometer for social advancement, those Victorian declarations became modern circumscriptions confining black women to roles designed by and for their mothers, now largely devoid of their female-centered self-determinative power. Race motherhood was not a New Negro update of Victorian black feminism but a discourse confining black women's subjectivity, identity, and activity to others' support and use.

Some New Negro women nevertheless traded on race motherhood to endeavor to make a place for their continued self-determination. Madam C. J. Walker utilized race motherhood to justify her entrepreneurial independence and to offset the potentially glamorous effects her cosmetic products offered black consumers. Her promotional materials suggested that she was not in business to enrich herself or to empower black women on multiple levels but was on a mission to advance the race's health and liberation. Social worker, teacher, and essayist Elise Johnson McDougald used race motherhood as a criterion by which to judge New Negro women's progress and contribution to racial advancement, celebrating those whom she deemed exemplary in their selfless service to the race's future and thus carving a place for them in New Negro visions of liberation. Yet Walker's and McDougald's efforts reinforced race motherhood discourse through their very use of it. The discursive formation of a modern, independent, anti-patriarchal black woman's self-determination would be several more generations in the making.[25] Meanwhile, the renewed masculinist focus on men's perspectives and well-being motivated an emphasis on the instatement of a black patriarchy and the achievement of black men's liberation as goals for racial advancement efforts. According to the New Negro vision, the race would be liberated through the alleviation of black men's oppression. Black women would profit only contingently, through their connections to black patriarchs.

As a result, women did not benefit in full measure from the era's commitment to self-determination and the opportunities New Negroes were creating. Relegated to limited race mothering roles, they were to dedicate themselves to others and remain subordinate to man-centered, patriarchal visions of racial self-determination and opportunity, or forfeit the benefits and protection of racial solidarity and social acceptance. Ma Rainey might assert her absolute independence from the burdens and obligations of conventional gender prescriptions, but her radical sexual independence had a price. The protective benefits of solidarity did not extend to those who shamed the race or undermined its advancement, even when that advancement was envisioned in masculinist terms. Rainey's audacious song, celebrated in the sex-race marketplace, ultimately failed to declare her emancipation but instead confined her in the grips of salacious, primitivist immorality and deviance.

As the great migration and converging economic and technological changes precipitated the formation of the sex-race marketplace that would shape the course of twentieth-century race politics and racialized popular culture, so too did that modern racial discourse motivate the development of an intra-racial discourse of race motherhood. Together, they rendered black women largely invisible, their subjectivities flat and inhuman, for the greater part of that century.

RACIAL AND SEXUAL MEANINGS IN TRANSITION

Prove It On Me is a discursive history of the meanings dominant society, New Negro politics, and black women themselves made and attempted to make out of black women's subjectivities and of the social forces shaping those meanings. It is not a narrative of black women's quotidian experiences or of their triumph over adversity against the odds. Rather, it is an elucidation of how those odds shifted, of how the changing discourses of gender, sexuality, race, and economics affected the kinds of opportunities black women found available to them, a discussion of the nature of oppression in its complexity and dynamism. This book recovers the contentious nature of historical change and the discursive battles Americans have waged and continue to fight over sex and race as they are integral to the very concept of American-ness. The book shows how Americans, black and white, male and female, used race and sex in the interwar period.

In its method and mode of analysis, this history owes a great deal to black feminist literary criticism, gendered cultural histories of race, and black women's histories.[26] In order to re-create the transitional racial world of the 1920s, *Prove It On Me* deciphers a broad range of the cultural texts produced in the period—including film, print media, music, images, and literary fiction—and also considers the backgrounds and motives of their producers. The explication of such texts in the historical context of their production and according to the motives of the scholars, artists, performers, authors, and corporations that created them reveals the discourses shaping the culture of the era. By considering several kinds of cultural productions, taking a broad, national perspective, and utilizing the analytical tools of multiple disciplines, *Prove It On Me* provides a glimpse of transformation in action and a better understanding of how notions of race, gender, and sexuality, and the power relations shaping them, shifted for both the nation and African Americans even as white supremacy persisted.

Through this broad, multidisciplinary approach attendant to discourse as evidenced through cultural productions, then, *Prove It On Me* describes the discourses shaping the whole of a New Negro *era* rather than detailing any particular New Negro "movement," which is an effort to achieve a stated set of goals and objectives. This book does not ask whether a New Negro "movement" succeeded or failed but investigates the cultural significance of the racial and sexual transformations that occurred across this dynamic period.

Because the New Negro era was not confined to any particular place, such as Harlem or Chicago, but was an aspect of the entire interwar social fabric and its racial politics, *Prove It On Me* moves beyond regional boundaries, while maintaining an awareness of the significance of distinctions such as rural and urban, Northern and Southern, and de facto and de jure segregation. In recovering the discursive terrain of the New Negro era as a whole, this book posits gender and sexuality as primary elements of African American racial identity and racial advancement politics and fore-grounds the sexual aspects of white supremacy's social functions and effects on black lives. It furthermore studies the implications of the inter-sections of race, gender, and sexuality for the historical operation of race itself. It is a history of how prevalent aspects of U.S. culture functioned through discursive investment in African American women's bodies and racialized sexual politics.

Each chapter of *Prove It On Me* addresses an aspect of the popular cul-ture New Negroes produced in the interwar period and the dynamic transi-tions under way in discourses of race, sexuality, and gender as African Americans and U.S. popular culture invested in black women. The book opens with an analysis of Oscar Micheaux's second film *Within Our Gates*, officially released in 1920, and the shifting, gendered terrain of African American anti-lynching ideology and strategies in the context of the bur-geoning sex-race marketplace and rising race motherhood. Ostensibly a film about the romantic tragedies and ultimate marital triumph of the fic-tional Sylvia Landry, a New Negro woman teacher whose family was lynched, *Within Our Gates* is actually a highly gendered call for an un-daunted African American patriarchal leadership. It is equally a demand for the recognition of lynching as a criminal act of savagery practiced upon black men and women in order to maintain economic and political white supremacy, not as punishment for rape. While they lynched black men, women, and children to stymie African American courage and potential, according to Micheaux, white people raped and abused black women and girls to satisfy their own carnal lusts, express their dominance, and terrorize black communities. In depicting all this in stark, black and white cinematic realism, Micheaux adapted the Reconstruction generation's Victorian black feminist anti-lynching ideology for modern audiences and yet, in his call for black male leadership, presaged the New Negro generation's masculinist agenda for racial advancement. With this film and the anti-lynching politics surrounding it, the racial and sexual transitions that marked the New Negro era were well under way.

Chapter 2 further explores the parameters of the era's intra-racial gen-der discourse through the activist scholarship of New Negro sociologists E. Franklin Frazier and Charles S. Johnson and the reports and articles written by New Negro women social workers and other professionals. *Opportunity: Journal of Negro Life*, which Johnson founded and edited from 1923 to 1928, is the cultural site of this chapter, as its content included the broadest array of opinion and types of artistic and scholarly production on race politics produced in the period. The magazine itself is an example of the

New Negro effort to intervene in the restructuring of racial discourses. Publishing reports of their efforts and strategies in *Opportunity*'s pages, New Negro progressives sought to ready the African American masses for urban life, industrial work, and civic responsibility. Much of this effort focused on critiquing and changing black women's mothering habits as well as on stemming the tide of women's potential independence through the vote, increased education, migration, and industrial and professional employment. In the scholarship of Frazier and Johnson as well as in the pages of *Opportunity*, the race motherhood ideals of womanly self-sacrifice and deference to male authority, a man-centered perspective on the effects of racial oppression, and the advocacy of the establishment of black patriarchy as a primary goal of racial advancement are repeated over and over again. They appear in sociological treatises, social workers' reports and recommendations, and the various notices about employment openings, educational opportunities, and the race's needs that the magazine included. Women as well as men espoused the race motherhood discourse.

Chapter 3 turns to black women's efforts to gain their share of New Negro self-determination and modern liberation through entrepreneurship, performance, and consumption, despite the prevalence of the race motherhood discourse and in the midst of ongoing white supremacist exploitation of black images and sexuality. This chapter details the machinations of the sex-race marketplace through the inter-war world of advertisements for cosmetics and blues records directed at black consumers through black periodicals like the *Chicago Defender*. At the intersection of the discursive sex-race marketplace and the material reality of goods for sale, black female bodies were manifested as both figurative and actual commodities. The commodified New Negro woman was sold to both black and white consumers who bought race records, cosmetics, and concert tickets and sported the fashions, hairstyles, and makeup the blueswomen popularized. This chapter posits the sex-race marketplace as the new, popular racial discourse that shaped and fed the primitivist predilection for the exotic black and thereby yielded the cultural space for the emergence of black bodies (as opposed to caricatured, minstrel images) in popular culture and yet relentlessly dehumanized those bodies. While New Negro consumers, performers, and entrepreneurs looked to the sex-race marketplace for various degrees and kinds of self-determination— from the thrill of donning a modern, alluring style to the opportunity to earn their own money, and the satisfaction of seeing their very own names in lights—liberation via the marketplace was ultimately ephemeral. And yet the satisfactions of participating in it remained real. Even as New Negro women asserted their modernity and challenged conservative gender ideals and outmoded racial representations through their participation in the marketplace, the marketplace succeeded in co-opting their efforts to the service of ongoing racial and sexual oppression.

In the New Negro era, there was a small cadre of women who recognized the dangers of seeking self-determination in the sex-race marketplace as well as the circumscribed opportunity for self-determination offered them by the prevailing race motherhood discourse. Chapter 4 considers their recorded words. Women such as Jessie Fauset, Nella Larsen, Marita Bonner, and Elise Johnson McDougald dared, to varying degrees, to criticize and even challenge the patriarchal ideals and masculinist vision of racial advancement that reigned in the New Negro era. They were bold enough to reveal their private, emotional, and sexual selves in order to explore the intimate effects of combined racial and sexual oppression. The published words of these authors are set alongside correspondence and oral histories relating the perspectives and recollections of other New Negro women whose experiences exemplify the personal quandaries and racial conundrums the writers set forth in their stories and essays. Although there was no concerted New Negro feminism advocating a woman-centered racial advancement effort or openly confronting intra-racial masculinism and patriarchy, there was among New Negro women a muted dissatisfaction with the limitations prescribed by race motherhood and a nagging frustration with the oversimplified, extreme, inhuman representations proffered within the sex-race marketplace. Chapter 4 probes New Negro women's words for signs of the effects of the commodification, proscription, hyper-sexualization, and subjugation wrought by society's cultural investment in black womanhood. It reveals the articulation of an alternate New Negro woman's subjectivity drawn from a black female perspective on the racial and sexual transformations churned up during the New Negro era.

Ultimately, the great migration, the struggle for African American self-determination, the emergence of new technologies of culture, the rise of economies of mass consumption, and the myriad other social transformations that converged to form the New Negro era produced a reconfiguration of racial politics and discourse that would shape the twentieth century. The New Negroes firmly established the legitimacy of their claim to an active role in the formulation of national racial politics and the representation of their bodies, culture, and lives. In this tumultuous period, the sex-race marketplace arose to mediate the dissemination of racialized representations and would continue to do so—with the addition of innovative technologies such as radio and television—as the century evolved. The New Negroes' masculinist vision of racial advancement formed the foundation of a twentieth-century freedom movement that went a long way toward achieving African American access to the formal, constitutionally guaranteed rituals of democracy and that still shapes African American gender politics and racial identities.

During the interwar years, white people continued to wield the lion's share of the power, including that most mighty of discursive implements, the power to name and to declare the truth. But New Negroes held at their disposal some new and useful tools and succeeded as African Americans had not before in inserting some of their own ideas into the stew of popular perception and racial discourse. They gained access to film, advertisements, music and the images associated with it, activist scholarship, and mass publication. Through these media, they waged interracial and intra-racial battles over the meaning of blackness, the measure of manhood, the ideal of womanhood, the significance of race, the value of independence, and their own humanity. Neither won nor lost, these battles mark the dynamic, roiling shifts in popular culture, politics, and the meaning of black womanhood that *Prove It On Me* recovers.

Ma Rainey's challenge still stands. Echoing up from the early years of the last century, her edgy voice still demands the proof of her guilt and her innocence, her value and her worthlessness, the uses to which society put her words, her image, and her very body—the efficacy of her battle to determine her own identity and destiny.

CHAPTER 1

✺

Oscar Micheaux's *Within Our Gates* and the Emergence of the New Negro

In her "My Thrills in the Movies" series, which was published in the weekly *Pittsburgh Courier*, star New Negro actress Evelyn Preer recounted some of her experiences working with the famous New Negro filmmaker Oscar Micheaux to make his films *The Homesteader, Birthright, The Brute, Deceit,* and *Within Our Gates*. Throughout the several installments, Preer's tone and language suggest her to have been a sweet, slightly silly, confidently popular glamour girl or flapper. "You see I must have my thrills," she wrote.[1] Yet Preer's light, teasing tone both promised more intimate knowledge than she intended to provide and belied the depth of insight she brought to her performance as Sylvia Landry in *Within Our Gates*, arguably the most controversial race film of the New Negro era.

In her series, Preer implicitly declined to satisfy her fans' curiosity regarding her more personal thrills and tastes. She quoted one admirer as asking, "Miss Preer, what male lead do you enjoy working with the best?" but she did not respond directly. Rather, she interpreted the question as "show[ing] the general interest in the movies" and went on to explain that "in this series I will try to answer some of these questions which both feminine and male admirers of a movie heroine might ask."[2] She discussed her work experiences, not her personal relationships. Indeed, in recounting her interactions on the set, Preer was quite circumspect, even downplaying the experience of enacting an attempted rape. Although she considered the scene of *Within Our Gates* in which Sylvia Landry fought off her attacker "the best [she] ever played in," Preer did not elaborate on the emotional impact of this work or her view of its political significance. She simply called the scene a "grand fight" in which she and her fellow actor "turn[ed] over tables, chairs and other furniture in the room."[3]

Preer first came to prominence through her leading roles in Oscar Micheaux's popular and controversial silent race films, especially his infamous second production *Within Our Gates*. Born on July 26, 1896, in Vicksburg, Mississippi, Preer was raised in Chicago.[4] Although Oscar Micheaux would later claim that he gave Preer her start in acting, she actually developed her interest in theater, in the form of popular minstrel comedies and black vaudeville revues, while still a schoolgirl when she began performing in the Lady Amateur Minstrels. After her graduation from high school, she toured the Pacific coast's Orpheum circuit as prima donna with a vaudeville team led by Charley Johnson.[5] Thus, Preer already had a great deal of experience as a professional performer when she met Oscar Micheaux in Chicago in 1917. She made her film debut in the producer's first work, *The Homesteader*, and remained his leading lady through eight more films. After appearing in Micheaux's *The Spider's Web* in 1926, Preer turned her attention to opportunities in Hollywood and her other theatrical endeavors.[6]

Despite the apparent success of her collaboration with Micheaux, Preer never confined her professional activities to her work with him. She joined the Lafayette Players, the first "serious" all-black theatrical troupe in the United States, in 1920, becoming the leading lady of its traveling circuit by 1924.[7] While on tour that year, Preer married her leading man, Edward Thompson, and the couple had one daughter born in April 1932 and named Edeve. With the Lafayette Players and other groups, Preer performed in many of the major theatrical events of her time, including *Salomé, Porgy, Paid in Full, Dr. Jekyll and Mr. Hyde,* and the Broadway productions *Lulu Belle* and *Shuffle Along*. A versatile and extremely popular performer, Preer also recorded blues songs, sometimes using the name "Hotsy Jarvis," and appeared with Ethel Waters and others at Sebastian's Cotton Club in Los Angeles during 1930 and 1931. Perhaps part of her reason for ceasing her work with Micheaux was the possibility of becoming a mainstream actor in Hollywood productions. In the late 1920s and early 1930s, Preer took small roles in films produced by Paramount, Metro-Goldwyn, and Warner Brothers studios.[8]

A migrant from Mississippi to Chicago and later Los Angeles, a former vaudeville performer, an actress in "serious" film and theater, a blues singer, and an aspiring integrator of Hollywood, Evelyn Preer embodied the mixture of incredible success, beauty, fashion, sophistication, and fortune that constituted the glamorous side of New Negro representations of black womanhood. Her stylishly draped clothes, bobbed haircut (which she wore from about 1921 onward), cosmetics, and light complexion all indicate her success in embodying the interwar era's standards for high fashion and feminine attractiveness. Her career and aspirations, furthermore, suited the facet of New Negro politics that sought racial advancement through demonstration of African American talent and intelligence in the arts.

The adoring critic Floyd Calvin described Preer as "a pioneer in the cinema world for colored women."[9] The New Negro press proudly owned her as one of its own preeminent race stars, "the Colored Queen of the Cinema," as the *Pittsburgh Courier* termed her. Yet even as she and her husband posed for photos displaying their Christmas gifts and allowed the press to announce the birth of their baby as if she were a princess, Preer deflected fans' and reporters' attempts to pierce the shiny bubble of her public persona. In her efforts to shape her popular representations, Preer endeavored both to shield her private life from public scrutiny and to maintain her popularity. Winding her way between the press's apparent adoration, her fans' curiosity, Micheaux's efforts to claim her stardom as one of his own creations, competing New Negro artistic and political imperatives, and her own aspirations, Preer exemplified the New Negro woman's negotiations of exploitative impulses and efforts for racial and individual self-determination in the era's sex-race marketplace.

Preer's performances, too, shaped and were shaped within the period's racial and sexual discourse. As Sylvia Landry in *Within Our Gates*, Preer epitomized the New Negro race mother, committed to advancing the race through her maternal dedication and fostering the development of a strong New Negro patriarchy. Preer and her character Sylvia seemed nearly diametrically opposed in affect, character, and ambitions, yet they were linked through their race and their womanhood and the vastness of their images projected on the silver screen. They were bound as twin sides of a coin in the logic of the marketplace offering flat, cardboard cutouts of black women for the public's edification, delectation, and consumption. With their second film, Micheaux and Preer utilized that simplistic dichotomy of black female subjectivity to disrupt the racial politics of the interwar period, advancing a New Negro discourse of gender ideals, sexual mores, and racial relations to rival the contemporary sexualized white supremacist regime and rally African Americans to a modern racial identity and vision of the race's future.

SPEAKING TRUTH TO POWER: MICHEAUX ON RACE POLITICS, LYNCHING, AND CENSORSHIP

With his ambitious and controversial 1920 film, *Within Our Gates*, Oscar Micheaux produced an entry point for the New Negro contribution to the burgeoning sex-race marketplace of perceptions, representations, and fantasies about blackness, race, and racialized bodies. The film was banned in several cities across the nation, especially in the South, and it was unpopular with many white and black audiences where it was shown, perhaps because it was rife with themes of racial and sexual oppression, readily depicted the violence necessary to maintain white supremacy, and was intended, according to its advertisements, to "make [viewers] grit [their] teeth in deepest indignation."[10] The film served as an undeniably militant opening to the cultural productions and politics of the New Negro era, and it encapsulates the particular contentions around gender, race, and sexuality that the New Negroes asserted in the course of the 1920s.

A popular production surrounded by controversy and protest, *Within Our Gates* exemplified the emergence of the New Negro. The film's release marks a moment in which African Americans began to dare to speak out in newly militant, demanding voices against the white supremacist bigotry and violence oppressing them. Through film and a multitude of other media, New Negroes began in this period not only to counter white supremacist assumptions but also to achieve the successful distribution and acceptance of new perceptions of black and white character, the nature of oppression, and national destiny. From that moment on, the oppressed would have a greater role in the formation of racial discourse and their own cultural representations. Although that increased power would be continuously and sometimes violently disputed, it would gain strength, clarity, and increasing adherents. In this way, *Within Our Gates* represents popular New Negro Renaissance art, serving notice of black people's determination to participate in the formulation of the nation's racial discourse.

Oscar Micheaux was a child of the Midwestern great plains. Born in 1884 to former slaves in Metropolis, Illinois and one of eleven children, he was ironically a fiercely independent loner. A failed South Dakota homesteader turned self-published novelist by 1918, Micheaux began his filmmaking career on impulse. Once prompted, he immediately recognized the potential of the genre as a means to further assert his particular perspective on race politics. Micheaux's prompt came from black filmmaker George P. Johnson of the Lincoln Motion Picture Company. Johnson had read Micheaux's novel *The Homesteader* and wrote to Micheaux inquiring about obtaining the rights to produce it as a feature film. Johnson advised, however, that he would need to work with Micheaux to excise the question of interracial marriage from the plot as he considered such a theme too controversial to suit the white theater owners and audiences he sought to court. Rather than flattered or thrilled by this offer, Micheaux was skeptical and stated several stipulations, including that his novel be made into a lengthy six-reel epic rather than the typical three-reel feature and that the interracial theme be retained. As Micheaux and Johnson continued to correspond and

Johnson attempted to impress Micheaux with his greater experience, Micheaux managed to cajole from Johnson many details about the business of filmmaking and distribution. In the end, Micheaux declined to work with Johnson and declared his intention to make his novel into a film himself. He promptly incorporated a new organization, the Micheaux Book & Film Company, and began seeking investors. Thus began the career of the New Negro era's most prolific, independent, and controversial filmmaker. Beginning with *The Homesteader* (1919), which turned out to be eight reels long, Micheaux wrote, produced, and directed thirty-seven films in the interwar period.[11]*Within Our Gates*, one of only three extant Micheaux silent films, is an example of his best and most racially provocative work.

In advertisements, *Within Our Gates* was repeatedly described as "A Story of the Race with an All-Star Colored Cast featuring Evelyn Preer and other capable artists" (see Figures 1.1 and 1.2). Preer was indisputably the premier artist of the film. From her work in Micheaux's previous popular film *The Homesteader* as well as her prior experience as a vaudeville performer, Preer was already well known to black audiences. Micheaux and his network of distributors used her name and, more important, her face to draw the crowds to this "masterpiece" of a "preachment against race prejudice."[12]

Because Sylvia Landry is the leading character and the plot follows her fortunes and fate, *Within Our Gates* might be said to be a story about the New Negro woman. Indeed, when distributed in Spain some time in the 1920s, it was retitled *La Negra*, or "The Negro Woman."[13] Viewers followed Sylvia from the home of her cousin in the North to her position as a teacher at the Piney Woods School in the South, back to the North where she mounted a fund-raising bid to save the school and met her hero Dr. Vivian and, finally, into flashbacks depicting Sylvia's family history where they encountered horrific scenes of lynching and rape, scenes that continued to terrorize Sylvia in the film's present and shape her character. However, the resolution of Sylvia's story, which is of course accomplished through her marriage, is not ultimately the point of *Within Our Gates*. Instead, the film uses her narrative to prescribe education and the ascension of a black patriarchy as means to advance the race. Along the way, Sylvia is demoted from race leader teaching and fund-raising in the tradition of the women of the Reconstruction generation to race mother serving as "tender wife" to her New Negro husband. Rather than to tell a story of the New Negro woman, then, the larger point of the film was to announce the arrival of the New Negro—a modern type of black man ready and willing to lead the race out of degradation—and a new order of African American gender relations to accommodate him.

Figure 1.1 Typical advertisement for *Within Our Gates*. The *Chicago Defender* simultaneously advertised the film's appearance at various theaters in separate cities. *Chicago Defender*, 31 January 1920, 8. Reprinted by permission of ProQuest, LLC and The Chicago Defender Newspaper.

Micheaux produced *Within Our Gates* in the midst of a fundamental, gendered transition in anti-lynching ideology. This emphatically political and propagandistic filmic story of race relations and lynching marks a transition from the activist ideology and strategy of the older generation of racial spokeswomen and volunteer community organizers who had formed the National Association of Colored Women (NACW) to the younger set of federal lobbyists, mass leaders, and professional social workers exemplified by the activists of the National Association for the Advancement of Colored People (NAACP) and the National Urban League (NUL). This younger generation of men reformulated the African American racial advancement rhetoric and anti-lynching strategies that had been initiated by Ida B. Wells in the early 1890s and that had been first supported by

Figure 1.2 Advertisement for *Within Our Gates* featuring Evelyn Preer. *Chicago Defender,* 31 January 1920, 8. Reprinted by permission of ProQuest, LLC and The Chicago Defender Newspaper.

the NACW. Drawing upon the older generation's woman-centered ideologies for its depictions of lynching and its sentimental, romantic themes, the film nevertheless presaged the masculinist, law-and-order concept of antilynching the new generation would emphasize.

Within Our Gates was released just after the U.S. victory in World War I had devolved into the violently racist urban riots of the Red Summer of 1919. Lashing out against signs of black economic advancement and competition as well as the sight of returning black soldiers in uniform, white men and women had taken to the streets in Charleston, South Carolina; Longview, Texas; Washington, D.C.; Chicago; and other cities, beating black men and women with fists, bricks, and other objects, shooting guns, and setting fire to their homes. Undaunted, the black victims of these attacks had defended themselves, vigorously fighting back, returning gunfire, and seeking to protect their families, homes, and property.[14] This new fighting spirit, engendered in men and women who had braved the battle fields of Europe and summoned the bold courage to leave familiar rural homes for the uncertainties of city life, declared the arrival of the New Negro, a savvy, spirited individual unwilling to bow easily to the demands of white supremacy.

With his second film, Micheaux captured the spirit of this new African American personality and displayed it on the big screen in idealized, bourgeois, venerable male and female forms. Micheaux's ideal New Negro man and woman were fixed paragons unassailable by the temptations of urban life and protected by their "intelligence" from the worst ravages of racial oppression. With these paragons, Micheaux intended to counter the unrelenting stereotypes proffered as black characters in Hollywood films and popular theater and to provide images African American audiences might venerate and emulate. Although Micheaux succeeded in capturing the spirit of his race in this initial era of migration, urbanization, and burgeoning political agitation, his film was unevenly received by the population whose experience it purported to reflect. Perhaps "8000 feet of sensational realism" was too much reality to serve as a satisfying evening's entertainment.

Micheaux's film heralded the emergence of the New Negro ethos, one that emboldened black men to directly confront white supremacy and fearlessly lead the way forward to racial advancement. Like the New Negroes who battled whites in the new form of racist terror, the urban race riot, and the men in Claude McKay's poem who pledged to die "pressed to the wall . . . but fighting back," Micheaux dared to confront and confound white supremacist truth.[15]

"THE MOST SENSATIONAL STORY ON THE RACE QUESTION SINCE UNCLE TOM'S CABIN"

Within Our Gates has long been celebrated as Micheaux's militant and timely reply to the immensely popular and rabidly white supremacist D. W. Griffith production The Birth of a Nation. The black filmmaker sought to provide a filmic representation of both the reality of African American life under racism and the truth of white supremacy and race relations in the United

States. Micheaux's depictions of rape and lynching, which detailed white brutality against African Americans, reversed the images of brutal black rapists attacking innocent white girls that justified the ravages of the Ku Klux Klan so vividly illustrated in Griffith's film. Indeed, the depictions of race relations and African American character in *The Birth of a Nation* had proved foundational to mainstream U.S. cinema. The 1915 film "constitutes the grammar book for Hollywood's representation of Black manhood and womanhood, its obsession with miscegenation, and its fixing of Black people within certain spaces, such as kitchens, and into certain supporting roles, such as criminals, on the screen." The genre of "race films," of which Oscar Micheaux's second feature is one of the earliest and best examples, was developed in direct contradistinction to these representations and suffused with the effort to overcome Hollywood's racism.[16]

Micheaux's audiences appreciated *Within Our Gates* as an answer to the horrifically popular Reconstruction drama presented as national history in *The Birth of a Nation*. One viewer observed that while "*The Birth of a Nation* was written by oppressors, to show that the oppressed were a burden and a drawback to the nation, that they had no real grievance, but ... [that] they were as roving Huns seeking whom they might devour, *Within Our Gates* is written by the oppressed and shows in a mild way the degree and kind of his oppression." The same viewer further observed that for all the controversy surrounding it, the film "only mildly portray[s] southern treachery and villainy" but is nevertheless "a quivering tongue of fire" and "constitutes a favorable argument against southern mobocracy, peonage and concubinage."[17] *Within Our Gates* was indeed considered a protest film against the realities of lynching, the economic oppression of black agricultural laborers, and the sexual exploitation of black women. Another reviewer proclaimed, "There is nothing in the picture but what is true and lawfully legitimate."[18] "This is an attraction that everyone should see," announced another reviewer, "The story deals with Negro life as we find it at the present day."[19] Yet another defended the film against disapproving censor boards by stating "The new picture deals with the present unrest of the races in America, showing things as they exist, and suggests a remedy."[20] Not only was Micheaux praised for portraying the actuality of the black experience under white supremacy but he was also lauded for prescribing a solution to the ills plaguing the race. Ultimately, it was acknowledged by reviewers to be a film, in the words of the Associated Negro Press, "calculated to arouse public sentiment against injustices, as 'Uncle Tom's Cabin' aroused public sentiment against the evils of slavery."[21]

Within Our Gates was immensely controversial, banned in many places and sometimes adamantly disliked, but the controversy seems only to have fueled the interest of the public, for large audiences greeted it almost everywhere it was shown. Micheaux had a great deal of trouble obtaining censors' approval to show this film, and he may have edited it several times to suit various audiences and the censor boards of multiple locales.[22] The film's premier in November 1919 in Chicago was received with shock and scorn by the city's censor board, and it "was at first turned down flat." However, Micheaux was able to induce the censor board to screen his masterpiece a second time and stocked the audience with "a number of prominent people" who would "express opinions on the possible effect that would be had on public sentiment." The Associated Negro Press reported that many in this second audience feared the film would incite "another 'race riot'" like the one that had ravaged the city the previous summer. However, "those who reasoned with the knowledge of existing conditions, the injustices of the times, the lynchings and handicaps of ignorance, determined that the time is ripe to bring the lesson to the front" of public consciousness, and "a permit was finally granted." The controversy was not yet over, though. Several of those who had wished to deny the permit "got busy among the churches" and organized protests "from those within the Race" against the film which were "carried on until the hour of the opening of the theater" for the first public showing. However, the protestors, who also sent white and black representatives from the Methodist Episcopal Ministers' Alliance to plead their case with the mayor and the chief of police, acted to no avail. *Within Our Gates* played its entire week-long engagement in Chicago, "and people [were] standing in the streets for hours waiting for an opportunity to get inside" the theater to see it.[23]

The New Orleans superintendent of police, Frank T. Monney, also objected to the racially explicit film and worked to ban it in his city. His captain, Theodore Ray, reported that, per Monney's instructions, he had "advised" two successive managers of the Temple Theatre in that city "to discontinue showing the picture 'Within Our Gates' owing to the race condition as [it] existed at that time." His discussion with the second manager of the theater, "Mr. Hammond, white man," who had described the film as "demonstrating the treatment during slavery times with which the negroes [sic] were treated by their masters," led Ray to conclude along with his superintendent that "it is a very dangerous picture to show in the South."[24]

However, theater owners in major Southern cities did manage to show the film. It played for short engagements of two to three days—a week at the most—in Chattanooga, Tennessee; Columbus, Georgia; Mobile, Alabama; and New Orleans. It also played throughout the Midwest in Sioux City, Iowa; Detroit, Michigan; and Omaha, Nebraska.[25] By playing the film for brief periods and advertising in New Negro weeklies with national audiences like the *Chicago Defender* rather than local papers, the theater owners and managers perhaps avoided the reprisals of disapproving local officials while satisfying the surrounding black communities' appetite for a viewing of this infamous production.

In this way, *Within Our Gates* was seen by a multitude of audiences not only in the New Negro hotspots of New York and Chicago but also in the various cities and towns across the nation to which African Americans had migrated. Although it was often seen, however, it was not always enjoyed. The controversy surrounding the film drew crowds to its initial engagements, but it was too realistic to suit some people. "The Public [*sic*] does not like the Race propaganda regarding lynching, especially here, as it is too realistic of what happened here in the city last year," advised Micheaux's distributor in Omaha, Nebraska.[26] The film was too reminiscent of the Red Summer's racial terrorism to suit viewer's desires for lighthearted entertainment. So decided were some viewers' objections that "quite a few walked out."[27] Audiences in other cities may not have reacted so vehemently, but it seems clear that *Within Our Gates* stirred the blood of its audiences, its faithfulness to their experiences perhaps cutting too close to the bone.

Micheaux remained unperturbed. "It is true," he commented in response, "that our people do not care[,] nor the other race for that matter, for propaganda as much as they do for all story. I discovered that the first night The Gates was shown. Still, I favor a strong story at all times, since I believe that every story should leave an impression." He went on to discuss the promotion of his next film, *The Brute*, and his upcoming national tour to promote both films. "I am going to New York," he stated. "I expect to bring back some fat contracts, having been working this up on the Gates which met with great approval down there, so expect to compel [*sic*] all to pay off handsomely."[28] Although detested in Omaha, *Within Our Gates* was apparently a great success in New York City. Building on that success and all but ignoring the objections of the fainthearted and squeamish, Micheaux was evidently determined to continue producing and promoting his films and "strong stories" his way.

The objections to *Within Our Gates* centered on its ready depictions of the "truth" of the violence perpetrated against African Americans by white people. *The Birth of a Nation* had been heralded as a historic epic for its gory images of African American brutes attacking struggling white Southerners and those whites' rightful, justified retribution. By contrast, Micheaux's reversal of these themes, his revelation of white brutality in the service of ongoing white political and economic dominance and the admirable struggle of African Americans to survive and improve themselves under these conditions, was a disgrace to be hushed up, a dangerous spectacle to be shut down. In challenging established racial discourses and asserting a new truth of racial power and relations, *Within Our Gates* surely threatened the white supremacist status quo.

The following three sections analyze the cultural and political implications of this groundbreaking film and New Negro anti-lynching politics. The first section turns to the gendered themes apparent in "the story," as Micheaux termed the romantic plot, while the second addresses the anti-lynching praxes Micheaux marshaled as he used this film to disseminate racial advancement "propaganda." The third section analyzes the changing anti-lynching politics surrounding the film as the work of racial advocacy transitioned from the women-led volunteer activism of the NACW to the masculinist, professional efforts of the NAACP.

THE STORY: SYLVIA LANDRY AND THE
ARRIVAL OF THE NEW NEGRO

In the midst of all of the controversy over the realistic depiction of racial violence and white supremacy and the formulation of a modern anti-lynching strategy, only one reviewer of *Within Our Gates* mentioned, seemingly as an afterthought, that "a beautiful romance is carried throughout the picture."[29] An example of black cinematic realism depicting the "truth" of contemporary race relations, *Within Our Gates* was also a melodramatic romance featuring Evelyn Preer as its star attraction. Alongside the headlines pitching sensationalism and promising indignation, her photograph—a headshot emphasizing her light skin and femininity—graced all but the tiniest of the advertisements for the film (see Figure 1.1). Her beauty and popularity served to temper the shock and emotional disturbance the headlines announced the film would induce. Readers of the film's advertisements in periodicals like the *Chicago Defender* were invited to see a film that not only told about the ravages of racism but that also related the story of this attractive, compelling woman. Potential viewers might be compelled to endure the emotional difficulty of watching the film in order to understand her story. Perhaps they were even inspired to survive the physical and psychological effects of racist terrorism as her character would do in the course of the film.

Micheaux's depictions of African American character and life were as significant an aspect of his vision as his pointed political statements. His heroine, Sylvia Landry, and her leading man, Dr. V. Vivian (played by Charles D. Lucas), are educated, genteel, extremely attractive and very light-skinned people whose ambitions focus squarely on contributing to racial uplift. Such characters themselves defied the degraded depictions of African Americans, often actually white actors in blackface paint, advanced in popular film and theater.

When Sylvia Landry is introduced, busily scribbling at a desk in a well-appointed middle-class parlor, she is quite explicitly described as a quintessential New Negro woman, "typical of the intelligent Negro of our times."[30] To signify her purity of heart and status as the film's heroine, she always wears white, except when very stylishly turned out in a tasseled traveling dress, fur stole, and modish wide-brimmed hat for her meetings and fund-raising engagements. The first section of the plot is set forth in the North where "the prejudices and hatreds of the South do not exist—though this does not prevent the occasional lynching of a Negro." With this intertitle, Micheaux foretells the revelations of Sylvia's tragic family history that will constitute his political message against lynching and racial oppression in both their Northern and Southern manifestations. Through the misadventures of this typical, educated African American heroine, *Within Our Gates* explores and displays the plethora of circumstances, moral failings, and violent prejudices besetting African Americans and retarding their progress as a people.

As the film opens, we learn that Sylvia is writing a reply to a letter from her fiancé Conrad Drebert who is living in Canada. Sylvia is visiting in the home of "her northern cousin," Alma Prichard who, we soon learn, is a divorcee anxious to "give marriage another try" by stealing Conrad away from Sylvia. Alma wears black, signifying her immorality, willingness to betray her cousin, and polar opposition to Sylvia. Alma's gambling and murdering stepbrother, Larry Prichard, who desires Sylvia, schemes with Alma to separate the worthy couple, going so far as to woo Sylvia despite his knowledge of her engagement. Subsequently, Conrad arrives at Alma's house to find Sylvia in the embrace of an unknown white man. Although she is clearly trying to escape the stranger's grasp and to decline whatever offer he appears to be making, Conrad assumes the worst. In a rage, he chokes Sylvia and throws her to the floor, storms out, and refuses to hear her explanation. Thus, at the outset of the film, we find the romance and laudable intentions of "intelligent" African Americans thwarted not only by the scheming selfishness of immoral family members but principally by the presumption that a black woman found in the embrace of a white man must be guilty of having an illicit sexual relationship with him and of being a lascivious character. Even in the minds of black men, the film shows, black women are presumed to be dishonorable.

In the course of the plot, Sylvia returns to the rural South, a place "far from all civilization . . . where ignorance and the lynch law reign supreme," and finds work as a teacher at the Piney Woods School, to which poor black Southern farmers flock in droves. They come "so's [their] children c'n get schoolin' 'n' be useful to society." Although providing an essential service desired by the surrounding population, the school soon runs out of funds and plans to close. After hearing this, Sylvia spends a sleepless night "think[ing] of nothing but the eternal struggle of her race and how she could uplift it" and arises with the determination to go north to raise the funds necessary to save the school. "It is my duty and the duty of each member of our race to help destroy ignorance and superstition," she informs her employer, the venerable Reverend Wilson Jacobs. Thus fortified with the mission of racial uplift, Sylvia travels to Boston where she intends to solicit funds from liberal-minded, wealthy white people.

In Boston, Sylvia finds salvation for both herself and her school. Robbed upon her arrival by the loafing black man from whom she had asked assistance, Sylvia is rescued and her purse returned by Dr. V. Vivian, a race man as "passionately engaged in social questions" as Sylvia. Before witnessing the theft, he is pictured in an office studying the race question—in the form of an article on the federal government's responsibility to provide funds for colored schools—at his rolltop desk. The two are instantly attracted to one another, and a second scene in Dr. Vivian's office shows Sylvia flirting prettily as she plays with his stethoscope and other articles she finds there.

However, Sylvia is not so easily distracted from her task and soon identifies a possible benefactor in Mrs. Elena Warwick, a wealthy white woman, who pledges to do all she can to save the school. Unfortunately, Mrs. Warwick is nearly dissuaded from her laudable intention to give the Piney Woods School $5,000 by her Southern racist and anti-suffragist friend, Mrs. Geraldine Stratton. Rather than support the school, Mrs. Stratton urges Mrs. Warwick to give $100 to her favorite black preacher, Old Ned, who "will do more to keep Negroes in their place than all your schools put together."[31]

At this point, the film cuts to a depiction of the preacher Old Ned himself. Besides the inflammatory lynching scenes shown later in the film, these portrayals of black clergymen through the folly of Old Ned were the most objectionable to black audiences and white censor boards, North and South. In his sermons, Old Ned rails against black efforts to gain education and start independent businesses, admonishing his flock that "the vices and sins of the white folk will end them up in Hell. When the Judgment Day comes, more Negroes than whites will rise up to Heaven" because white people have more sinful sophisticated knowledge than black people and use it to make more money. Beyond this, he is quite plainly a fool and the servant of white men who pay him for his services in maintaining the racial status quo. After paying him his pittance, they jokingly kick him in the butt and ridicule him as he obligingly dances a jig for their entertainment. The existence of leeches like Old Ned, who live off poor black people while working to help maintain their oppression, is as much of an impediment to Sylvia's mission as Mrs. Stratton's influential racism. However, despite Mrs. Stratton's efforts, Mrs. Warwick maintains her conviction of the worthiness of the Piney Woods School and gives Sylvia an incredible $50,000 to save it.

All is not yet well for Sylvia, however. She returns to teaching only to find her criminal suitor Larry Prichard pursuing her once again. This time, he threatens to tell her friends and employers at the school of her shameful past if she refuses him. Rather than either marry a criminal or stay to be humiliated, Sylvia flees the Piney Woods in the night. Meanwhile, her hero Dr. Vivian has sought her at her cousin Alma's home. Suffering from a guilty conscience, Alma confesses her role in driving away Sylvia's fiancé and goes on to relate her cousin's whole history. In a series of flashbacks, we finally witness the revelation of the closely guarded secrets that have dogged Sylvia since the film opened.

In a twist of fate common to the "race melodrama" genre of which *Within Our Gates* is a part, it turns out that the Landrys are not Sylvia's real family at all.[32] Rather, Jasper Landry and his wife, whose deaths by lynching we witness in the flashbacks, are merely her adoptive parents. Sylvia happens to escape the lynch mob because she slips out of the family's hiding place in the woods and back to their home to refresh their provisions. While gathering food and supplies, she is attacked by a white man who would have raped her had she not fought valiantly and had the attacker failed to notice a mark on her breast. Inexplicably, he desists and slinks away in mortification. It turns out that this white man, Armand Gridlestone, is Sylvia's real father, who knowingly married a black woman in defiance of racial mores. He is the same white man whose unwanted embrace so enraged Sylvia's former fiancé Conrad at the beginning of the film. Although innocent of any wrongdoing and the daughter of a legitimate marriage, Sylvia is apparently so shamed by these facts that she flees the Piney Woods School, a place she had worked diligently to preserve, rather than suffer their revelation. Perhaps Conrad's hasty, lascivious assumptions and violent reaction taught Sylvia to dread the disclosure of her history. Perhaps she blames herself, her womanhood, or her mixed racial heritage for the violence she has suffered at the hands of men. Perhaps she understands that the victims of sexual violence, especially if women of color, are usually presumed to have been at least partially responsible for the acts perpetrated against them. Sylvia assumes that she is somehow wrong and that her friends and colleagues will judge her unfavorably.

The precise source of Sylvia's profound shame remains unclear. And the words Dr. Vivian speaks to her, which he seems to intend to assuage her pain, are just as ambiguous. Apparently having found one another again, Dr. Vivian and Sylvia sit together and talk over the personal history he has just learned. Dr. Vivian embraces Sylvia, caresses her, and pats her hand.

Yet, the intertitles seem strangely incongruous with these actions. "Be proud of our country, Sylvia," he admonishes her. "We should never forget what our people did in Cuba under Roosevelt's command." He goes on to list battles from the Spanish-American War and World War I in which black men fought. He emphasizes that African Americans "were never immigrants" and again urges her to "be proud of our country, always!" He tells her he knows she "has been thinking deeply about this" but that her thoughts "have been warped." He goes on to say, "In spite of your misfortunes, you will always be a patriot—and a tender wife." With this patriotic proposal, Dr. Vivian apparently wins Sylvia's hand in marriage. The film closes with a scene of the couple embracing as they walk to a lighted window in a well-appointed bourgeois parlor. The final intertitle reads, "And a little while later we see that Sylvia understood that perhaps Dr. Vivian was right after all." Together, they look out the window and turn to one another, intertwine their hands, and smile. With Sylvia's marriage to this right-thinking, progressive man, the poor, shamed orphan has found a worthy place in the world, and her story concludes. The screen goes dark.

On the surface then, Micheaux's "masterpiece" can be viewed as a politically provocative, but ultimately simple love story happily concluding as expected with the marriage of the troubled heroine. However, a few questions remain. Why is the doctor's speech emphasizing black men's heroism in military service a fitting conclusion to a story about the New Negro woman, as *Within Our Gates* might be considered to be? And why would such a speech double as a marriage proposal? Dr. Vivian's final speech and odd proposal provide a profound comment on the contemporary emergence of the New Negro era and modern African American gender relations. Although the plot of *Within Our Gates* is driven by the story of a quintessential New Negro woman, and its melodrama is based on the revelation of her woeful past, the themes of the film center on the character and abilities of New Negro manhood.

All of Sylvia's decisions and actions are motivated by the needs, demands, or aspirations of the black men surrounding her.[33] When we first meet her, she is dreaming of marriage to Conrad, but this dream is thwarted when he beats and strangles her and refuses to hear her explanation of her apparent betrayal of him with Armand Gridlestone, her real father. Because of this disappointment, she flees to the South where she dedicates herself to Reverend Wilson Jacobs's Piney Woods School. When the school's future is endangered, she determines to raise the funds necessary to continue its mission of uplift out of her newfound sense of duty to her people. Sylvia's people, the race as a whole, are represented by a black man, the lone father who brings his children to the school to receive an education. Thus the black race whose cause inspires Sylvia is masculinized. In Boston, the existence of black men like the dishonest preacher Old Ned, who actively subverts racial progress and is rewarded by white racists for doing so, nearly thwarts Sylvia's one chance to succeed in her fund-raising effort. Once the school has been saved and she has returned to her work there, Sylvia is again forced to act when the criminal Larry Prichard threatens to reveal her secrets if she refuses to marry him. In the flashback sequence, Jasper Landry's need for help in calculating his yearly earnings and his determination to request his rightful due from the planter Philip Gridlestone put him in the wrong place at the wrong time, while the servant Efrem's self-aggrandizing perfidy focuses the anger of the lynch mob on Landry's family and Sylvia with them. Sylvia is forever pleading with, assisting, running from, or otherwise reacting to a man whose forthright actions on his own behalf, whether right or wrong, work to forward her plot.

In this way, *Within Our Gates* is not about Sylvia at all. It is not a film about the New Negro woman. It neither works to explain her perspective on events nor celebrates her as a heroine on behalf of racial advancement and uplift. Indeed, Sylvia's subordination in marriage to the scrupulously honorable, educated, suave, dedicated race man Dr. Vivian—rather than any sort of revelation or liberation for her as an individual—is the culmination of the film. The film recommends the subordination and protection of black women in the properly patriarchal homes of educated, sophisticated, respectable black men as part of the solution to the race problems occurring "within our gates." Furthermore, the film celebrates the arrival of such New Negroes, in the form of Dr. Vivian, as a significant moment of hope for the future of the race.

In his speech concluding the film, Dr. Vivian emphasizes black men's ability and willingness to defend the nation as proven by their military heroism in the last two major wars, the SpanishAmerican War and World War I. The intertitles read, one after the other,

> Be proud of our country, Sylvia. We should never forget what our people did in Cuba under Roosevelt's command.
>
> And at Carrizal in Mexico.
>
> And later in France, from Bruges to Chateau-Thierry, from Saint-Michel to the Alps!

These words have been read as an assertion of black people's belonging to the U.S. nation-state.[34] "We were never immigrants," the doctor goes on to assert. In addition to its insistence on black citizenship rights, however, Dr. Vivian's speech also establishes a tradition of black men's capable participation in one of the seminal proving grounds of manhood—war. World War I in particular afforded "black people an opportunity to challenge pejorative conceptions of black masculinity, while at the same time upholding and vindicating the broader manhood of the race through the heroic valor of military service."[35] Although denied the vote and access to equal opportunities in education, business, and the other institutions supporting society, black men have been soldiers, brave warriors fighting and willing to die for their country. They not only belong to the nation-state, but, as worthy and capable men, have done battle in defense of its "gates." Thus, within those gates, they have earned the right to participate as equal men, equally qualified patriarchs.[36]

Sylvia is to be "proud of our country" because black men have taken the trouble to defend it. As the doctor pats Sylvia's hand and holds her close, he indicates that she is to take not only pride but also comfort from her knowledge of black men's warrior heroism. Capable of defending the nation, they are as capable of defending her. Dr. Vivian goes on to chide Sylvia. Although he knows she has "been thinking deeply about this," he asserts that her "thinking has been warped." She was wrong to feel compelled to flee from pillar to post in search of security; she was wrong to take the leadership and uplift of the race onto her shoulders; she was wrong to allow her horrific experiences of lynching and attempted rape to make her ashamed of her past and distrustful of father figures and potential husbands. Dr. Vivian is the antithesis of the other men in the film. Fools like Old Ned and Efrem, abusive, thoughtless men like Conrad, scheming criminals like Larry, and well-meaning but uneducated and thus vulnerable farmers like Jasper Landry—leeches, lackeys, brutes, and victims—are no longer representative of black manhood.[37] Modern black men are educated, gentlemanly, honorable New Negroes like Dr. Vivian, champions of the race. Dr. Vivian embodies the capable, principled, patriarchal New Negro his speech celebrates. There in the flesh, he is ready to take Sylvia into his arms and under the sheltering roof of his protection. The New Negro has arrived.

In addition to his gentlemanly patriarchal capabilities, this New Negro man also evinced a stalwart, determined, militant advocacy of African American racial advancement. Micheaux's early twentieth-century radicalism functioned by asserting that modern African American men were as worthy as their white counterparts of the rights and responsibilities of patriarchy and by insisting upon their consequent entitlement to an equal place within the victorious nation-state. Micheaux's version of racial militancy was common to the race leaders of the New Negro era. W. E. B. Du Bois expressed it in his editorial "Returning Soldiers." "This is the country to which we Soldiers of Democracy return," he wrote after describing the nation's failures in "lynching, disfranchisement, caste, brutality and devilish insult."

This is the fatherland for which we fought! But it is *our* fatherland. It was right for us to fight. The faults of *our* country are *our* faults. Under similar circumstances, we would fight again. But by the God of Heaven, we are cowards and jackasses if now that that war is over, we do not marshal every ounce of our brain and brawn to fight a sterner, longer, more unbending battle against the forces of hell in our own land.

We *return.*

We *return from fighting.*

We *return fighting.*

Make way for Democracy! We saved it in France, and by the Great Jehovah, we will save it in the United States of America, or know the reason why.[38]

Thus, a few months ahead of Micheaux, Du Bois, too, heralded the arrival of the New Negro and identified him with the new fighting spirit of the soldiers and the migrants. These sons of the "fatherland" were worthy patriarchs and therefore rightful heirs of the nation's civil and material wealth. Such New Negro militants waged a war for the honest and equal implementation of the nation's stated ideals of democracy and freedom.

With the arrival of the New Negro, always implicitly if not explicitly gendered male, the concomitant modern, intra-racial discourse of race motherhood emerged.[39] A principal tenet of race motherhood was the New Negro patriarchal mandate. This formulation dictated that black men win the economic opportunities, civic rights, and social potency that would enable them to act as patriarchs in their homes and in society. This achievement of patriarchal authority on the part of black men would advance the whole race as black women and children were protected and provided for by their husbands, fathers, and brothers. This new discourse of patriarchal gender ideals and a sexual politics based in masculinism and respectability is well expressed in the themes of the film. Indeed, we witness Sylvia's subordination to race motherhood in the final scenes. Dr. Vivian has not only healed Sylvia's wounds by reminding her of her reasons to take pride in her race and nation. He has also rather adamantly asserted that her gender and racial "thinking has been warped." As the couple gazes out of the window, presumably into a brighter future, the intertitles tell us that Sylvia eventually "understood that perhaps Dr. Vivian was right after all." Dr. Vivian, not Sylvia, is the right-thinker. He is the modern New Negro race leader who will extend the strength of his protection and escort Sylvia, and the race, into the better day glimpsed through the window.

The happy ending of this film does not reverse Micheaux's incisive political commentary nor negate the continuing savagery of lynching in favor of a facile, accommodationist patriotism, as some critics have asserted.[40] Neither does Micheaux advocate a woman-led mission of racial advancement through Sylvia as a representative New Negro woman.[41] Sylvia's struggles have been nearly too painful and arduous for her to bear. She has only narrowly escaped the major pitfalls of rape by a white man and a coerced marriage to an unworthy black man and many smaller dangers. Although intelligent, capable, and dedicated, she has been in constant need of a strong protector and is not suited for race leadership. Her future role will be to support Dr. Vivian's rightful leadership as his "tender wife." [42]

Thus, Sylvia's story culminates in her marriage to Dr. Vivian not simply because of romantic convention but more pointedly because his speech ushers in the New Negro—with the doctor as its paragon—and establishes the New Negro's ability to act as her protector and provider, subordinating her to a helpmate, race mothering role in both her personal life and her participation in racial advancement. Through Sylvia's adventures in *Within Our Gates*, we witness a microcosm of both the gender ideals of intra-racial relations and the gendered politics of racial advancement that would prevail in the New Negro era. Perhaps even more than Micheaux knew or intended, his "8,000 feet of sensational realism" was emblematic of his times. His rich, detailed depiction of lynching and the social world in which it happened, too, formed a portrait of the shifting and dangerous terrain the New Negroes navigated.

THE PROPAGANDA: "THE GLARING INJUSTICES PRACTICED UPON OUR PEOPLE"

Although the lynching sequence in *Within Our Gates* is a minor point in the plot and occurs within a flashback near the conclusion, the film was suffused with the national scandal of racialized violence.[43]Advertised as a timely story of race relations and their effects on African American lives, the film would hardly have been complete without some references to lynching. What is more, it emerged in the fall of 1919, just a few months after the travails of the Red Summer during which several major cities had exploded in race riots. Micheaux's film reflected the new fighting spirit, the will to fight back against racist attacks, whether mounted in the streets, in print, or on the screen.

Within Our Gates was primarily promoted, not through its melodramatic romance advancing themes of modern African American gender ideals, but through its realist comment on national race relations. The gendered themes of the plot and the controversial representation of lynching politics are intertwined but separately expressed, and the story of the film's characters and their experiences is distinct from the anti-lynching propaganda of the film, which proceeds along its own trajectory. The scenes displaying the heinous details of lynching—the capture and torture of the victims, the sexual nature of many of these tortures, and the ultimate barbaric desecration of the corpses—serve as the definitive climax of the propagandistic statement Micheaux sought to make. While relating the story of Sylvia's travails and travels, the film explores the contemporary racial politics of the nation North and South and, intertitle by intertitle, reveals the national system of economy, influence, white supremacy, and immorality that supported and justified lynching. It is this theme that most pointedly renders *Within Our Gates* an anti-lynching protest film, a militant manifestation of the New Negro ethos, and an intervention in the sex-race discourse emerging in these years.

In the film, Micheaux shows how lynching happened with impunity, not just on the spot and according to the circumstance of a particular case but as an integral aspect of the contemporary system of U.S. race relations, power, and economy. For him, "ignorance" and "superstition" were the mainstays of that system. He showed how these failings ultimately converged to create and justify heinous murders of black people. The first intertitle of the film, which appears before any of the other filmic images, introduces Micheaux's emphasis on lynching and simultaneously splits the nation into regions according to their relationship to black advancement and victimization. "At the opening of our drama, we find our characters in the North, where the prejudices and hatreds of the South do not exist—though this does not prevent the occasional lynching of a Negro," this first intertitle reads. Micheaux exhibits an ironic wit undermining the North's reputation for sober liberal-mindedness when he contradicts the assertion of the North's lack of prejudice with the recognition that lynchings occurred in Northern states every now and again. Although conditions may have been comparatively better in the North, no region was guiltless and therefore neither was the nation.

Already condemned as a region of "prejudices and hatreds" in the first intertitle, the South is later further described as a place "where ignorance and the lynch law reign supreme." Here, "the lynch law" is coupled with an "ignorance" identified with the region as a whole and said to "reign supreme" there. Indeed, as she departs to raise money for the Piney Woods School, Sylvia identifies the battle against ignorance as the primary objective of African American advancement efforts. "It is my duty and the duty of each member of our race to help destroy ignorance and superstition," she declares.

Having identified the black advancement struggle as a battle against ignorance through Sylvia's declaration, Micheaux uses a series of scenes in the middle of the film to detail an array of obstacles confronting the race and the means by which those obstacles converged to facilitate white supremacy and its extreme expression in lynch law. The powerful arm of Southern ignorance reaches Sylvia and retards her struggle even in the liberal bastion of Boston, locus of the antebellum anti-slavery movement. The

"rich Southerner passing through Boston," Mrs. Geraldine Stratton, represents the white upper-class version of her region's ignorance. She not only
opposes woman's suffrage "because it appalls her to think that Negro
women might vote" but when we first meet her is also shown nodding
approvingly while reading a newspaper article entitled "Law Proposed to
Strip Negroes of the Vote." When Mrs. Warwick naïvely requests her advice
as a Southerner, Mrs. Stratton adamantly opposes Mrs. Warwick's declared
intention of contributing money to the Piney Woods School. She insists
that "it is an error to try and educate" black people and furthermore that
"they don't want education" but instead desire "to belong to a dozen lodges,
consume religion without restraint, and, when they die, go straight up to
Heaven." Rich, white, and well respected, Mrs. Stratton has the power to influence the institutions of society and government. Through this character's
opinions and actions, Micheaux demonstrates how the funds and power
to improve and protect themselves were deflected out of African Americans'
hands. Mrs. Stratton nearly succeeds in dissuading Mrs. Warwick from contributing to the Piney Woods School.

To further illustrate the operation and ill effects of ignorance and superstition, Micheaux includes scenes featuring the preacher Old Ned, the
favorite of Mrs. Stratton whose sermons equate "schooling" with sin and
vice and ignorance with purity of soul. Old Ned takes bribes from white
men for his services in preaching such sermons, which work to maintain
the ignorance and behaviors confirming Mrs. Stratton's notions of foolish
black people who reject education outright and whose only ambitions are
lodge membership, church attendance, and entrance to heaven. In this way,
the influence of people like Mrs. Stratton is shown to reach even into
the self-conceptions of black people, creating a cycle of racial prejudice
and confirmation that discourages the respectful assistance of those, like
Mrs. Warwick, with the means to intervene and those, like Sylvia, with the
determination to uplift the race.

Micheaux was lambasted by black clergymen for his implication of their
participation in the maintenance of racial oppression, but these scenes from
Within Our Gates seem rather to point to the malevolence and pervasiveness of a white supremacist discourse that worked to oppress black people
and to justify their lowly status.[44] Every character in these scenes, except our
crusading heroine Sylvia and learned hero Dr. Vivian, is guilty of one form
of ignorance or another. Even Mrs. Warwick is ignorant or naïve enough to
ask Mrs. Stratton's advice and to trust her blatantly prejudiced assertions.
This is the system that fostered the ignorance and superstition that bred and
justified lynchings and kept black people vulnerable to the mob's assaults.

Thus, in *Within Our Gates*, education is not merely a noble cause of racial
advancement but the core of anti-lynching efforts. If the South was a region

ruled by lynch law because it was a land of ignorance and superstition, lynch law was to be eradicated through education. Sylvia, whose life has been so deeply affected by the lynching of her adoptive parents, struggles in behalf of a school endeavoring to educate poor, rural black Southerners. Dr. V. Vivian, so "passionately engaged in social questions," is studying articles about education, not lynching. According to the film's logic, it is education and the creation of a race of learned, sophisticated, determined men like Dr. Vivian—and worthy women like Sylvia to support him—that will free black people from the threat of lynching. This education will also eliminate the other effects of white supremacist-supported ignorance, such as poverty, criminality, and vice, which are exemplified by characters like the criminal Larry Prichard, the feckless Alma, and the foolish Efrem, whose stories seem tangential to the main plot but function to demonstrate this point.

As Micheaux is at pains to show us—displaying scenes of his characters hard at work reading and writing—both Dr. Vivian and Sylvia are "intelligent Negro[es] of today." This very intelligence, gained through the education the director advocates, was itself a challenge to the white supremacy African Americans endured. In fact, the lynching sequence in the flashback is set into motion by the revelation of Sylvia's intelligence. Having been sent away to school, Sylvia possesses the knowledge to correctly tally her stepfather's earnings for the year, and she thus helps him determine that he has earned enough to free himself from the cycle of debt that made tenant farming a new form of enslavement for the descendants of the freedmen and women.

Landlord Philip Gridlestone's personal servant, Efrem, freely reports the Landry's imminent success to his employer. Advising his mean-spirited boss that Sylvia Landry had been sent to school, he plants the idea that Gridlestone will no longer be able to "cheat" Jasper Landry because she keeps her father's books. Gridlestone then says "Just as I imagined it," and pictures Sylvia sitting with her family while Mrs. Landry tells her husband, "She is as educated as white girls now—so when you go pay the boss you tell him that." Gridlestone imagines that Sylvia and her family seek to best white people, that Sylvia, daring to compare her education to that of white girls, will denigrate the general superiority of white womanhood. For Gridlestone, Sylvia becomes a symbol of audacious black aspiration that threatens white supremacy by directly challenging the white monopoly on the ideal of feminine refinement. Gridlestone further imagines that Landry intends to gloat about these achievements and to embarrass him, to force him to acknowledge Sylvia's equality and thus his own failed posture of superiority. With this simple intertitle and scene, Micheaux details the gendered nature of the operation of white supremacy and an aspect of the impact of racism on black women.

However, the film reveals that "what they really said was: you should keep an account of all your purchases, sales, and debts so that when you go to the Gridlestone house you can take the accounts and settle without argument." The Landrys seek only to transact the business at hand in a rational manner and thereby achieve their small goals. This very ability, earned through education, to conduct business rationally, however, challenges Gridlestone's mastery. He cannot cheat as he is accustomed to do. He cannot win by default. He must earn and maintain his higher economic and social position through fair capitalist enterprise and competition. And, the thought whispers in the back of his mind, he might lose. Such a possibility, however remote, is insupportable. In this way, Micheaux not only details the gendered and sexual aspects of white supremacy but also the beginnings of white resentment of black economic advancement that so often built until culminating in a lynching or an urban race riot.

Gridlestone expresses his resentment and suspicion in rude and racist haughtiness. When Landry comes to settle accounts with him, the landowner replies, "You're gettin' mighty smart, eh? But I'm on to you. And remember that the white man makes the law in this country!" The drunk Gridlestone then pulls a revolver to demonstrate his point—as the lawmaking white man, he can kill Jasper Landry and any other black man at will. Landry grabs his hand in an effort to divert his shot. At the same time, a white man whom Gridlestone had offended appears at the opposite window, aims his shotgun, murders Gridlestone, and sneaks away without leaving a trace of his presence. Gridlestone falls to the floor dead, while Landry is left holding the revolver. The spying, perfidious Efrem concludes, "Landry done killed Gridlestone!" and proceeds to spread this false news throughout the town in an effort to aggrandize himself. Efrem runs from shop to shop in town urging his white neighbors to amass to capture the so-called murderer. The man who actually shot Gridlestone is an early member of the gathering lynch mob.

White women are also a prominent, active presence among the marauders. Through this unflattering depiction of white womanhood, Micheaux positions Sylvia as the only demure, polished, gentle "lady" in the flashback sequence and thus reverses the supposed gender politics surrounding lynching. The black woman and future victim is the lady whose honor is threatened, while the white women rampage along with white men in a thoroughly uncivilized manner. The director further emphasizes this reversal by leaving the question of whether black men rape white women out of the film entirely. Jasper Landry is not accused of raping a white woman but of "savagely" murdering Philip Gridlestone in cold blood for no reason. Rape is left entirely to white men as represented by Armand Gridlestone's attack on Sylvia later in the flashback. Far from delicate victims of rampant black lust needful of white men's belligerent protection through extralegal acts, white women appear in the lynching sequence as members of the lawless mob who are as brutal and bloodthirsty as their male counterparts.

Micheaux's reversal of the gender politics of white supremacy and his exploration of its effects on black women are extensive. He also includes a short sequence focusing on Mrs. Landry as she is hiding in the swamps with her fugitive family. He introduces the segment with the statement, "Meanwhile, in the depths of the forest, a woman, though a Negro, was a HUMAN BEING." Mrs. Landry is shown with her hair down sitting in their hidden camp under a makeshift tent looking sorrowful as she combs her hair and reads her Bible. She starts at some passage she finds there and exclaims, "Justice! Where are you? Answer me! How long? Great God almighty, HOW LONG?"

The next frame shows a proclamation written by "The Committee" advising that the citizens of Lawrence will bring the murderer Jasper Landry "to the place of execution" since he has been captured and has confessed to the crime of killing Philip Gridlestone. A crowd of white men, women, and children are shown to read the proclamation and respond with enthusiasm. Next is an intertitle reading simply "Sunday," suggesting that Southern white people are so immoral that they commit murder on the traditional Christian day of worship. In the next frame, the lynch mob, with clubs raised as weapons, descend, crazed, upon the Landrys, chasing them across a field. They throw Mrs. Landry to the ground and strip her to her underwear. Mr. Landry attempts to choke one of the men in retaliation for this dishonor but is pulled away by the other members of the mob. We then see the scaffold and nooses that have been prepared for the hanging. The mob takes hold of the Landrys, ripping young Emil from his mother's arms, and hangs nooses around their necks. In the confusion, Emil Landry escapes and rides away to safety on a stolen horse. We then see Mr. and Mrs. Landry standing under the scaffold, the nooses around their necks, and the members of the mob gathered around preparing to hoist them. We are not made to endure a depiction of the actual suspended bodies, however. Instead, Micheaux shows us the ropes moving over the crossbar of the scaffold and smoke wafting up from below, presumably from the burning of the bodies. The scene is nevertheless acutely graphic: the viewers' imaginations provide more horrific detail than Micheaux might have dared to supply. Indeed, his audiences might have drawn images of similar scenes from their memories rather than their imaginations.

Such masterfully suggestive scenes of the lynching of the Landrys are interspersed with scenes depicting Armand Gridlestone's attempted rape of Sylvia "that same afternoon." Micheaux tells us that "not satisfied with the poor victims incinerated in the bonfire, Gridlestone has come searching for

Sylvia." Scenes extracted from the lynching sequence—of the bodies being cut down from the scaffold, of white men preparing the bonfire that would later burn the Landrys, of the mob hunting the forest during the night with torches—punctuate the rape sequence, suggesting that Micheaux intended to equate the two acts as twin instances of violence working in tandem to maintain white supremacy.[45]

In fact, the coincidence of lynching and the rape of black women as forms of racist terror was almost always highlighted in traditional black anti-lynching arguments. This was the argument advanced by clubwoman and race leader Mary Church Terrell in her published articles decrying the injustice of vigilantism. First, Terrell challenges the pretext that lynchings are precipitated by rape, stating that "out of every 100 negroes [sic] who are lynched, from 75–85 are not even accused of this crime." Then she goes on to attack the racially oppressive presupposition that the call for racial social equality incites unruly black men to assault white women. "The alleged fear of social equality has always been used by the South to explain its unchristian treatment of the negro [sic] to excuse its many crimes." However, she points out, "the only form of social equality ever attempted between the two races, and practised [sic] to any considerable extent, is that which was originated by the white masters of slave women, and which is perpetuated by them and their descendants even unto the present day." She goes on to explain more explicitly that "throughout their entire period of bondage colored women were debauched by their masters. From the day they were liberated to the present time, prepossessing young colored girls have been considered the rightful prey of white gentleman in the South, and they have been protected neither by public sentiment nor by law. . . . White men are neither punished for invading [the negro's home] nor lynched for violating colored women and girls."[46] As Micheaux would do some fifteen years later, Terrell inverted the rape-lynch discourse, accusing white men of the brutality of systematic sexual assault on defenseless black women. Quickly dismissing the fiction of black men's rape of white women, Terrell identifies white men's rape of black women as a long-standing aspect of racist oppression both within slavery and beyond it. Not only were white people guilty of the brutality of lynching in Terrell's formulation but they also displaced their own heinous sexual behavior onto black people and violated the very ideals of veneration of womanly virtue and the sanctity of the home they claimed to defend. Drawing upon this tradition in African American anti-lynching ideology, Micheaux recreated this argument in vivid visual detail.

The rape sequence is perhaps more graphic than the lynching scenes because of the fervent interaction of the two characters. Sylvia fights valiantly—turning over chairs, climbing upon tables, pulling Gridlestone's hair and necktie, brandishing a knife she finds on the table—while he tears her hair from its tidy bun, leaving it to fall around her face in wild hanks, and rips away the bodice of her dress revealing her underclothes. Sylvia eventually tires, and Gridlestone finally overpowers her. His hand moves menacingly toward her breast, and it seems that he will molest her before violating her completely.

Suddenly, we are returned to Alma's parlor in the North and realize that she has explained all of these events to an intently listening Dr. Vivian. Alma concludes the story of Sylvia's near defilement, saying "A scar on her chest saved her because, once it was revealed" under Gridlestone's intent study of Sylvia's bosom, "Gridlestone knew that Sylvia was his daughter—his legitimate daughter from marriage to a woman of her race—who was later adopted by the Landrys." When the next scene returns us to the flashback, we witness Sylvia fainting away as Gridlestone finds the scar on her breast. We are then returned to the present to see Dr. Vivian rise from his seat and shake his fist in angry determination, and we next find him advising Sylvia to be proud of her country and to remember black soldiers' brave feats in battle "in Cuba under Roosevelt's command." The revelation that Sylvia suffered a sexual assault at the hands of a white man becomes an occasion for Dr. Vivian to celebrate black men's militaristic bravery and manly success. Micheaux has fully demonstrated the race's need for principled, educated, and brave New Negro patriarchal leadership.

Touting education as the means to redeem the race, Micheaux sought to educate the populace about the real reasons for lynching and the operation of racist oppression. As the original work of an aspiring race leader disseminating his opinions regarding the race's present and future through the newly popular technology of film, *Within Our Gates* itself might be described as a form of mass protest against lynching. The plot of the film works, in part, to display the egregious wrong of vigilante "justice." But beyond this, the concerted effort to win its approval by the multitude of local censor boards, particularly the first in Chicago—to win the right to publicize and popularize a New Negro point of view on white behavior not only in words but, more important, in stark, clear, emphatic images—struck a blow against the white supremacist monopoly on truth and information. Then, too, the participation of the audiences in viewing the film formed a kind of mass protest, a communal sharing and affirmation of their truth. Indeed, the film's reviewers called upon potential audiences' race pride and commitment to racial advancement when they urged their readers to the theaters. "This is an attraction everyone should see," wrote one reviewer.[47] Another advised, "People interested in the welfare of the Race cannot afford to miss seeing this great production."[48] Micheaux and the reviewers of his "masterpiece" called out the masses to bear witness to the white supremacist practices besieging them and the resulting vices retarding their progress. He called upon them to learn the remedy he prescribed—the emergence of the strong, capable, intelligent New Negro. Ultimately, he exemplified the ethos marking the arrival of the New Negro his film celebrated. In producing and successfully distributing *Within Our Gates*, Micheaux, like the migrants, like Du Bois, like Claude McKay, fought back against the forces of white supremacy.

WOMEN'S WORK NO LONGER

Micheaux's *Within Our Gates* exemplified not only the transitions in racial advancement strategies during the New Negro era but also the gendered elements of the modern racial discourses the New Negroes were helping to craft. As they sought to intervene in racial politics and shape more balanced representations of themselves in popular culture, New Negroes like Micheaux also articulated a set of gender ideals and intra-racial prescriptions that venerated patriarchy and required women's subordination to it both in their homes and in the work of advancing the race's interests. Just as Dr. Vivian silenced Sylvia—declaring her thinking "warped" even as he offered her the strength of his arm—so did the emergence of the New Negro in modern culture and politics, although hailed as a triumph and ushering in a new day of self-determinative agitation against white supremacy, work against the concomitant emergence of an independent New Negro womanhood.

When *Within Our Gates* premiered as a valiant critique of contemporary white supremacy in the fall of 1919, ushering in the era of the New Negro and a concomitant race motherhood discourse, the NAACP had already begun to reformulate anti-lynching strategies, participating in the construction of emergent racial discourses through political activism, lobbying, and revealing the violent foundations of white supremacy. Daringly, the organization sent undercover observers into local communities after especially noteworthy instances of vigilantism to conduct interviews, take photographs, and record information about the causes and "reasons" for lynchings and race riots and then publicized this information in the pages of *The Crisis*.[49] The publication of this information, designed to shame the locality and indeed the whole nation that permitted such atrocities, was akin to Ida B. Wells's early strategy of pamphlet distribution and the one the NACW had used from the 1890s forward. The women's organization passed resolutions against lynching at each of its national conventions, which served to rededicate the membership to anti-lynching work and uplift, and successive NACW presidents, beginning with Mary Church Terrell in the 1890s and continuing on to Mary B. Talbert in the 1920s, published articles denouncing the crime and explaining its complexities.

In the beginning of the struggle in the 1890s, black women incorporated anti-lynching into the women's work of racial uplift and imbued anti-lynching ideology with the Victorian black feminism they developed to support that work. The educated black women leaders who founded the NACW and were henceforth known as clubwomen adhered to the Victorian black feminist ideology of anti-lynching developed by Ida B. Wells as she furiously published pamphlets and engaged in a flurry of national and international speaking tours to denounce lynching.

Wells's discourse of anti-lynching recognized the crime as an act of terrorism perpetrated by white Southerners to maintain their economic and social dominance over African Americans. Although Southern white apologists insisted lynching was righteous punishment meted out for the sexual violation of women, Wells researched the facts and wrote polemics to refute this argument. She found that most victims of lynching were not even charged with committing rape and that women as well as men were victims of mob violence. Furthermore, she found that any sexual contact between black males and white females, consensual or not, was decried as rape and used to justify lynching as a defense of virtuous Southern womanhood. On the other hand, sexual contact between white males and black females, no matter how coerced or brutal, was never defined as rape and was never legally or extralegally punished as such. Thus, the assertion that lynching was a chivalrous and manly act of retribution for the sexual defilement of virtuous women was utterly false. When the women were black, they were not extended the chivalrous protection of Southern manhood. Rather, Southern manhood, black as well as white, enjoyed unfettered sexual access to black women.

Simultaneously, Wells wryly suggested, the steadily rising numbers of lynchings supposedly enacted to punish those who dared to sexually accost Southern white women began to call into question the virtue of those white ladies it claimed to defend. Was all of this interracial sex really to be understood as rape? In her own words, Wells leveled "a defense for the Afro-American Sampsons who suffer themselves to be betrayed by white Delilahs," or scheming women who lie with men in the night only to despise them in the morning.[50]

Through Ida B. Wells's incisive analysis, then, advocates of racial advancement came to accept that the accusation of black men's sexual contact with white women, which was always read as rape, was an excuse for the perpetuation and brutal expression of white supremacist oppression of all black people. They further understood that white Southerners' rhetoric about the chivalrous protection of women against brutal sexual attack was false because this protection did not extend to black girls and women. Men were neither expected to defend black women nor punished when they attacked black women. Beyond this, the explanation both for the failure to include black women in the chivalrous defense of Southern womanhood and for the assumption that all black men were potential rapists derived from the sexist and racist assertion that black women were sexually immoral, therefore had no honor to be defended, and were incapable of instilling morality and self-control in their children. Their daughters and sons, the racist logic asserted, thus inevitably grew up to be whores and rapists.[51]

The National Association of Colored Women and the Victorian black feminism practiced by the clubwomen were founded out of the necessity of defending black women from such sexist and racist conceptions as a means to refute the allegations that justified lynching. The clubwomen's anti-lynching discourse invariably included, not just the acknowledgment that black women suffered racial oppression and were often lynched alongside black men, but also the indictment of lynching as a crime of patriarchal white supremacist oppression that was based in and perpetuated deleterious assumptions about black women's sexuality and morality.

In speaking out against lynching according to her understanding of its sexist-racist origins, Wells sought to expose the brutal hypocrisy of Southern whites and turn national and international public opinion against them. Her actions aroused a storm of defensive protest on the part of U.S. whites. James Jacks, president of the Missouri Press Association, sought to denounce Wells and discredit her campaign by insisting that all black women were "prostitutes and natural liars and thieves."[52] Thus, Wells was not to be believed, and the justifications for white supremacy and lynching were reinforced. Jacks's explicit denunciations of their morality and denials of their ladyhood were circulated among educated black women. Mobilizing to refute the charges, the national community of educated black female leaders founded the National Association of Colored Women in 1896 with Mary Church Terrell as its first president.[53] Organized to demonstrate the falsity of Jacks's libelous words specifically and the sexist-racist understandings of black women that justified lynching and racial oppression generally, the NACW was literally founded as a result of Ida B. Wells's anti-lynching campaign.[54] Furthermore, the clubwomen imbued their ideology of racial uplift, including their anti-lynching discourse, with Victorian feminist understandings of the links between the uplift of black women and the advancement of all African Americans.

Clubwomen would not allow white racist apologists for lynching to presume all black men to be immoral potential rapists of white women without raising the issue of white men's immoral and non-chivalrous sexual access to black women. If it was true that lynchings occurred because African Americans lacked the moral sense to respect women, Terrell contemptuously stated, "the South has nobody to blame but itself" because it silently condoned the sexual harassment and assault of black women. Lynchings, she insisted, were not precipitated by rape but were "due to race hatred."[55] Terrell's unflinching pronouncements recognized lynching as a sexualized issue that equally, though distinctly, furthered the racial oppression of black women as well as men. Following Ida B. Wells's arguments, NACW club-women incorporated anti-lynching into their Victorian black feminist ide-ology of racial advancement and claimed the anti-lynching struggle as women's work.

As they evolved in the course of the 1910s and 1920s, the NAACP's arguments and strategies would come to differ substantially from those of the NACW, and the race's anti-lynching ideology in general would de-emphasize black women's central place in the rape-lynch discourse and thereby lose the incisive edge of turning the moral tables on the mob and its apologists. Instead of righteously and repeatedly inverting the rape-lynch discourse by emphasizing white men's sexual violation of black women, the NAACP developed a pragmatic law-and-order ideol-ogy of anti-lynching that called upon the power of the federal govern-ment rather than the moral outrage of the nation's citizens to halt the crime. Furthermore, the organization utilized the new urban masses of African Americans to display the strength and determination of African American protest against lynching. The 1917 Negro Silent Protest Parade in New York was the first mass street protest on behalf of African Ameri-can racial advancement, the first civil rights march. As part of the protest, NAACP leaders, including political activists James Weldon Johnson and W. E. B. Du Bois and entrepreneur Mme. C. J. Walker, "representing the colored people of New York and the sentiment of the people of Negro descent throughout the land," presented a "Petition re Lynching" to "The President and Congress of the United States." In it, they decried the lynching of "2,867 colored men and women" since 1886 and declared,

> We believe that this spirit of lawlessness is doing untold injury to our country and we submit that the record proves that the States are either unwilling or unable to put down lynching and mob violence.
>
> We ask, therefore, that lynching and mob violence be made a national crime punishable by the laws of the United States and that this be done by federal enactment, or if necessary, by constitutional amendment. We believe that there can be found in recent legislation abundant precedent for action of this sort, and whether this be true or not, no nation that seeks to fight the battles of civilization can afford to march in blood-smeared garments.[56]

In the midst of World War I, these daring activists insisted that a nation mighty enough to pledge to defend democracy and "civilization" overseas ought not to be so hypocritical and weak as to condone uncivilized lawlessness within its borders.

In the years following the release of *Within Our Gates*, the NAACP built further upon the growing urban populations of African Americans who could vote and whose small but growing disposable income might be used to aid the race's progress if directed in the right vein. Through the push to gain passage of the first of many federal anti-lynching bills, the organization raised its membership rolls and therefore its resources in cities across the nation.[57] Micheaux had displayed the horrors of white supremacy and incited the masses' ire. Now the NAACP would provide a useful outlet for their indignation. The organization lobbied both houses of Congress and the president of the United States to criminalize mob violence on the federal level and empower federal forces to investigate and prosecute offenders within the states. For the NAACP, interested in providing an expedient definition of the problem and identifying a pragmatic, workable solution, the convoluted crisis of lynching boiled down to a simple question of law and order.

The NACW, too, adopted this method. As the NAACP increasingly took the lead in the early 1920s, the elder women's organization, led by its president and NAACP board member Mary B. Talbert, sought to utilize its network and resources to support the struggle and formed a group committed to that purpose.[58] Working as an ad hoc committee uniting the efforts of the NAACP and the NACW, the Anti-Lynching Crusaders acknowledged, even emphasized, the fact that black women were also the victims of lynch mobs, but they did so to prove that rape was not the justifiable cause of lynching rather than to discuss black women's oppression. "Since 1889," they stated in their pamphlet, "eighty-three women are known to have been lynched." They provided the details of some of these crimes. Surely, black women could not have been lynched in retaliation for raping white women, they implied. The Crusaders publicized the murder of one black woman in particular, describing its especially heinous brutality. Mary Turner, who had "threatened to have members of the mob arrested" when they came for her husband, "was in the eighth month of pregnancy" when

> the mob of several hundred took her to a small stream, tied her ankles together and hung her on a tree downwards. Gasoline was thrown on her clothes and she was set on fire. One of the members of the mob took a knife and split her abdomen open so that the unborn child fell from her womb to the ground and the child's head was crushed under the heel of another member of the mob; Mary Turner's body was finally riddled with bullets.[59]

Such a horrible story was calculated to disturb the minds and open the hearts of potential allies among white women, thus exciting their moral and monetary support for the NAACP and its anti-lynching bill. With this strategy and the ultimate goal of the passage of a federal anti-lynching bill in mind, the Crusaders trod softly. They neither stridently accused white women of immoral, consensual sexual congress with black men as Wells had done, nor harangued white men and the whole of the white South for their sexual exploitation of black women as Terrell had done. Instead, they muted these arguments, letting the facts in the brief biographies they related and the statistics they provided speak for themselves. Such pragmatism was savvy and absolutely necessary if the Crusaders were to have any chance of winning the sympathy and support of their white counterparts. However, combined with the NAACP's law-and-order approach, their pragmatism began the process of obscuring the complexities of black women's stake in the crime of lynching and rendering obsolete and unintelligible the sophisticated anti-racist feminism of their arguments against it. Over the course of the decades to follow, lynching would come to be understood as a crime against black men and the free expression of their manhood—and continue to be misunderstood as a crime punishing black men's sexual interest in white women—while black women would disappear from the story altogether.

Through both its gendered story heralding the arrival of the valiant New Negro and its sensational propaganda exposing the structures of white supremacy and the sexualized injustice of lynching, *Within Our Gates* epitomized the race motherhood discourse that shaped intra-racial gender ideals and sexual politics throughout the 1920s. In defining the ideal New Negro woman as a race mother, a woman devoted to the race's interests, even to the exclusion of her own aspirations, this intra-racial discourse countered the images of servile mammies and selfish, over-sexed divas that were proliferating in the burgeoning sex-race marketplace. Rather than seek to lead the race as her foremothers in the Reconstruction generation had done, and rather than serve in white people's kitchens or expose herself to their fantasies in the glaring spotlight of the entertainment stage, the race mother of the New Negro era assisted New Negro patriarchal leadership in achieving the new day of black advancement and interracial harmony.

While Oscar Micheaux presented this ideal through the fictional exploits and ultimate marital protection of Sylvia Landry, New Negro activist-scholars E. Franklin Frazier and Charles S. Johnson, along with a cadre of social workers and other professionals, sought to recreate actual black women, workers, and mothers according to its parameters. Such women would not only submit to worthy black patriarchs but also devote their lives, work, and very bodies to the amelioration of the race's problems and the betterment of its children.

CHAPTER 2

❦

Mothering the Race

New Negro Progressivism and the
Work of Racial Advancement

In the first issue of the National Urban League publication *Opportunity: Journal of Negro Life*, social worker Edith Sampson related some of her experiences in assisting families to provide proper care for their children. She told the story of "Annabelle" who was raised as the only poor black child in her relatively affluent, integrated Chicago suburb. Annabelle was unable to make friends with the white and black children around her because they "had had the advantage of much more education and contact with the world. They went to parties, occasionally to the movies, had nice clothes and above all the constant supervision of their parents."[1] Lacking these advantages because her mother worked as a maid and her father was "trifling," Annabelle relied on her long-standing friendship with the white neighbor boy Joe. He "sympathized with her and urged her to place her confidence in him. Within a short time Annabelle suddenly realized that she was about to become a mother."

Annabelle's pregnancy became the object of a small dispute in the pages of the magazine. In continuing the narrative, Sampson related that Annabelle decided not to rely on her parents' help but instead moved to the city and went to work to support herself. As her pregnancy advanced, she "got in touch with the Child Placing Society" and requested their services in providing for her during her confinement and in caring for her child. "Finally a lovely baby arrived and Annabelle knew that the child would have to be given for adoption because Joe had turned from her and there was no chance of a marriage between them. . . . Although it was very attractive[,] Annabelle could not be persuaded to keep the child. She gave it to the Society for adoption."[2] Thus, twenty-year-old Annabelle decided she did not want to be a mother, at least not at that time in her life. But her decision worried some of the magazine's readers, and their comments demonstrate how the personal, life-shaping decisions of women like Annabelle fed the frenzied collection of preconception and anxiety, misinformation and fantasy forming the sex-race marketplace and the race motherhood imperative.

Students at the Atlanta School of Social Work, which E. Franklin Frazier directed, had used Sampson's reports of her case work as object lessons in their studies, and they wrote to *Opportunity* to share their opinion. In discussing her case, the students determined that "Annabelle was sinned against in several ways."[3] They felt that she was neglected by her community, which should have either assisted her father in becoming "less trifling" or granted her mother some reprieve so that she might have cared for her daughter more diligently. Of course, they also condemned Joe's treatment of her and questioned the stated respectability of his family. However, they particularly worried that Annabelle was apparently coerced into giving up her baby for adoption. They felt that

> the final unfortunate thing happening to this girl was the loss of her baby. The Child Placing Agency seems to have been lukewarm in its efforts to insist that she keep it, for we read:—"Finally a lovely baby arrived and Annabelle knew that the child *would have to be given for adoption* (Italics ours) for Joe had turned from her." How did Annabelle know that? And we question further, Was the baby placed in a boarding home without its mother? As Annabelle was a healthy mother[,] should she not have nursed the baby through its first year? Would she not have loved the baby and wished to keep it with her from the hour of its birth until she went home to her parents? Was her final refusal to keep the child based in any way upon the knowledge that the society would place it if she did not keep it?

The Atlanta School students could not imagine that Annabelle might not have been devoted to her baby. Apparently, they felt that the Child Placing Society ought to have "insisted" that she keep and raise her baby herself. Instead of noting the hard economic facts of Annabelle's life, these students appear to have been guided by romantic notions of ideal motherhood as they listed their objections. According to their own standards, however, Annabelle was herself neglected as a child, and she may not have had any suitable home to which to take her baby. Furthermore, these students attributed a great deal of supposedly instinctual motherly affection to this young woman when there was no reason to believe she felt any such emotion. Their comments evidence the contemporary presumption that motherhood was and ought to have been a paramount role for women and girls. They also assume that motherly love—ostensibly an emotion that sprang up spontaneously upon conception—ought to dictate the terms of women's decisions regardless of their circumstances.

Unlike the actress Evelyn Preer, who participated in the manipulation of her media image as an aspect of her professional work, Annabelle may never have even known she had become a public spectacle. Consciously or not, both women, like all New Negro women, lived within and understood themselves through the prevailing sexual and racial discourses of their time, which operated according to a particular, interwar mix of racism and sexism and New Negro efforts to advance the race. Whether Annabelle's decision was purposefully defiant or not, in flouting the prevailing dictates of racial unity and respectability she shows how powerfully race motherhood pervaded New Negro discourses. Ultimately, in the pages of *Opportunity*, Annabelle's story came to illustrate not the progressive liberation of a young, single mother or even primarily the triumph of a social worker's efforts but instead the magnitude of emphasis New Negro discourses placed on motherhood and the effort to reshape and control it.

As Oscar Micheaux produced films depicting the patriarchal New Negro as the race's future hero and James Weldon Johnson led the NAACP's efforts to promote a masculinist, law-and-order anti-lynching strategy that clouded black women's stake in the rape-lynch discourse that surrounded the issue, New Negro progressives worked diligently to disseminate a modern, rational analysis of the race problem and its solution. These New Negro progressives, including professional racial advocates, sociologists, psychologists, ministers, teachers, and a rising army of social workers, developed an approach that placed a premium on women's maternal roles in ideally patriarchal black families and communities and obfuscated the need for the redress of black women's particular oppression.

NEW NEGRO PROGRESSIVISM AND RACE MOTHERHOOD

As African American migrants descended upon Northern and Southern cities, the leaders and spokesmen among them reformulated racial advancement ideologies in recognition of their new urban, industrial circumstances. Within New Negro progressivism, the migrants' self-determinative efforts were partly, sometimes wholly, submerged. The New Negro progressives actively sought to subdue those impulses they found detrimental among individual migrants and to define a common racial self-determination to challenge white supremacy, reform African American morality and habits, and facilitate integration. New Negro progressivism combined the strategies of modern social science, industrial engineering, and social work with the politics of urban social improvement through professional advocacy, education, and training. This was a strategy focusing on the urban, economic issues of employment, working conditions, housing, health, and family structure.

The progressive strategy New Negroes promoted continued the fight against white supremacist terrorism and combated racial oppression through careful social scientific analysis of African Americans' Southern and Northern urban circumstances in housing, labor, and health and through practical, professional intervention to improve those circumstances. This ideology of racial advancement was the purview of social scientists, social workers, industrial educators, teachers, educated ministers, and the philanthropists who funded their organizations and projects. Together, these New Negro progressives aimed to demonstrate African American humanity and worthiness for full sociopolitical inclusion by documenting the effects of oppression. Rather than a backward race inherently unsuited to the exigencies of modern life and the responsibilities of political participation, African Americans were to be understood as the victims of historical and contemporary circumstances outside their control. If those unfavorable circumstances could be ameliorated and the race given the opportunity to overcome their consequences, African Americans would contribute worthwhile and unique cultural, economic, and social benefits to the nation.[4]

In many ways, this progressive version of New Negro racial advancement ideology constituted an evolution of the previous generation's uplift strategy. Leaders of the Reconstruction generation had founded volunteer clubs and associations through which they channeled funds, materials, and their own energies to raise their fellow African Americans to their ideal of bourgeois, genteel Christian morality and Victorian codes of conduct. The proponents of New Negro progressivism updated this strategy, insisting that this necessary work must be carried out by paid professionals with specialized training and using modern, scientific methods of analysis and intervention. Yet the younger generation retained their elders' conviction that the masses of African Americans were an ignorant, backward, pitiable lot much in need of the progressives' beneficent efforts to transform their lives, morals, and habits. This aspect of New Negro racial advancement exhibited a deeply entrenched class bias. In the progressives' view, the migrants were largely unready for full sociopolitical participation and incapable of self-determination.

New Negro progressives acted and wrote with an acute awareness of the stereotypes of African American laziness, immorality, vice, and contamination against which they labored. They were also conscious of the real and crippling poverty, disease, and lack of access to social institutions like regular schools and adequate health care most African Americans suffered, especially in the rural South. Consequently, much of their work came to focus on the family as the primary institution transmitting African American values and morality, forming the migrants' habits, and motivating their behaviors. The health, structure, and "organization" of the family were the subjects of countless articles in this period. In the course of this research and activism centered on the black family, New Negro progressivism participated in the development and dissemination of an intraracial discourse overwhelmingly binding black women's identities to motherhood. Whether they were mothers rearing their own children or childless women supporting themselves, black women were expected to devote the whole of their energies and talents to the betterment of the race's opportunities through the successful reproduction and training of the next generation.[5] They were, essentially, to mother the race.

As they drew upon and extended race motherhood, New Negro progressives sought to diagnose the reasons that black women failed to achieve the mothering ideal and went on to prescribe the best means of helping them reach it without reference to black women's prerogatives or recognition of their human complexity. Race motherhood worked to excise, belittle, and criticize the other aspects of black women's identities and daily lives as tragic, detrimental, or irresponsible. Seeking to overturn rather than buttress deprecating stereotypes, New Negro progressives refrained from openly criticizing African American women. Race motherhood was never explicitly stated in New Negro publications but was everywhere implied by the nearly absolute absence of commentary on black women's personal experiences and lives independent of black men or children and by the overwhelming coverage of infant mortality, children's health, child labor, and the progress of social work focusing on black families and children's education. When black women were the exclusive focus of an article or report, the theme was discussion of their employment circumstances, and the author inevitably bemoaned their inability to be good mothers as a result of the necessity that they work for pay outside of the home. Mention of black women in the rhetoric of New Negro progressivism almost always returned to their motherhood and by extension to the expectation of their selfless service to the race and their ideal subordination to strong, benevolent, capable black patriarchs.

As the previous chapter detailed, New Negroes in the arts and those working for racial advancement through other venues also evinced a masculinist discourse circumscribing women's opportunities and emphasizing motherhood. Race motherhood permeated the New Negro era. From Marcus Garvey's Universal Negro Improvement Association to A. Philip Randolph's Brotherhood of Sleeping Car Porters, New Negroes high and low sought to promote a black patriarchy relegating women to helpmate roles in the work of racial advancement and the rearing of the next generation.[6] More than a strategy for assimilation or a gender ideal, race motherhood encompassed identity, standards of respectability, sexual mores, and obligations of racial solidarity. Sharing in the discourses of their era, understanding themselves, and conceiving of racial advancement through those discourses, New Negro progressives acted as professional exponents of race motherhood.

During the 1920s, a rising army of New Negro professionals, largely women, disseminated the word of racial advancement through progressivism. Themselves imbued with the necessity and efficacy of race motherhood, this phalanx of social workers, nurses, and teachers enacted its precepts and enforced its tenets as they interacted with their clients, patients, and students.[7] In their racial advocacy work, these professional women were guided by social scientists like E. Franklin Frazier and Charles S. Johnson, whose scholarship and directorship of modern institutions like the Atlanta School of Social Work and the National Urban League's (NUL) *Opportunity* magazine made their voices particularly powerful. Even then, in the early stages of their illustrious careers, Frazier and Johnson were among the architects of New Negro progressivism and the concomitant discourse of race motherhood.

The remainder of this chapter explicates the progressive articulation of race motherhood discourse in two sections. The first section focuses on the racial and gender discourse Frazier professed in the scholarship he produced while working in Atlanta, teaching other New Negro scholars and professionals. The second section investigates the gender dynamics of the progressive racial advancement work New Negro social workers accomplished as they reported on their activities in the pages of *Opportunity* under Charles S. Johnson's editorship.

A NEW NEGRO ANALYSIS

In 1927, Frazier, having recently been relieved of his duties as the head of the Atlanta School of Social Work and professor at Morehouse College, published a radical, provocative article. "The Pathology of Race Prejudice" equated the irrational biases, petty etiquette, and terrorism required for the maintenance of white supremacy with a form of insanity plaguing the whole of the white South. Using the jargon of psychology and the rational methodologies of modern social science, Frazier diagnosed the white South as suffering a "Negro-complex" that had "the same intense emotional tone that characterizes insane complexes." "The behavior motivated by race prejudice," he argued, "shows precisely the same characteristics as that ascribed to insanity."[8] He proved his thesis with a series of examples comparing insane behavior with racist behavior. "Just as the lunatic seizes upon every fact to support his delusional system," he wrote, "the white man seizes myths and unfounded rumors to support his delusion about the Negro."

Frazier went on to analyze the sexual aspects of white supremacy by arguing that "the energetic measures white Southerners use to prevent legal unions of white with colored people look suspiciously like compensatory reactions for their own frustrated desires for such unions." According to Frazier's formulation, white men desired to continue to "use colored women" "arbitrarily and without censure" as they had in the past, but such liaisons were becoming taboo. Therefore, they increasingly accused black men of desiring white women, thereby projecting their own "insistent desire [for interracial sex] upon the Negro." Because of these only partially repressed, taboo desires on the part of white men throughout the region, "in the South, the white man is certainly a greater menace to the Negro's home than the latter is to his."[9] Frazier thus denied black men's supposed desire for white women and denounced white men's subversion of black men's patriarchal prerogatives over their own homes and families.[10]

The most provocative of Frazier's assertions focused on white women's projected repressed sexual fantasies and desires for black men.

> Perhaps more justly to be classed as symptoms of insanity are those frequent hallucinations of white women who complain of attacks by Negroes when clearly no Negroes are involved. Hallucinations often represent unacceptable sexual desires which are projected when they can no longer be repressed. In the South a desire on the part of a white woman for a Negro that could no longer be repressed would most likely be projected—especially when such a desire is supposed to be as horrible as incest. It is not unlikely, therefore, that imaginary attacks by Negroes are often projected wishes.[11]

Here, Frazier updated and extended Ida B. Wells's assertions regarding the multitude of black men lynched for the supposed rape of white women. Whereas Wells had used biblical references implying black men were innocent Sampsons betrayed by seductive, scheming white Delilahs, Frazier used explicit psychological jargon to directly accuse white women of so ardently desiring black men that they pretended to have been raped when they had not in fact even been touched.[12] Like Wells a generation before him, Frazier was run out of the South for daring to broach the subject at all.

When an unknown person, presumably an irate white Southerner, sent a copy of this article to the editors of the *Atlanta Constitution* and the *Atlanta Independent*, the whole city learned that the local black sociologist, Edward F. Frazier, who had just weathered one scandal involving a white woman and ending in his dismissal from his job, was the same bold upstart, E. Franklin Frazier, who dared to publish articles criticizing the Southern way of life, disapproving white treatment of African Americans, and advocating social equality.[13] Frazier and his wife Marie, who were already planning to relocate to Chicago where Frazier would begin his doctoral studies, were forced to flee Atlanta immediately for fear of being lynched. "The Pathology of Race Prejudice" became infamous as Frazier's "farewell to the South," a kind of parting shot much admired among New Negroes.[14]

Following the event, Frazier's fellow black sociologist and sometime competitor Charles S. Johnson wrote him to say that everyone he met as he traveled throughout the South that summer talked incessantly of the article and requested copies of it because "the newsstands have been exhausted of the issue." All wanted to share in Frazier's triumphant adventure in manly defiance. Frazier's friend Gustavus Steward jokingly congratulated him on his unwillingness or inability to perform "the proper amount of bootlicking" and refusal to be the "good nigger," a role that, if he were only willing to play it, would garner him much praise and reward, including "free trips to Europe thrown in occasionally."[15] Audacious, often embattled, and unyielding in his political commitments, Frazier was indisputably a man personifying the New Negro ethos, including its masculinism.

"The Pathology of Race Prejudice" is somewhat atypical of the measured, logical, scientifically grounded essays New Negro scholars such as Frazier normally produced as a form of progressive racial advocacy in the 1920s. Frazier later described his tone as "partly satirical," and his sardonic, biting wit is evident throughout the article.[16] Yet the piece demonstrates the bold determination and refusal to accommodate Jim Crow white supremacy that characterized the New Negroes as well as the emphatic rationalism they would use to formulate a modern ideology of racial advancement. Frazier's emphasis on manhood and defense of black men's patriarchal prerogatives and domains, including black women's bodies, were also emblematic of New Negro imperatives. Although Frazier might not have been entirely serious in his diagnosis of insanity in the whole of the white South, he was quite earnest, and clearly very angry, in his unrelenting denunciation of Jim Crow white supremacy and the inhumanity and terrorism necessary to maintain it.[17] His infamous article, therefore, stands as a particularly explicit and unequivocal expression of New Negro progressivism.

Like Micheaux and the other New Negro artists who sought to wrest back their representations from the fallacious images conveyed by white supremacists and to assert a strong New Negro manhood, Frazier joined his fellow academics in the first generation of African American scholarly self-determination in the endeavor to reformulate the terms of the race debate. He used the methods and rhetoric of social science to advocate African American humanity, good character, and fitness for an equal role in U.S. society. He always wrote with an awareness of white supremacy and offered a salient, though sometimes muted or implicit, criticism of its ill effects on African American lives and U.S. society in general.

While committed to securing an appropriate place in the academy as a reputable and qualified scholar through teaching and publication in scholarly journals, Frazier also published in popular New Negro periodicals like *The Crisis* and *Opportunity*. He sought to influence African American opinion and self-perception as well as to challenge white supremacy in popular assumptions and scholarly findings. He also put his scholarship to work at the Atlanta School where he directed the training of African American social workers, teachers, and ministers in "organized efforts to solve such social problems as those of race, poverty, and health, by the application of scientific methods" and in his later position as director of research for the Chicago Urban League.[18] Frazier was, in today's parlance, a public intellectual who would help to shape the ideology of New Negro racial advancement politics and activism.

In 1925, Frazier won first prize in one of the famous *Opportunity* literary contests for his essay "Social Equality and the Negro." In keeping with his pattern of dauntless publishing and penchant for issues that touched on black men's prerogatives, Frazier directly addressed one of the most heavily loaded terms in the lexicon of U.S. racial politics. As Frazier acknowledged, white people, especially Southerners, were alarmed by the term "social equality" because they mistakenly understood it to mean "familiar social intercourse" between the races and to imply black men's unfettered access to white women.[19] Consequently, African Americans habitually denied they sought social equality so as to assuage these fears while still seeking civil rights, equal employment opportunities, and an end to Jim Crow segregation. Frazier wrote to clear up the confusion and, in doing so, provided a reasoned argument advocating full racial integration and equal application of the law, denouncing white supremacy as inimical to democracy, and, ultimately, promoting social equality.

Frazier defined social equality as a "social ideal" that is the implicit goal of a democratic "commonwealth where there are no hereditary classes with special rights and privileges and all men are equal before the law." He observed that in contemporary U.S. society, there was "an approach to this ideal" that was stymied by class and race distinctions.[20] Over the course of the history of U.S. slavery and labor struggles, these distinctions made African Americans into a separate, culturally inferior "caste" differentiated by color and locked into a dependent, servile position relative to the white population.[21] With this observation, Frazier refuted the idea that there was something inherently or biologically inferior in African Americans that made them unworthy of proximity to white people. Their status was purely circumstantial and due to social factors. Furthermore, Frazier identified white supremacy as the basis for these circumstances and their mainte- nance. White people objected to black social equality because it threatened their economic and social dominance. To illustrate this claim, Frazier of- fered a few familiar observations. He noted that

> the presence of a dirty Negro in a menial position creates no resentment while a cultivated Negro of pleasing manners and features becomes offensive, especially to southerners, if he occupies any place where the superiority of the white is not asserted. A white girl who sits in the lap of the Negro servant who drives her home daily stands up from Washington to Philadelphia rather than sit beside a colored passenger. . . . [The southerner] maintains a benevolent attitude toward individual Negroes, while he opposes treating them as citizens. . . . [T]he southern white man boasts of his love for the Negro while denying him citizenship rights. Herein is clearly shown the difference between the benevolence shown a social inferior and the recognition of the rights of a social equal.

Despite their stated objections to social equality on the basis of fear of inter- racial sexual congress, white people opposed social equality because they knew it would threaten their absolute social and political control. In Fra- zier's estimation, white racists' paternalistic condescension betrayed their true motives. He explained that Jim Crow, excused as a system of separate but equal, was really a caste system affording whites the privilege of crossing the line if they chose but denying black people the same choice. Even in the North, where Jim Crow was not the rule, "the Negro's enjoyment of civil rights is limited" and "the limitations increase as the Negro population in- creases" because the threat to white dominance became all the more real as the presence and potential of African Americans multiplied.[22]

The solution to these problems was manifold. First, there was hope in the migration of African Americans from isolated rural areas to the cities and in their incorporation into the industrial classes by which they were joining the labor struggle. Thus, "if the struggle between capital and labor becomes intensified[,] the Negro may become an integral part of the prole- tariat, and the feeling against his color may break down in the face of a common foe." "Moreover," African American success in labor and business ventures encouraged society "to show some respect towards [the Negro's new] independent position." Besides economic advancement promoting the breakdown of racial barriers, African Americans would need regular in- teraction with white people, rather than any form of separatism, because "caste breaks down when social intercourse becomes general."[23] Such

"social intercourse" would promote the natural and desirable development of "group affiliations" based on "similarity of tastes and sympathy of
thought" and "similarity of character and talents" that was so crucial to the
recognition of African American humanity and white awareness of the
injustice of discrimination.[24]

In his scholarship and his training of social workers during the 1920s,
Frazier sought to promote among African Americans the economic success
and readiness for positive social intercourse he thought necessary. He
endeavored to accomplish this through his focus on the black family. Frazier had concluded that one reason for African Americans' low status as a
despised "caste" was that their "cultural level . . . [was] below that of
whites."[25] Thus, Frazier sought to show African American racial advocates
and social workers how to increase African Americans' "cultural level"
through the assimilation of dominant values, behaviors, and gender relations. As in "Social Equality and the Negro," Frazier always took pains to
point out the falsity of assumptions that African Americans were somehow
biologically distinct from whites or inherently unsuited to full assimilation
and participation in Western society and culture. Their degraded circumstances as a despised caste in U.S. society had simply left them ignorant,
unskilled, and unhealthy. Frazier's analyses purported to identify the reasons for these adverse circumstances and to prescribe a solution. African
Americans were to be educated not only in letters and job skills but also in
the "social intelligence" and values necessary to form and maintain "organized," patriarchal families.[26]

In his article "Psychological Factors in Negro Health," which might be
considered a sort of companion or coda to "The Pathology of Race Prejudice," Frazier found it necessary to first defend African Americans from the
idea that they had any inherent racial traits regarding disease, mental health,
or personality before beginning his analysis. Only after establishing African
American humanity in this way did he discuss "those conceptions concern-
ing the origin of disease which affect the health of the race" and "the prob-
able effects of the social environment upon the health of the Negro" in the
South. He then went on to point out some "primitive conceptions of
disease" emerging from African American religious faith and folklore. In
doing so, he belittled African American folklore and also indirectly criticized black mothers as the primary caregivers practicing these "primitive"
methods. The idea that "tea made from a hornet's nest" was a cure for a
child's whooping cough was simply foolish in his mind. The possibility that
this folk remedy might be based on some long-standing homeopathic
knowledge never entered his analysis. He considered those who practiced
this remedy to be at least as irrational and superstitious as those who considered it "a sort of impiety" or an attempt to subvert the will of God to

believe that "health is something that can be acquired by proper hygiene."
For Frazier, these were not useful home remedies or religious views but
simply fallacies maintained by African Americans' lower culture and the
"larger amount of ignorance" among them due to their isolated rural roots.
They were the sorts of problems that, once uncovered through social scientific research, might be solved through teaching and social work.[27]

Such instances of ignorance as they affected African American family life
and economic prospects soon formed Frazier's primary interest. Building
upon his investigations of the inadequacies of rural health care and psychology, he developed a scholarly focus on the African American family
and its fundamental problem of "disorganization."[28] Often impoverished,
frequently in poor health, and, most important, lacking a structure of patriarchal authority, the African American family was in dire need of assistance.
Frazier posited the family as the primary foundation of African American
life chances and social mores and so focused on it as the first locus of racial
advancement efforts. Frazier asserted, "I have emphasized the problem of
family disorganization because I feel it lies at the basis of many of the
Negro's problems."[29]

In Frazier's estimation, the black family "has been touched by all the factors operating to destroy the semi-patriarchal family in America." First, the
black family in particular had been "burdened with 250 years of promiscuous sex relations," presumably the inability to marry under slavery and
congress between white men and black women under slavery and Jim Crow.
Then, "just at the time the Negro was struggling to build up regulated sex
relations, there were assaults upon the only marital relation according to
which he could model his own family life." That is, the paradigmatic white
patriarchal family was itself becoming "disorganized" in the turbulence of
modernizing society. "These influences, such as the growth of modern in-
dustrialism, the decay of religious control, urbanization and the larger freedom of women have all affected Negro families." Among other modern
transformations revolutionizing society, Frazier found women's greater autonomy and increased choices regrettable since they meant women were
less inclined to restrict their lives' activities to marriage and motherhood.

Frazier was aware of contemporary arguments against patriarchy and for
the formulation of alternative family structures, but he remained committed to male dominance in families as the ideal "norm" to which African
Americans ought to aspire rather than develop alternative configurations
more suited to their circumstances. "While we appreciate the position of
those who feel that because the Negro is not over-burdened with an out-
worn tradition he might contribute to a more rational attitude towards sex
relations," he wrote, "it cannot be denied that at the present time the normal
functioning of the family is necessary in order to save us from many of our

problems."[30] His refusal to seriously consider alternative family structures, especially given the well-known necessity of black women's labor outside of the home to support their dependents, is curiously myopic. This myopia indicates the extent to which masculinism shaped Frazier's ideology of racial advancement. When he spoke of "the Negro," he was referencing black men, and his use of the masculine "his" and "he" when referring to "the Negro" was not simply generic.

Indeed, much of Frazier's discussion of white supremacist oppression emphasized its effects on black manhood. When analyzing African American psychology, he diagnosed "fear," "helplessness," and "repression" as symptoms of a "psychology of the sick" wherein black people were forced to defend their self-conceptions from disintegration by ascribing their inactivity to illness. "Subjectively, [this psychology of the sick] affords the Negro that defense against self-depreciation that is intolerable. A sick man is not expected to assert himself. Objectively considered, he will elicit pity rather than resentment from the dominant race." Better to be pitied for an imaginary illness or to be suspected of laziness than to be forced to recognize the extent of the social restrictions on one's prerogatives. However, a pitiful man is not a respected man. The fear and repression instilled by white supremacy forced black men to represent themselves as or even believe themselves to be sickly and ineffectual. Frazier "noted on more than one occasion that even in cases where physical superiority counted, the Negro hesitated to 'let himself go' lest he appear to challenge the superior social position of the white man."[31] Frazier concerned himself primarily with the psychological and social effects of white supremacy on black manhood, especially as they related to black men's ability to equal white men in patriarchal prerogative and respectability.

Frazier knew economic forces and the ill effects of white supremacy were largely outside African American control. Thus, he focused on those circumstances and habits that black people could control, and their relations with one another lay at the heart of these. If nowhere else, within their families black men ought to assert themselves as dominant and capable. Frazier observed that black men did not do this and sought to identify the reasons this was so. He assumed that the "lack of social intelligence" that constituted African Americans' "ignorance" translated to their lack of sufficient fortitude to withstand the difficulties of their circumstances or to maintain their commitments.[32] The average "Negro family" suffered an "incomplete assimilation of western culture" with all of its ideals and mores.[33] At the same time, Frazier denied that the frequency of desertion among African Americans, for example, was due to "some inherent lack of certain moral fibre [sic]."[34] Thus, black people were capable of benefiting from education, the efforts of social workers, and exposure to worthy influences, and these would teach them to value and seek to emulate the patriarchal "norm." Frazier sought to promote and incorporate such educational and progressive efforts into the mission of racial advancement.

Frazier analyzed the characteristics and problems of black families from the perspectives of would-be patriarchs and of children, but not of women. When discussing an aspect of family "disorganization" such as desertion, Frazier empathized with black husbands. "With people living on such a level [of dire poverty,] the slightest cessation of income brings a crisis in the family. Even the heads of families with more moral support than the head of the Negro family finds and has within himself, will often throw up the whole matter and desert." Not only poverty but also the fecundity of black women was a problem precipitating men's desertion of their families. "Many heads of Negro families in spite of their proverbial optimism, see only an untoward Providence piling up liabilities. A railroad ticket gives an easy release." Frazier fails to mention the willing role black men must have played in the creation of this "untoward Providence" of children. Neither does he recommend the use of birth control as a means of reducing the birth rate in black families. Perhaps this was an aspect of the "larger freedom of women" he thought so detrimental to the family.

Even when he directly referenced black women's circumstances, Frazier did not incorporate their perspectives. Rather, they were one of the sources of the problem. "Another economic factor helping the disorganization of Negro family life is the large number of Negro women in gainful occupations," Frazier wrote. Rather than in the effect of these circumstances on black women's lives and prospects, he was most interested in the fact that nearly half of the women working for pay outside the home "had children." He bemoaned the fate of such children: "It is only when we face the situation of hundreds of homes in every city where the children are locked out or in the house until after the father or mother returns in the evening that we get a true picture of this situation."[35] Frazier would have his readers understand the frustration and humiliation of men unable to support their families and so excuse their desertion. His audience was to imagine forlorn children left to their own devices for long hours in the evenings and worry over their bleak futures. But he urged no similar empathy for black women. This omission in Frazier's analysis implies an indictment of black women's role in their families' "disorganization," however unintended or unavoidable that role might have been.

Frazier battled white supremacy and justifications for Jim Crow segregation by refuting racist notions of inherent African American "primitiveness" or incapability to learn and practice Western cultural habits and mores. He used rational social scientific methods to prove that African

Americans were not inherently backward. Rather, their degraded condition was the result of historical and contemporary oppression. To Frazier's mind, the deleterious effects of white supremacy were manifold, but their most debilitating result was the fracture of the African American family. Thus, he considered the salvation of this family the foundation of any racial advancement effort. Any progress in other areas of the struggle would "be of little consequence as long as we permit the fundamental social unit in our society to go to pieces."[36]

Frazier not only discounted women's perspectives on family organization but also wholly ignored black people's human desires and motivations as he purported to analyze their private lives and intimate relationships. Their culture, in his eyes, was a less-developed, lower version of white American culture, a hodgepodge of stupid misconceptions, quackish home remedies, and immorality, all the result of stultifying oppression. He never addressed the motivating forces of love and lust, the pain of marital abuse and filial disappointment, the joy of fantasies, or the fun of irrational aspirations. In his zealousness to prove black equality and potential for successful integration and assimilation, Frazier dismissed the very traits and impulses that made African Americans human.

The problems Frazier identified among black people were real and entrenched. Without question, the great majority of African Americans were mired in poverty, and the white supremacist oppression they endured did injure their self-conceptions as well as it severely handicapped their efforts to improve their prospects and livelihoods. Yet Frazier diagnosed and prescribed partial solutions to these problems with little reference to black women's perspectives. Indeed, he considered black women's increased but still uncertain access to some forms of self-determination inimical to his vision of racial advancement in the New Negro era. Through his analysis of black family disorganization and his focus on the family as the primary locus of racial advancement efforts, he advocated the institution of patriarchal "family control" and a masculinist idea of racial progress.[37] Frazier was aware of contemporary arguments against patriarchy and for alternative family structures, but he rejected them. Instead, he bemoaned the plight of the black "head of household," the fact that black mothers worked outside the home for pay, and the purportedly inevitable gloomy fate of their children. Although he focused much of his research on the circumstances of black mothers and their resulting inability to properly rear their children, he did not consider the welfare of black mothers as women in their own right. His masculinist approach reinforced race motherhood as black women were to be subordinated under men's authority within the family and devote themselves to the welfare of children.

OPPORTUNITY AND THE WORK OF RACE MOTHERHOOD

While Frazier worked to build the Atlanta School of Social Work and pub-lished his earliest articles prescribing patriarchy as a solution to black deg-radation, his colleague and sometime competitor Charles S. Johnson spent the greater part of the 1920s working for the National Urban League as di-rector of its research initiatives and editor of its *Opportunity* magazine. Through the latter position, Johnson succeeded in developing a modern discourse on race that centered on black industrial and professional em-ployment and the health and prospects of black men, women, and children. However, under his editorship, *Opportunity* became much more than a journal for social workers, social scientists, and supporters of the National Urban League.

While maintaining his commitment to coverage of scientific and profes-sional racial advocacy work, Johnson made *Opportunity: Journal of Negro Life* live up to its full title by using its pages as a site for the publication of New Negro art, literature, and literary and political essays. Articles on New Negro theater, reviews of the latest fictional and social scientific publica-tions, and images celebrating African American culture and history, as well as the poetry of New Negro Renaissance luminaries like Langston Hughes, Countee Cullen, and Ann Spencer, were to be found in the pages of *Oppor-tunity*. Added to these was the multitude of articles submitted by social sci-entists and National Urban League employees and social workers' reports of their progress and cutting-edge strategies as they met the new challenges presented by urban overcrowding, the uneven industrialization of black workers, and the effects of ongoing racism. Thus, the magazine evolved into a forum for the debate and analysis of the variety of African American life and politics through multiple media and a diversity of voices. It reached a wide range of readers and joined *The Crisis* as one of the leading publica-tions advancing the artistic production and political agendas of the era.[38] With Johnson at the helm, *Opportunity* served as a politicized and powerful voice advocating New Negro racial advancement.

Rather than rail against the injustices of white supremacy and indict white racists for their self-serving perfidy and hypocrisy as Frazier often did, Johnson set out on a course of quiet and slow but steady chipping away at the foundations of white supremacy and digging the trenches in which later, more explosive battles would be fought. He prided himself on his ability to illuminate the issues and problems engendered by racial oppres-sion without setting any telltale fires. He intended "to create more light with no more heat than is necessary for warmth."[39] He laid the foundations of gradual systemic change upon which he expected future generations to build. Johnson was no radical or revolutionary. Yet he was visionary enough to see both the necessity of applying modern paradigms to the new forms of entrenched social problems and the efficacy of engaging a variety of viewpoints and methods to provide the "light" he knew to be invaluable. Johnson's commitment to social scientific approaches, his sponsorship of the New Negro Renaissance, and his open-mindedness—his modernism—made him a New Negro, and the magazine he founded and guided to prominence reflected those values.[40]

Johnson "tried to assemble in [*Opportunity's*] columns the best minds this country [would] yield in its dispassionate assault upon the traditional errors of our tangled relations, in its equally dispassionate quest for truth, and in its revelation of the neglected aspects of Negro life."[41] His editorials were sober, deliberate contributions to this mission. He intended his several editorial essays on black women's work and their role in the African American family to enhance the magazine's coverage of the full breadth of African American life. With such editorials, Johnson provided a large proportion of the magazine's coverage of black women's experiences. He recognized their essential role in racial advancement, but he saw that essential role as limited to motherhood.

Johnson did not consider women inherently inferior to men. He ridiculed the notion that women lacked "reasoning capacity" due to smaller brains than men as "a species of arrogance" and "puerile sophistry." He regretted that "even in this enlightened age scientists are trying to find some justification for the very convenient status to which [women] have been relegated." He wryly observed the "most uncanny similarity between the charges made against the mentality of women and those made against the mentality of Negroes" and reminded his readers that "none of them can be successfully established" with sound scientific evidence.[42] Rather than a sexist belief in women's inherent inferiority, Johnson evinced a masculinist understanding of the African American racial situation that relegated black women to the home and children's care.

In editorials on women workers, infant mortality, and mothers' mortality over the course of the 1920s, Johnson identified working women as a curse on the black family. "Mortality among Negro women at childbirth is increasing," he reported. "These deaths have been found to be most common among mothers who are forced to work and where proper medical care cannot be secured."[43] He did not celebrate black women's increasing employment in industry, although it was generally better paid and offered more regular hours than domestic service. Instead, he lamented that "of the married Negro women 15 years of age and over, 44.9 per cent must work" and that "marriage ... does not offer any significant change in the status of Negro women."[44] Furthermore, "the Negro group stands at the peak with an infant mortality average 129% higher than the native-born [white] group." Black mothers' failures were to blame. "Diarrhoeal diseases" in black infants were "very largely due to bad feeding habits," and "developmental disorders . . . result[ed] from the lowered physical condition and habits of the mother's living before childbirth." Johnson followed this statement with a list of statistics confirming black mothers' high rates of employment relative to "native whites of native parentage" and other groups.[45]

Overall, Johnson announced that "working mothers can neither give the maximum vitality to the children to whom they give birth, nor a reasonable measure of care to their health and education after they are born."[46] Therefore, they should not work at all. Rather than seeking to improve women's employment conditions or remuneration or urge the organization of community or institutional services to assist black families in child-rearing and education, Johnson advocated the augmentation of black men's employment prospects. "It seems reasonable to urge that this waste of life could be avoided if the heads of families could earn enough to provide for their families," he wrote.[47] Ultimately, the opportunity Johnson, his magazine, and the New Negro politics he helped to define sought to create on behalf of the race was "the opportunity of the father to earn a decent livelihood."[48]

In this way, Johnson turned articles ostensibly focused on the experiences and chances of black women into statements on behalf of black men's increased opportunities. Such masculinism in discussions of the family echoed Frazier's focus on black men's and children's perspectives over women's. And the minimal focus on women, as opposed to industrial work, the family, and children's health, in the magazine's articles and reports offered little to balance that masculinism. The New Negro vision of racial advancement was closely tied to men's opportunities for self-determination and remunerative employment. Furthermore, New Negro progressivism considered women's employment a detriment. Rather than out working for wages or pursuing their own visions of self-determination, whatever those might have been, women were to remain at home, their energies concentrated on their children. If they did work, moreover, their employment must benefit the greater racial good. One way or another, black women's lives were meant to revolve around the achievement of others' self-determination, not their own.

Ideal New Negro women fulfilled the expectations of race motherhood, if not in their family lives, then through their work. The paradox of race motherhood was its exposition by New Negro women themselves, especially the professional women whose work in counseling, teaching, guiding, and nurturing black families, children, and workers, often under the direction of more respected and better paid men, exemplified its tenets. Women's racial advocacy and respectability, their loyalty to the race's interests, even their very identities, were measured, prescribed, and evaluated in terms of race motherhood. Social workers like Elise Johnson McDougald, Helen Sayre, and Eva Bowles mothered the race through their progressive, professional labors. Their reports of their strategies and successes, published in the pages of *Opportunity*, perfectly fit Johnson's editorial goals. Through their work and the publication of their endeavors, they helped to maintain and extend the discursive power and reach of race motherhood.

Even if they forsook the service-oriented professions of teaching, social work, and nursing, educated black women were expected to contribute to the cause of racial advancement. Those working in business, for example, were to consider themselves engaged in "actual service in freeing a race burdened by economic oppression."[49] When working in black-owned businesses, their male employers found black women "to be efficient, willing and capable workers." Such companies benefited from the fact that "a woman of equal training and ability of a man . . . can be obtained at a lower wage, for it is presumed, justly or falsely, that a woman does not have family obligations." In mentioning this point, author Sadie Tanner Mossell hints at her disapproval of such sex discrimination in black-owned companies, but quickly moves on to emphasize that "women . . . will more readily than men recognize authority and accept dictation. . . . They are less likely to seek to undermine the established position of a man." Thus, "Negro businesses were convinced of the efficacy of using women in their enterprises."[50]

In spite of the well-known fact that most black women worked out of the necessity of supporting not only themselves but also older and younger dependents, black-owned businesses such as the North Carolina Mutual Life Insurance Company exploited women's need for employment by paying them less than their male counterparts. Furthermore, they depended on these women's feminine hesitancy to challenge authority and their good deportment to confirm black male employers' manly authority in the office. In this way, educated black women workers were expected to buttress the development of black patriarchy and embody race motherhood, even to their own detriment.

In describing the increased employment opportunities for educated colored women, Eva Bowles evidenced her commitment to race motherhood. Before listing the various professions, she observed that "in past generations the thought of a proper career for a woman was a home and the rearing of children. Who would vouchsafe to say that the present day woman should not feel this first and foremost?"[51] Bowles confirmed that her list of professional opportunities was not meant as an alternative to marriage and motherhood. Black women should put such familial obligations first among their aspirations. However, for single women seeking employment before they settled down to their true life's calling, there was work to be done on behalf of the race.

Bowles's article was part job posting and part celebration of the successes of black women in capacities formerly closed to them due to racial discrimination and lack of training. "Barriers have been breaking away," she exulted, "and by degrees [the colored woman] has achieved success in avenues of life where formerly she dared not approach. She has not been wanted, especially, but she was needed." Even more qualified black women were needed to fill posts in teaching, social work, and nursing where they would serve the cause of racial equality by evidencing black people's abilities to fulfill responsible positions and participate in the all-important endeavor of improving the education, welfare, and health of the race. While acknowledging that the vast majority of black professional women were educators, Bowles urged her readers to go into teaching, especially in the elementary grades "where experience and character [were] needed in moulding [*sic*] the youth of the race."[52] Deans of Women were being hired in some of the black colleges, and Bowles hoped the rest would follow suit, providing such exemplary women to their student bodies "as an inspiration in the developing of Negro womanhood."

Bowles spent the majority of the article discussing the great variety of positions and specialties available in the field of social work through organizations such as the NUL and the Young Women's Christian Association. Especially necessary were trained social workers willing to toil in the most challenging areas of the rural South. "While the social consciousness has developed more rapidly in Northern cities, our Southern communities are fertile fields for well equipped and conscientious women social workers." Such work challenged "the Negro woman of the best calibre [*sic*] in equipment to meet these tangible, social and economic problems." Although Bowles mentioned the increasing number of black women in professional positions of authority such as lawyers and physicians, she emphasized social service-oriented roles. She advised that "there is a possibility of a career in combining the profession of medicine with the technical aspect of social work, child welfare, community health and positive health measures particularly." And she stressed that "too much encouragement cannot be given to the nursing profession."[53] Such professional women would not only handle cases of families in need and assist doctors in providing medical care but would also train the women of the communities in which they worked in better cooking methods, nutrition, hygiene, sexual health, home economics, the proper care of children and other issues of which they were considered ignorant.[54]

Under Johnson's editorship, *Opportunity* promoted race motherhood throughout its discussions of black women's employment circumstances and prospects. This discourse worked against black women's participation in the "opportunity" the magazine touted as the hallmark of the era.

Black women were not to seek to determine their destinies independently of the greater racial good nor take advantage of their increased employment opportunities to create lives that excluded or decentralized their mothering potential. Furthermore, they were to promote New Negro patriarchy by serving in subordinate, helpmate capacities to professional black men in business and medicine and by accepting less payment than their male counterparts.

According to race motherhood and within New Negro progressivism, particularly as it was delineated in the pages of *Opportunity*, social workers held a special place. Their work formed the backbone of the NUL's progressive racial advancement efforts, and they often reported their accomplishments in the organization's magazine. These black women social workers performed the work of race motherhood in their daily lives. The reports and articles they published in the magazine reflected their willingness, if not to endeavor to exemplify race motherhood completely, then to uphold its tenets in their discussions of their work.

Discernible between the lines of the exalted, self-congratulatory language in the social workers' reports and underneath their didactic rhetoric was a clash of competing self-determinative impulses. In moving to the city, African American migrants had sought to remake their lives and find some degree of fulfillment according to their own ideals and fantasies. New Negro progressives sought to prescribe a plan of common racial self-help and model behavior that would, they thought, not only improve the migrants' health and financial prospects but also relieve the whole race from deleterious stigmas of laziness, immorality, and contamination. Sometimes, the migrants' sense of self-determination, which the progressives saw as waywardness, was wholly obscured in the articles and reports. As they reflected on their efforts to advance the race's interests in education and industrial work, the social workers often readily dismissed the migrants' desires and motives, assuming them to be ignorant, "disorganized," and immoral.

Industrial social worker Helen Sayre reported on her work reforming the black women laborers at the Nachmann Company, which manufactured "spring filled cushions used for automobile seats, mattresses and furniture." Her mission was to change the work habits and increase the efficiency of the black women employees because the company was considering dismissing them all and excluding black women from future employment. "The large labor turn-over, lack of punctuality and general irregularity in attendance of the colored workers had created a bad situation."[55] These deficiencies seem momentous until one reads that "the sewing of covers, inserting of springs and tying [were] paid for on a piece work basis."[56] The workers were not paid regular hourly or incremental wages but received payment according to the number of pieces they completed. So, instead of working the hours prescribed by the company for its benefit, the workers were toiling according to their own schedules, attending work when they thought necessary, and producing only enough finished pieces to earn the money sufficient for their needs. Perhaps they spent the rest of their time caring for their children or laboring at other jobs to supplement their earnings.

For Sayre, then, "the most important task . . . was that of developing in the worker's mind her personal responsibility to become a regular and efficient employee and of showing her the requirements and standards of satisfactory service." In exchange, Sayre did acknowledge that "next in importance was the question of wages, because it is only reasonable to assume that if a girl is to be stimulated to put out good work[,] she must have tangible encouragement in her pay envelope." Ultimately, Sayre's priority was to demonstrate the potential fitness of black workers for industrial employment on behalf of racial advancement. This required her to evaluate the workers and their conditions from the employers' points of view and to develop a program of action that benefited the race's prospects in industry over the needs of the individual workers in a particular factory. Thus, she deplored the work habits she found at the Nachmann Company. "This class of workers," she lectured, "is largely responsible for low averages in industry by colored workers." The NUL and its staff of industrial social workers had their work cut out for them. "If we can educate the workers as well as give them evidences [*sic*] of appreciation for loyalty and good work, we have gone a long way towards making factory work attractive and colored workers efficient."[57]

Laboring within race motherhood, social workers attempted both to augment the education of black schoolchildren by supplementing their mothers' inadequate knowledge of hygiene and nutrition and to re-educate the mothers so that progressive methods and attitudes to health would spread and they would more closely resemble the ideal. Jane Harvey reported that social worker Madeline Tillman had great success in leading "a health campaign . . . [consisting] of a number of health stories and plays in which the children were not only interested listeners but active participants."[58] By inspiring the children to change their habits and appetites, she also aroused the curiosity of their mothers, an even greater coup. The mothers "want to know about these rules that are being taught at school, so where the health work is being carried on in the schools of a district it is also developed in the parent-teacher meetings, churches, and community centers." In these venues, Tillman gave lectures and held "Supper Clubs" in which she demonstrated the preparation of a "well balanced meal." Harvey also praised Tillman for influencing the local teachers along her circuit. "As a result, they [the local teachers] themselves are taking over gradually the main body of the health teaching." Tillman thus succeeded not only in improving the knowledge and habits of her assigned pupils but also in spreading her influence to the communities surrounding the schools in which she worked. Both local mothers and teachers absorbed the standards of progressivism and became better mothers of the race.

Similarly, *Opportunity* published social worker Elise Johnson McDougald's speech relating her activities developing vocational services for elementary and junior high school students in New York City. She considered this work "simply a phase of the big struggle of the modern era—the struggle of the Common Man for fullest development."[59] In assisting black children to find their vocational niches, she considered herself to be bringing their parents' migratory aspirations to fruition. Her work was precipitated by the social transformation occasioned by African Americans' movement. "After years of patient endurance, the Negro by migrating has made the problem of education and vocation, a national, rather than a sectional one." Extrapolating an assumption of the migrants' individual aspirations from her knowledge of the lesser educational opportunities in the South, McDougald devoted herself to shaping those presumed aspirations into a program of advancement for the greater racial good. She would train and guide the migrants' children toward appropriate, remunerative employment in the fields open to them.

In developing programs to train female students in domestic work, cafeteria work, and household management skills, McDougald recognized that the majority of black girls would have to work outside their homes to support themselves. She sought to prepare them for the inevitable. Yet she joined Johnson and Frazier in lamenting that economic necessity and its effect on black families. "The tendency in industry to force the Negro downward is most noteworthy for a body of social workers," she observed.

> It is at the root of many of the problems which the social worker is called upon to help solve. In passing, consider just one; because of it, the women of the Negro race are compelled to supplement the low wage of their men. They enter the laundries, shops and factories, or, continue to labor in the homes of the more fortunate women, to the neglect of their own. This forced neglect of the home during the day necessitates undue freedom for the children and lack of care as to feeding, recreation and discipline.[60]

The improvement of black men's employment prospects and wages would ameliorate the situation for the whole group. Black mothers could then remain at home with their children and give them the proper guidance, McDougald implied. In the meantime, however, she took the pragmatic attitude that since black women must work, they might as well do so to their greatest advantage and ought to receive the appropriate training, support, and guidance.[61] McDougald thus refrained from blaming black mothers for racial retardation or advocating a focus on black men's employment prospects. She

did not evince the same level of masculinism as the leading black male sociologists of her time, nor, however, did she challenge that masculinism. She
worked within race motherhood.

The black women who filled the race-serving roles in teaching, social
work, and nursing were not necessarily exemplars of race motherhood. Their
individual lives and personalities may not have conformed to its self-
negating, compliant, maternal parameters. Yet women like Elise McDougald, Helen Sayre, and Eva Bowles did feel responsible for the welfare of the
race, and they believed in the efficacy of their efforts to intervene in the lives,
culture, and habits of the black communities they served. They joined Johnson and Frazier in regretting the necessity of black women's work outside of
the home. They assumed that black women ought to stay home to devote
themselves to their children and to assist in the development of black patriarchal organization. Their publications in *Opportunity* represent their satisfaction in the small, daily successes they had in working toward these goals.

Elsewhere, however, they sometimes hinted at dissatisfaction or a lack of
fulfillment from their roles as race mothers. In her essay for Alain Locke's
The New Negro, Elise McDougald extolled the virtues of those progressive
New Negro women who blazed trails in professional and industrial work as
well as the vast and increasing numbers who, like herself, toiled on behalf
of racial advancement in teaching, social work, and nursing. However, she
divulged, "We find the Negro woman figuratively struck in the face daily by
contempt from the world about her. Within her soul, she knows little of
peace and happiness."[62] Even for the most progressive of New Negro
women, the satisfactions of mothering the race were not all they were purported to be.

LIMITED OPPORTUNITIES

The content of *Opportunity* serves as a window on the ideology of New
Negro racial advancement during the 1920s. New Negro progressivism was
a particular, class-inflected, professionalized method of prescription and
diagnosis operative within the multiple, overlapping methods of advancing
the race and achieving various visions of liberation in the era. As Charles
S. Johnson and Oscar Micheaux understood, politics, artistic production, labor struggles, and popular culture all inevitably intertwined and affected one another. Furthermore, these movements were united by their
militant insistence on achieving some level of self-determination, and they
all evinced similar understandings of the gender ideals that ought to prevail in modern African American life. Movements as seemingly divergent
and even antithetical as James Weldon Johnson's progressive anti-lynching

campaign through the NAACP, socialist A. Phillip Randolph's labor union the Brotherhood of Sleeping Car Porters, and Marcus Garvey's international and imperialist Universal Negro Improvement Association (UNIA) all envisioned African American advancement in terms of the achievement of patriarchy for black men and the subordination of black women in concomitant supportive roles.[63]

The gender discourse evident in New Negro progressivism permeated the overall meaning of racial liberation and progress during the era. The organizations and activists struggling on behalf of African American self-determination in labor, the arts, politics, consumption, and business assumed that their success would be indicated by African American men's enjoyment of the prerogatives and social power of patriarchs. According to this masculinist vision of New Negro racial solidarity, African American women's ideal roles, both in the racial struggle and in the future they worked toward, were subordinate. Black women were not to win their own self-determination but to assist black men in the effort to achieve theirs. Black women were to mother the race, to devote themselves to the maintenance and welfare of the greater black family, gladly serving everyone except themselves. The proliferation of this gender discourse worked against black women's realization of the opportunities for independence and self-determination that migration, urbanization, the Nineteenth Amendment, industrialization, and city life should have made possible. Ultimately, it muted black women's voices and circumscribed their opportunities. It did little to eliminate the particular oppression that continued to assault them, and it failed to provide them a full measure of fulfillment.

Although the problems New Negro progressives identified were very real and truly dire, their sense of responsibility was overblown. Even as the New Negro progressives sought to wrest the power of social analysis and the pronouncement of African American destiny from white paternalists' and racists' hands, the masses of African Americans were already on the move. As they migrated, they re-created themselves as savvy, urban, politicized New Negroes. The competition between divergent strategies of self-determination was repeated in the sex-race marketplace of popular culture, entertainment, and fashion. In this marketplace, New Negroes consumed commodified versions of their own ideologies and subjectivities, many of them shaped by or against race motherhood.

CHAPTER 3

✧

Consuming the New Negro

The Whirlpools of the Sex-Race Marketplace

I n one of her publicity photographs (Figure 3.1), the blueswoman Ethel
Waters is displayed in a costume she wore while performing in Paris in
the mid-1920s. Her dress seems a curious cross between an elegant satin
gown and an eroticized European fantasy of African or Asian "tribal" dress.
The satin bodice is lined with sparkling jewels, as are the headdress and the
buttons on her satin pumps. She wears shimmering hose and shows off her
legs in a pose seemingly designed to display her in the midst of a dance. Her
arms and fingers, too, sparkle with jewelry. Yet the straw- or feather-like material of her skirt and the plume of her hat bespeak a Western notion of
primitive womanhood made available for white delectation through Waters'
performance. This costume and the photograph of Ethel Waters wearing it
conjure the primitivism born of modern longings for the imagined simple,
natural life of "native" peoples, nostalgia for the days of unchallenged white
dominion over "the darker races," and the fantastic allure of dark-skinned,
nubile bodies.

Born in 1896, raised in small-town Pennsylvania, and later a migrant to
Philadelphia, Ethel Waters claimed a miserable, loveless, poverty-stricken
childhood during which she entertained and ran errands for the neighborhood prostitutes in exchange for nickels and dimes and much-needed affection.[1] The product of her mother's rape, Waters married at the age of thirteen
to escape her abusive family. When her husband, too, proved abusive, she
left him and supported herself by working as a maid in Philadelphia hotels.
It was during this period of her life that her talent was discovered when she

Figure 3.1 Ethel Waters in Paris costume. Photographs of Blacks Collected by James Weldon Johnson and Carl Van Vechten, James Weldon Johnson Collection, Yale Collection of American Literature, Beinecke Rare Book and Manuscript Library, New Haven, Connecticut. Reprinted with permission of the Frank Driggs Collection.

performed for friends at a party. She began working the vaudeville circuit and soon graduated to club performances in cities such as Chicago, Atlanta, and New York. In 1921, she recorded her first song for a small, unknown label and then moved on to the New Negro company Black Swan Records, which merged with Paramount in 1923, and also recorded for Columbia Records, moving between competing labels for much of her recording career. Drawing on her vaudeville roots, Waters also acted on stage and screen throughout her career. Known as "Sweet Mama Stringbean" and "Queen of the Blues singers," Waters was one of the most popular, versatile, and long-standing stars to emerge out of the sex-race marketplace.

The inscription on the photo indicates that Waters was aware of and amused by her status as a prized commodity in the early twentieth-century marketplace of fantasy, racial tropes, power politics, and erotic delectation. She merrily wrote, "To Carl Van Vechten[,] Ethel Waters now dressed to go back where I stayed last nite [*sic*] & shake that Thing so 50 more million Frenchmen can go wrong." She reveled in her power to tantalize and seduce and to earn a very ample living doing so. Readers of this inscription might laugh along with Waters and applaud her wit as well as her success, as her friend Van Vechten likely did. Her fans then and now might even glory in her apparent ability to make Paris bow to her will. But this cannot be an entirely lighthearted thought. What work, other than ill-paid domestic drudgery, could a beautiful and talented, but uneducated and originally bitterly poor, black woman imagine for herself at that time, besides some form of seduction, some form of fantasy provision?

Ethel Waters's representation in this photo encompasses the conflicts and contradictions surrounding black women of the New Negro era. Evident here is Waters's effort to mold and control her own image and the pleasure she took in using it to entertain and manipulate her audiences. Yet, as she was apparently well aware, her image, like the representations of the New Negro women who inspired and imitated her, also fed the fantasies and predilections of an oppressive, dominant culture with the power to exploit her body and to suppress the independence of her voice. Within the sex-race marketplace, black women's sexuality, talents, and aspirations were never entirely their own.

Ethel Waters's music, performances, and glamour bespoke the dreams and experiences, the trouble, the pain, and the fun had by thousands of black women. She is an exemplar of the blueswoman, the greatest icon emerging out of the whirlpools of early twentieth-century sociocultural transitions, the rising popular culture industry, and the cultural investment in black womanhood. Not simply formed from her own talent, ambition, audacity, and roots in African American musical styles, the blueswoman emerged from a fusion of growing consumer and entertainment markets— especially the recording and advertisement industries and the spectacular fun of urban nightlife—as well as the era's startling tendency to display the body, celebrate the personality, and privilege the exotic.[2] As much as she was her own creation, formed as she built upon many of the same shifting gender discourses and sexual mores that inspired her white counterpart, the flapper, the blueswoman was also a beneficiary of the era's eroticization of the primitive.[3] Ultimately, the blueswoman was not only a woman who performed and recorded the popular black music of the Mississippi Delta and of the urban migrants. She was a particular manifestation of New Negro womanhood, an iconic image of modern, performative black womanhood born in and made possible by the sex-race marketplace. Shaped in the marketplace that consumed and produced popular knowledge of black womanhood, the blueswoman was in many ways emblematic of all black women. She was the New Negro woman writ large—larger than life, larger than reality.

COMMODIFYING THE NEW NEGRO WOMAN

Although, as the New Negro progressives constantly lamented, newly urban African Americans were most often employed in the dirtiest, most dangerous, and lowest paying jobs at the bottom of the employment scale, they nevertheless made more money than ever before. Even those, like the majority of black women migrants, who were denied industrial work and took jobs as domestics in white urban homes, earned more than they had in the rural South.[4] Despite the higher cost of living in the cities, African Americans as a group had a much larger disposable income as a result of the migration.[5] By 1929, economist Paul K. Edwards estimated that urban African Americans spent "31.9 percent" of their income "for miscellaneous items," including luxuries such as outings, entertainment, records, and cosmetics. This 31.9 percent equaled approximately "$99 million."[6] Clearly, the migrants had money to spend, and, despite their hardships and the disapproval of people like E. Franklin Frazier, they spent a great deal of it enjoying their new lives in the city and re-creating themselves as New Negroes. It was through the purchase of clothes, cosmetics, race records, and other luxuries and entertainments, as much as through travel, work, and politics, that African American migrants became urban, sophisticated, undaunted New Negroes. As much as any other factor, the clothes and the cosmetics, the music, and the nightlife helped them forge new identities, develop new attitudes, and shape their destinies in this period.

Around the New Negroes' conspicuous and growing presence in the cities and their burgeoning power as a consumer market as well as the nation's social transformations in this period, a new popular racial discourse emerged that was reflected in the early twentieth-century marketplace. The logic of primitivism made blackness itself a spectacle and the revelation of attractive black women big business. Increasingly, rather than by comedic and insulting blackface minstrel characters and vaudeville skits, blackness was represented by real black bodies—bodies that were entertaining precisely because they seemed to be newly revealed and therefore exotic, and erotic. Entertainments like the blues and the adventure of "slumming" to witness blackness in action were publicized and disseminated to white America via the emergent recording, film, cosmetic, and publishing industries, which were becoming the powerful primary arbiters of social trends, cultural conception, and popular comprehension. Professionals in all of these industries consciously sought to harness the new blackness—the New Negro—to increase the sales of their products. They used advertising as a means of manipulating the public, both white and black, through familiar, established tropes and subconscious perceptions.[7] This manipulation of race and sex in the early twentieth-century market worked to compromise the self-determinative efforts of the popular New Negro public figures of the era and the masses of African Americans who consumed their images and the products those images sold. The New Negro was commodified.

Yet modern popular culture did not function only to exoticize and dehumanize African Americans. The New Negroes, too, utilized the marketplace to forward sociopolitical agendas, disseminate cultural productions, and reformulate the concepts of race and African American character. Filmmaker Oscar Micheaux, professional activist James Weldon Johnson, and magazine editor Charles S. Johnson all exploited the rising interest in black people and engagement with racial politics to sell products, whether film tickets or political stratagems, and thereby to distribute and popularize their particular outlook on American racial destiny. Indeed, performers like Evelyn Preer and Ethel Waters habitually used and promoted their commodification to sell tickets to shows, records, and their own images to make their livings. On the whole, New Negroes, acutely aware of the sex-race marketplace and its machinations, sought by various means to use their commodification to their own advantage.

Through the rising culture industries of film, recording, and advertising, the sex-race marketplace embodied and distributed ideologies and fantasies about blackness, femininity, sexuality, pleasure, corruption, and desire. The marketplace was both made from and expressed in the pages of multiple periodicals, all replete with advertisements offering entertainment and self-improvement, articles and editorials pronouncing the state of the race, reviews of performances on stage and screen, and a multiplicity of images displaying the pleasure and shame and grandeur of the lives of unknown people in unglimpsed places who were nevertheless familiar in their hopes and miseries. This marketplace existed and was further expressed in the performances and performers of the period. Their revues, vaudeville acts, plays, films, concerts, and race records were also business ventures catering to the tastes of customers. The sex-race marketplace offered cosmetics, tickets, records, clothing, jewelry, and a multitude of other items. It offered knowledge of other realities, new fashions, nostalgia, fantasy, escape, and the makings of reasoned plans and goals. The marketplace was also made up of the assumptions and aspirations, the desires and dreams of those who browsed and shopped it, seeking not only tangible objects but ephemeral satisfactions as well.[8]

Black women were not simply objectified by the sex-race marketplace but participated in it on many levels. They were producers of tangible commodities such as Madam C. J. Walker's shampoo and intangible ideas like Elise McDougald's pragmatic adaptation of race motherhood that fed racial discourses. They were performers like Evelyn Preer depicting idealized, didactic characters such as her Sylvia Landry. They were also unwitting, perhaps unwilling, objects of scrutiny and scorn such as the unfortunate Annabelle. Indeed, black women's participation in the sex-race marketplace was complex and multifaceted, reflecting the swirling vagaries of the marketplace itself. It would prove to be a simultaneously liberating and constricting space, one through which black women played a part in the formulation and dissemination of modern subjectivities and ideals of femininity and were also consumed as racialized, dehumanized objects of desire and derision. This chapter will concentrate on black women's roles as performers, or commodified images, and consumers in the marketplace through a focus on advertisements aimed at and depicting them.

The meeting of the mass media and New Negro popular culture in the market created multiple commodified versions of New Negro womanhood that were used to sell products. Unlike the Mammy figures created to facilitate white consumption of pancake mix and household cleaners, the advertisements directed at New Negro audiences were complex representations of iconic blackness crossed with modern and nostalgic, rural and urban impulses.[9] They reflected interracial and intra-racial struggles over the cultural meaning of blackness and the formulation of modern ideals of black womanhood. The race motherhood ideal was reflected in this complex marketplace. There too were commodified representations of New Negro women's attempts to accomplish sexual self-determination in the New Negro era.

The advertisement campaigns competing for the new African American consumer dollar and their representations of black women evince a facet of the struggle black women waged to create modern, independent subjectivities in the New Negro era as well as the discourse shaping New Negro conceptions of the relationships between race, gender, and sexuality. When considered in the context of the early twentieth-century sex-race marketplace, interwar advertisement campaigns also exemplify black women's objectification and the nearly immediate cooptation of their attempts at self-transformation. Seething and swirling like a whirlpool, the sex-race marketplace took back even as it seemed to give and ultimately maintained the racial and sexual status quo. Because of the insidious, cynical exploitations of the marketplace, black women's representations, while changing and modernizing, remained flat and one-dimensional, caught between the excesses of hyper-sexuality and the restraining impulses of the quest for respectability, while their real, complex, humanity remained obscure.

The remainder of this chapter explores three aspects of the sex-race marketplace. The first section focuses on New Negro women's entrepreneurship and attempts to control their representations in the marketplace through the sales strategies and advertisement campaigns of the Madame C. J. Walker Manufacturing Company, which utilized race motherhood discourses. The second section turns to advertisements for race records and cosmetics that feature black women performers, or blueswomen, and discusses the cynical circumlocutions of the marketplace as it manipulated blackness, sex, nostalgia, and race politics. Finally, the last section uncovers New Negro women's efforts at self-creation in the midst of the marketplace's unrelenting whirlpool through examination of publicity photographs of blueswomen alongside photographs of regular black women.

MARKETING RACE MOTHERHOOD: THE WALKER COMPANY'S CAMPAIGN FOR RESPECTABILITY

Reflecting on his years of editing the *Crisis*, W. E. B. Du Bois remarked that "pictures of colored people were an innovation" in the early New Negro era, and he observed that "in general the Negro race was just a little afraid to see itself in plain ink" at that time.[10] Representations of black people in realist or plainly human forms rather than in carefully crafted, idealized portraits, easily discernible blackface minstrel comedy, or cartoonish exaggerations— and the dissemination of these plain forms to nationwide and even worldwide audiences—were still new, still risky and daring, still in formation. The new visibility of African Americans was one of the defining factors of the New Negro era, and many members of the race were still uncomfortable with their sudden conspicuousness. They feared, often rightly, that images of black people would be used to further denigrate and exploit the race.

Advertisements for Madam C. J. Walker's products reflect the hesitation among the New Negro business class and other prominent people to see the Negro race "in plain ink" or in forms other than idealized representations, particularly through photographic images. The images and rhetoric the Walker Manufacturing Company developed to promote its products in the New Negro era express the company's conservatism and adherence to the long-standing culture of dissemblance dictating the representation of black women. [11] When black women, like Mme. Walker, could exercise control over their representations in the sex-race marketplace, the culture of dissemblance taught them to emphasize lady-like femininity and respectability over physical beauty and desirability. As the owner and primary promoter of the Walker Manufacturing Company, Mme. Walker followed these dictates in her advertisements and other promotional materials. As she did so, she utilized and extended the discourse of race motherhood to justify her promotion of her own and other black women's economic independence and to coat the beauty her products would provide with the sheen of race-serving respectability. Rather than glamour, urbanity, and individuality, consumers of Walker products were urged to buy into racial advancement through adherence to a modern version of the long-standing "culture of dissemblance" dictating the representation of black women and the tenets of race motherhood.

Mme. Walker's business and the use of the products she sold through it greatly augmented the self-determination efforts of black women in the early twentieth century. She self-consciously offered black women a kind of race pride by asserting that they could be beautiful if, of course, they grew their hair using the Walker method and products. The company's advertisements admonished consumers about the importance of good hygiene and advised them of the benefits of Walker Company products for the health and length of their hair. "Where the scalp and hair are given regular attention and care, with application of Mme. Walker's vegetable shampoo, the effect of the Mme. Walker Wonderful Hair Grower on the impoverished cells (Papilae) [sic] of the hair works like magic," reads a draft of a pamphlet published to advertise Walker products. [12] A 1919 ad advised potential customers,

proper shampooing is what makes beautiful hair. It brings out all the real life, luster, natural wave and color, and makes it soft, fresh, and luxuriant. Your hair simply needs frequent and regular washing to keep it beautiful, but it cannot stand the harsh effect of ordinary soap. . . . This is why discriminating people use Mme. C. J. Walker's Vegetable Shampoo for Beautifying the Hair. [13]

For Walker, selling beauty products was not simply a business enterprise but also a means of advancing the race through the improvement of hygiene and appearance.

Walker also offered black women economic independence by creating the opportunity for them to join the nationwide network of Walker agents who sold Walker products on commission and their services as beauty culturists. One Walker agent and "hair culturist," Mrs. B. F. Walker of Philadelphia, wrote to Walker's attorney and general manager F. B. Ransom relating the good news of her business's expansion. "I am now preparing to leave my business situated at my home and take a store front shop in the most poplar [*sic*] section of the colored people of South Phila[delphia]," she wrote. A savvy businesswoman, she used the remainder of her two-page letter to bargain for a reduction in wholesale prices for Walker Company products: "[A]s I handle and sell a great deal of Mme. Walker's goods," she wrote, "I would like to know if there could not be a reduction made to me by the dozen. . . . I can readily sell all the goods that I can handle, but I have not thought it worth my while to sell by the dozen for the same price I pay for it, I would only be accomadating [*sic*] others and not helping myself financially[.]"[14] Such sophisticated business dealings on the part of Walker agents indicate the readiness of black women to seize the opportunities offered in the New Negro era. They also demonstrate the agents' commitment to their individual financial well-being, over and above the company's mission of racial advancement.

Walker's advertisements often emphasized the strength of the company as a successful New Negro racial advancement endeavor, one progressive New Negroes ought to support and in which they should take pride. One full-page advertisement features a headline stating "The Spirit of Mme. C. J. Walker Lives On in Her 30,000 Agents All Over the World" and relates that "The preparations of the Mme. C. J. Walker Mfg. Co. are sold not only in the U. S. A., but also in Canada, Alaska, Mexico, Central America, So. America, West Indies & Africa." It further invites readers to read a "Spanish testimonial" sent from a satisfied customer in Santo Domingo reprinted in both the original Spanish and an English translation.[15]

The primary objective of the rhetoric and images Mme. Walker and ads for her products presented to the public was the establishment and maintenance of black respectability. Rather than black women's autonomy and empowerment as individuals or as a sex, Mme. Walker's company represented her primary interest as one of service to the race. Walker not only represented this goal through the language of her advertisements but also actively promoted it as she toured the nation's black communities in urban centers and rural hamlets. In this way, the Walker brand of the racial advancement ethos was disseminated through a network of women much like that of the National Association of Colored Women.[16] Local Walker agents proudly reserved a venue—usually the largest black church, sometimes a lodge hall—arranged for a host, and generated enthusiasm to secure a large audience to attend Mme. Walker's lectures on the benefits of her products and the importance of personal hygiene and maintenance of appearance for the good of the group. Her products and agents were to be means of racial betterment.[17]

Indeed, Mme. Walker likened her work to that of a missionary and encouraged her agents to do the same. In her "Instructions to Agents," a form letter mailed to each new Walker associate, Walker encouraged the new agent to "imagine [herself] a missionary and convert [the potential customer]" to the constant and proper use of Walker products.[18] In the company's "Short History of Madam Walker," Walker's distribution of goods is likened to Christ's conversion of the masses and, thereby, racial advancement work to missionary work: "Believing, as Christ converted the world by miracles He wrought before the Jews, by placing her hand in His, she might convert the world by the wonderful good she would do for her people. Hence, on September 15, 1906, she started out to place her goods on the market."[19] Here the money-making aspect of Walker's business is almost entirely obscured in favor of a description of the business as a boon for her people. Walker was mothering the race, working on behalf of others. According to its promotional rhetoric, the Walker Manufacturing Company was not so much a business enterprise as it was a missionary outpost on the quest for racial advancement. The service and use of Walker products would improve the image of black women, thereby allowing the race to appear more favorably in the nation's social consciousness, more worthy of acceptance. This insistence on advancement and race-serving economic achievement established by Madame C. J. Walker reinforced the discourse of race motherhood along with the dissemblance of black women's sexuality in popular representations. It remained the company's trademark long after Madame Walker's death in 1919.[20]

Walker Company advertisements did not utilize a model or black woman celebrity, besides Walker herself, to catch the eye of the reader, demonstrate the products' effectiveness, or provide the reader with a beautiful paragon to emulate.[21] Instead, a posed portrait of Madame Walker's face, representing unparalleled Negro wealth coupled with unquestionable respectability, rather than desirability, was the only photographic, human image decorating the company's advertisements in the 1920s. Instead of exhibiting black women's face and figure "in plain ink," Walker Company ads displayed the products themselves, emphasized their variety and worth, and suggested the company's apparent success and reliability.

The typical quarter-page ad in Figure 3.2 is rather simple. It emphasizes the fact that the company sold ten products in all and highlights the success of the company by intimating that the ten products are "sold everywhere" and that the company has "branches all over the world." The type face, rather than any image, does the work of expressing the delicate femininity and beauty the products would allow consumers to achieve.[22]

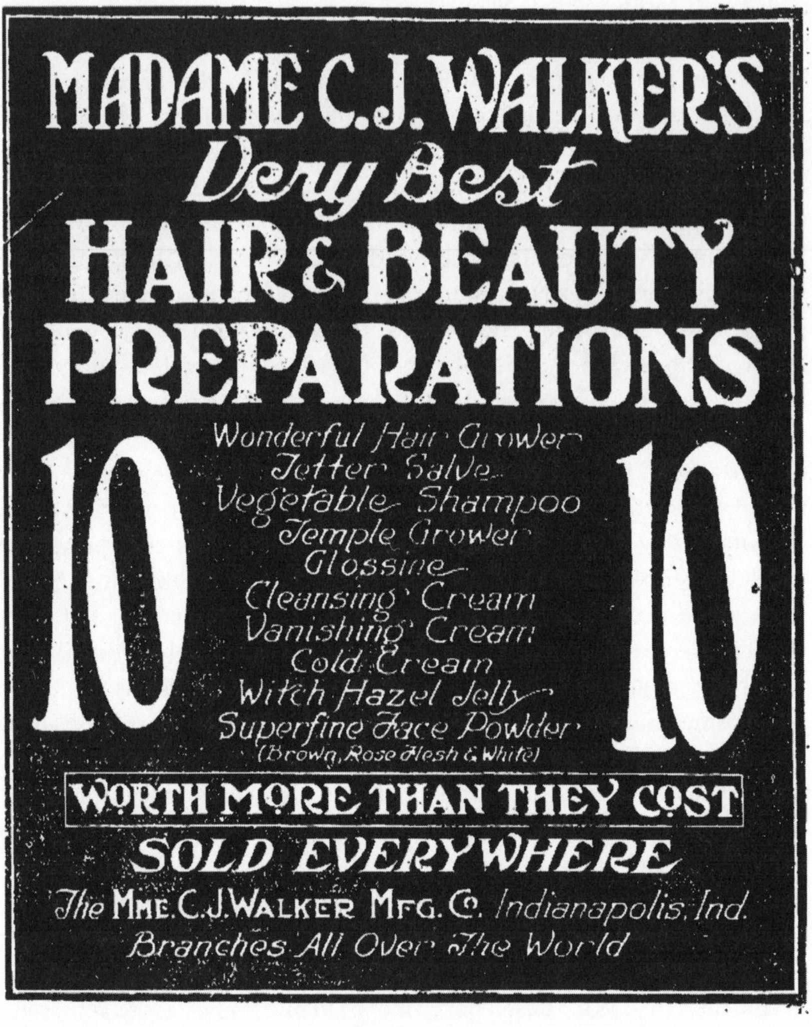

Figure 3.2 Walker Co. Advertisement for Ten Products, *Chicago Defender*, 12 July 1919, 6. Reprinted by permission of ProQuest, LLC and The Chicago Defender Newspaper.

In contrast to the first ad's feminine simplicity and given the company's resources and popularity, Walker Company ads could also be quite elaborate. The full-page ad shown in Figure 3.3 features extensive, detailed illustrations of the products in their packages. It also includes an illustrated tale of winged cherubim delivering the products to a fair, long-haired maiden, presumably the "queen" the products were "fit for," as if they were gifts from on high. Madam Walker's portrait is the centerpiece, serving to remind readers of her oft-repeated life story of rags-to-riches success through hard work, business acumen, and the blessing of a vision teaching her the recipe

Figure 3.3 Walker Co. Advertisement "Fit for a Queen," *Chicago Defender*, 10 January 1920, 5. Reprinted by permission of ProQuest, LLC and The Chicago Defender Newspaper.

for her products. The image itself, a headshot of Madam Walker with her hair arranged in a loose bun and dainty earrings dangling from her lobes, demonstrates her respectability. In the full version of this portrait, which was featured in other promotional materials such as the company's free instruction booklet, Walker wore an elegant white dress, which, though stylish, was by no means provocative or flashy. Using strategies such as these, Walker Company ads traded on the company's undeniable success and Madame Walker's reputation for wealthy respectability.

Although the Walker Company self-consciously provided black women with opportunities for financial and personal self-improvement, its advertising campaigns emphasizing the race mothering ideal through the missionary work of beautifying the race and the portrayal of respectable femininity de-emphasized one opportunity her products made possible. Madame Walker's products afforded black women the possibility to not only improve but also actually re-create themselves. Changing their hair and their appearance according to one of the several fashionable styles that came and went during the era allowed black women to become new versions of themselves. They could keep up with the latest fashions, feel beautiful, feel desirable, and, better yet, control their images—the face and figure they presented to the world. However, as noted, this last opportunity was one Mme. Walker refrained from emphasizing. Her promotional speeches and advertisements only hinted at the possibilities the products might offer for black women to increase something as salacious as their sex appeal and achieve something as radical as personal autonomy by creating new versions of themselves.

The Walker Company's promotional campaign demonstrates the effects of the utilization of race motherhood and the strategy of the culture of dissemblance. Although black women were afforded greater economic opportunities for self-determination, their independence was not wholly sanctioned within New Negro discourses and their humanity remained obscured. The Walker Company advertisements also point out how shocking and revolutionary were images of black women that flouted the rules of respectability. Accordingly, the Walker Company's decision not to use blueswomen like Ethel Waters as models and spokeswomen as other companies did indicate that its ongoing emphasis on respectability not only led it to highlight the carefully constructed image of the company founder but also to maintain a determined distance from association with "smut" and the questionable morality of lowdown entertainment like vaudeville and the blues.

Despite the conservatism and carefully molded ideals of New Negro womanhood presented by racial spokespersons like Madame Walker, black women did utilize such products to reinvent themselves. On the crowded avenues and streets of the cities, there walked black women who aspired to an ideal of New Negro womanhood quite different from the paragon the Walker Company sought to popularize. The migrants fashioned for themselves a New Negro woman suited for the vagaries and compromises, the machinations and negotiations of the struggle to not only survive but to enjoy life in the modern world of the industrial metropolis. This New Negro woman was not a paragon of respectability constrained by the culture of dissemblance. On the contrary, she sought the limelight and reveled in her visibility.

THE ILLUSION OF SELF-DETERMINATION:
MARKETING THE BLUESWOMAN

Walker Company advertisements were disseminated across the country along with other facets of the sex-race marketplace through black-owned and edited periodicals. These periodicals, such as the *Chicago Defender* and the *Pittsburgh Courier*, were distributed by black Pullman porters along the railway lines throughout the nation and eagerly read aloud and looked over in thousands of black communities large and small, thereby casting the ever-growing net of the sex-race marketplace far and wide.[23] Surely another motivation creating the great migration was the migrants' dreams of achieving the glamorous prosperity and living the exciting urban life reflected in those newspapers. Partially glimpsed through a sampling of the advertisements that crowded the pages of these New Negro era periodicals, the sex-race marketplace was constituted by a variety of fantasies and imagistic myths of New Negro womanhood. These fantasies and myths called upon both long-standing stereotypes and caricatures of nostalgic blackness and modern notions of black identity derived from the influx of African Americans into urban spaces across the nation and the consequent conspicuousness of the group and their perceived racial difference. Thus, the sex-race marketplace produced multiple versions of black womanhood—glamorous, ridiculous, sensual, ugly, caricatured, modern, and nostalgic.

This advertisement for Ethel Waters's race record "Heebie Jeebies" features an illustration of the blueswoman and her band in the midst of performance (Figure 3.4). The sharp lines and angles of the drawing all radiate from the depiction of a dancing Waters at the center. From her dynamic performing body, the rest of the band with their instruments seems to explode in a combustion of enthusiasm, action, and energy. Waters's short sleeveless dress, pointed-toe shoes, dangling earrings, and bobbed haircut convey her stylish, fashionable appearance, while the men's tuxedos and bow ties establish the whole group as upscale, high-quality performers.

Other illustrated advertisements followed a similar format of depicting the action or sensibility conveyed in the song's title or lyrics. A Paramount

heebie jeebies

Other Latest Columbia New Process Records

BESSIE SMITH
14147-D } Them "Has Been Blues"
10"—75c } Baby Doll

CLARA SMITH
14156-D } Whip It to a Jelly
10"—75c } How'm I Doin'

GEORGE WILLIAMS
14148-D } Levee Blues
10"—75c } Some Baby—My Gal

LEMUEL FOWLER'S WASHBOARD WONDERS
14155-D } Jelly Roll Blues
10"—75c } Frisky Feet

JOE JORDAN'S TEN SHARPS AND FLATS
14144-D } Morocco Blues
10"—75c } Senegalese Stomp

ROSA HENDERSON
14152-D } He's My Man
10"—75c } In That Apartment Upstairs

THE ST. MARK'S CHANTERS
14149-D } My Lord's Gonna Move This Wicked Race
10"—75c } Live Humble

As Only Ethel Waters Can Sing It

YOU all know the "heebie jeebies." Perhaps you've had them before. You just can't keep still. Here's your chance to get them in jazz form. When you hear Ethel Waters and Her Jazz Band warm up, you'll lay back your ears and go to it.

"Ev'rybody Mess Aroun'," on the other side, is a great jazz number, too. It's funny how Ethel does pick 'em. This record is another of her two-time, double action, sure fire hits. Play it for your friends before they play it for you.

No. 14153-D 10 in.—75c.

HEEBIE JEEBIES
EV'RYBODY MESS AROUN' }
Ethel Waters and Her Jazz Band

Columbia Phonograph Company — 1819 Broadway New York City

Other Latest Columbia New Process Records

ETHEL WATERS
14146-D } Sugar
10"—75c } You'll Want Me Back

DIXIE WASHBOARD BAND
14141-D } You for Me, Me for You
10"—75c } My Own Blues

PERRY BRADFORD AND HIS GANG
14142-D } So's Your Old Man
10"—75c } Just Met a Friend

MAGGIE JONES
14139-D } I'm a Real Kind Mama
10"—75c } I'm Leaving You

REV. J. M. GATES
14145-D } Death's Black Train Is Coming
10"—75c } Need of Prayer

JOHN ERBY
14151-D } Lonesome Jimmy Blues
10"—75c } Awfully Blue

BIRMINGHAM QUARTET
14154-D } Southbound Train
10"—75c } Birmingham Boys

NEW ORLEANS WANDERERS
698-D } Perdido Street Blues
10"—75c } Gate Mouth

Columbia NEW PROCESS Records

"Heebie Jeebies" By Ethel Waters and Her Jazz Band
Now in Jazz Form — Order This Record Today — It's Hot!! — 75c

On the Other Side Is "Everybody Mess Aroun'"
And It's a "Dinger"—75c

Order From

330 SOUTH STATE ST. **RIALTO MUSIC HOUSE** CHICAGO ILLINOIS

Figure 3.4 Columbia Records Advertisement for Ethel Waters' "Heebie Jeebies," *Chicago Defender*, 18 September 1926, 6. Reprinted by permission of ProQuest, LLC and The Chicago Defender Newspaper and courtesy of Sony Music Entertainment.

advertisement for Jimmy Blythe's song "Messin' Around," which featured "a vocal chorus by Trixie Smith," another popular blues singer, features a larger-than-life flapper whose swirling skirts and beads suggest she is messin' around to the rhythm of the tune (Figure 3.5). The female figure's rolled hose, revealed by the frenetic swirling of her skirts, the position of her legs,

Figure 3.5 Paramount Records Advertisement for "Messin' Around," *Chicago Defender,* 31 July 1926, 7. Reprinted by permission of ProQuest, LLC and The Chicago Defender Newspaper and with the approval of Jazzology Records.

and her pose all suggest her "messin' around" is more than a dance. The fact that her image surmounts Blythe's, whose song is the focus of the ad, communicate that the song's—and the ad's—intent is to create an atmosphere of sexual promiscuity and revelry in which women will be free to mess around for the benefit of onlookers.

Figure 3.6 Columbia Records Advertisement for "Whip It to a Jelly," *Chicago Defender*, 28 August 1926, 8. Reprinted by permission of ProQuest, LLC and The Chicago Defender Newspaper and courtesy of Sony Music Entertainment.

In contrast to the implied public nature of the sexualized activity in the advertisement for "Messin' Around," the ad for Clara Smith's song "Whip It to a Jelly," which describes the proper way to have satisfying sexual intercourse, is emphatically domestic (Figure 3.6). It is intended to belie the song's explicit sexual content by depicting the literal, rather than the metaphorical, meaning of the title. Here the blues singer Clara Smith is barely present. A portrait of her smiling face is included at the bottom right corner. Instead of to the blues singer herself, the act of whipping it to a jelly is ascribed to a smiling woman wearing an apron and pumps and busily preparing a bowl full of jelly. The New Negro woman is depicted, not as "the World's Greatest Moaner," as Columbia Records billed her, nor employed as a uniformed maid working in another woman's kitchen as most black women were, but as a happy, fashionably attired homemaker preparing a meal in her own kitchen.[24]

These advertisements utilize cartoons and illustrations to create an elaborate world or narrative to relate to viewers, many of whom may have been illiterate. As they looked, they were encouraged to buy access to an alternate life or identity—perhaps an alternate version of themselves—that permitted pleasures and luxuries heretofore only imagined or witnessed in someone else's life.

All of these advertisements also augmented the fantasy of the images by using racialized language in the text. This was language sellers presumed their potential customers wanted to hear—not necessarily language they assumed these customers spoke, but language that was intended to conjure a time, place, and personality that was identifiably black. "Boy-O-Boy how Clara Smith can whip it," Columbia Records announces in the advertisement in Figure 3.6. "And girls-O-girls how Clara does whip it. Before she gets through, it can't tell itself from a jelly roll. No record ever had anything on this latest one by Miss Smith. . . . When you hear her latest hit, you'll agree Clara does jes' fine."[25] Similarly, Columbia Records promises customers, "When you hear Ethel Waters and Her Jazz Band warm up, you'll lay back your ears and go to it."[26] Paramount, too, participates, claiming "Messin' Around" will "make your feet itch and quiver to hot-foot it on the boards. Look out you don't wear out your dogs a-dancing to it."[27] This racialized language moves readily from expression of an urban, savvy slang to a nostalgic rural drawl and droll expressions. Bespeaking two worlds at once—both of them fantastical—this two-tongued language equally addresses urban dwellers and those remaining at home in rustic communities and encapsulates the transition of the migrants, who remembered and perhaps longed for their rural roots even as they adapted themselves to city life.

Such racialized language was not politically benign, however. Even as it might have comforted homesick migrants and thrilled aspiring urban sophisticates, the language also caricatured, ridiculed, and blackfaced them. It helped to maintain the racial hierarchy and imbalance of power by returning African Americans to their accustomed cultural place as minstrel comedians and their social place as the stepping-stones of white supremacy. At times, this cultural power differential did not remain obscured in the text but was fully revealed as the theme of the advertisement itself.

In the text of their advertisement for Clara Smith's "Mean Papa Turn in Your Key," Columbia Records announces,

> Yes, indeed! Clara sure does sing with authority. . . . And when you play it, you're going to hear something special because there's the slickest guitar accompaniment you ever heard anywhere. Some of the plunks sound just like a bullfrog singing bass. No fooling.[28]

This racialized language is set alongside an image of a large, blackface caricature of a black woman who is holding out her hand, apparently demanding
her key, to a much smaller blackface caricature of a black man who wears a
loud checked suit, spats, and straw hat and carries a cane (Figure 3.7).
Drops of sweat seem to explode from his head as he reaches into his pocket
for the key. Given the title of the song and the import of most blueswomen's
lyrics about relationships, it is likely that this song describes a man who has
mistreated his partner, but the image suggests the *woman* is the strong, abusive, threatening element in the relationship, lording her power over her
much weaker, literally smaller, mate. The minstrel image used to advertise it
thus undercuts any woman-centered, feminist condemnation of marital
abuse Clara Smith might have intended to convey in the song, and it recalls
and re-establishes long-standing stereotypes about deviant black heterosexual relationships, akin to the same myth of black sexual deviance that
justified white supremacist terror.

In a similar way, Columbia Records' advertisement for Bessie Smith's
"Hateful Blues" features a caricatured black woman with a wide, minstrel
mouth and a mismatched outfit consisting of a checked skirt, striped stockings, and flower-print blouse brandishing a butcher knife as she chases a
man whose high-top hat, coattails, and spats are the only evidence of his
recent escape (Figure 3.8). Far from celebrating the independence and
self-confidence of a woman who refuses to tolerate an abusive lover who
"treated [her] wrong," as the lyrics of the song clearly intended, this advertisement, like the previous one, played upon and updated minstrel stereotypes of black women as overbearing shrews who dominate effeminate,
lazy black men.[29] A small circular portrait of Smith in a jeweled headdress
at the bottom left corner of the page is intended to insert the glamorous
sensuality "The Empress of the Blues" was to epitomize. But the juxtaposi-
tion of the two images—Smith and the caricatured minstrel woman—
deprecates Smith's image. She becomes equivalent to the stereotyped
minstrel woman in the ad, and her music is depreciated to give voice to the
violence and taboo relationships of stereotypically degraded and "disorganized" black gender relations rather than to black women's self-expression
in image and performance.

The racialized language and minstrel images in these advertisements
may have reflected something of black people's experiences, and even if
they did not, New Negroes might have appreciated and enjoyed their comedic intention. However, these images do more than entertain. They also
subvert the modernization process the migrants were undertaking in
becoming urbanized workers and savvy nightlife connoisseurs. The alter-
nately cowering and domineering creatures in these advertisements, in
their clashing outfits and unkempt hair, are rubes—coarse, unsophisticated,

Figure 3.7 Columbia Records Advertisement for "Mean Papa," *Chicago Defender*, 21 June 1924, 5. Reprinted by permission of ProQuest, LLC and The Chicago Defender Newspaper and courtesy of Sony Music Entertainment.

and unfashionable. The slang and minstrel images included in these advertisements reaffirm nostalgic notions of country black folk, foolishly squabbling over trifles and content to live ineffectual lives far from the centers of modern life and its sophisticated concerns, much like the anti-heroes Old Ned and Efrem in Micheaux's *Within Our Gates*. The sex-race marketplace offered the urbane allure of blues culture to all customers but also

Figure 3.8 Columbia Records Advertisement for Bessie Smith's "Hateful Blues," *Chicago Defender*, 19 July 1924, 5. Reprinted by permission of ProQuest, LLC and The Chicago Defender Newspaper and courtesy of Sony Music Entertainment.

circled back to disseminate nostalgic visions of its converse, ultimately servicing the formulation of a modern white supremacy steeped in primitivism that accommodated and appropriated the power of the potential revolution instigated by the emergence of the New Negro.

Although expanding black women's representations well beyond the Walker Company's constricted images of staid femininity, the advertisements promoting race records exploited the blueswomen's iconic status and contorted the self-determinative import of their art. In many ways, such advertisements exemplified the risks from which the Walker Company sought to shield black women's marketplace representations. Since the Walker Company continued its record of strong profits through direct sales, agent sales, training schools, and beauty shops, it clearly commanded the resources to finance a more dynamic, modern advertising campaign.[30] Yet, throughout the 1920s, the company declined to portray black feminine beauty through any lens besides respectability. Ironically, the Walker Company's fear of depicting the race "in plain ink" allowed white-owned companies, like the record companies discussed here and the cosmetic companies discussed later, to pioneer the photographic depiction of African American women's sexuality in the sex-race marketplace. These advertisements made even more explicit use of blueswomen's sexuality while also exploiting their iconic status and the idea of self-determination itself.

The Walker Company was not the only business marketing cosmetics to African American women during the New Negro era. Several entrepreneurs joined Mme. Walker in founding companies to sell hair products, skin treatments, and makeup to the fashion-conscious black urban populations. Chief among the multitude were Poro, owned and operated by Mme. Walker's former employer Annie Malone, and two white-owned companies, Golden Brown Beauty Preparations and Pluko Hair Dressing.[31] Oddly, Malone's Poro Company had relatively little advertising presence in national African American weeklies like the *Chicago Defender* during the 1920s, suggesting that Malone, too, adhered to the culture of dissemblance. Golden Brown and Pluko, however, produced a deluge of advertising copy, thereby establishing a powerful presence in the sex-race marketplace. These companies' advertisements often utilized photographs of black women performers to impress viewers with the "reality" and attainability of the fantasy they were selling. These images were sensual, sometimes adamantly sexualized, and depicted a very different New Negro woman from the one advanced by the Walker Company.

Pluko showcases a publicity photograph of vaudeville actress Katheryne A. Boyd in a quarter-page advertisement from 1926 (Figure 3.9). Quoted in the endorsement as stating that the product "is easy to use, keeps my scalp healthy, and makes my hair soft, straight, silky and glossy," Boyd is proclaimed as a sex symbol. Although her bobbed, wavy hair is certainly gleaming, her bare shoulder, neck, and back form the real focus of the photograph. Boyd is pictured smiling coquettishly and gazing fixedly over her left shoulder as if at a lover who has just entered the room. A fur coat or stole is bunched over her left arm as if it has just slipped from her shoulders. The fur, a string of pearls around her neck, and a strikingly large diamond ring are her only adornments. The viewer cannot tell whether Boyd wears a

Theater goers all over the country admire the beautiful hair of Miss Katheryne A. Boyd of the J. Lawrence Criner Company.

Miss Boyd says: "I often wondered how other women kept their hair looking so smooth and glossy until I started using Improved Pluko Hair Dressing. Then I knew the secret. This delicately fragranced, fine textured preparation is easy to use, keeps my scalp healthy, and makes my hair soft, straight, silky and glossy."

If everybody knew —

How easy it is to make their hair long, straight and glossy using Improved Pluko Hair Dressing, everyone would have beautiful hair that is easy to arrange in any manner and stays that way looking smooth and glossy; because this soft, daintily perfumed preparation is so economically priced everyone can afford to use it.

Improved **Pluko**

" ALWAYS THE FINEST HAIR DRESSING
NOW THE EASIEST TO USE "
Snow White 50¢ *Amber* 25¢

If your dealer can't supply you with Improved Pluko Hair Dressing, send his name to the Pluko Company, Memphis, Tenn., and for your courtesy they will send you a free copy of their book "Be Proud of Your Hair"

Figure 3.9 Pluko Advertisement featuring Katheryne Boyd, *Chicago Defender*, 25 September 1926, 4. Reprinted by permission of ProQuest, LLC and The Chicago Defender Newspaper.

backless gown or is completely nude under her fur, but the glamorous, sexually charged effect is the same either way.

Here, Boyd is utterly revealed for consumption. Stating that "this soft, daintily perfumed preparation is so economically priced everyone can afford to use it," Pluko clearly intended to market its product to the overwhelmingly young, working-class population of black migrant women and assumed they dreamed of looking like Katheryne Boyd. Such women attempted to claim and express their own sexuality and enjoy their beauty on their own terms. But the exploitation of the far-reaching sex-race marketplace meant that their sexuality was not wholly theirs. They did not completely control its sociocultural effects or the uses made of it.

Likewise, Golden Brown Beauty Preparations displayed Ethel Waters in a revealing spaghetti strap dress (Figure 3.10). Even more explicitly recommending its model as an icon of beauty and desirability, Golden Brown proclaimed in its half-page advertisement that "'Queen of Blues Singers' Ethel Waters tells how Madame Mamie Hightower's 'Golden Brown' beauty preparations have made her the most famous and beautiful of Our Race Stars." In her matching pearl earrings, bracelet, and rope necklaces and clingy, spaghetti strap dress, Waters epitomized the sexy, golden-skinned race woman Golden Brown thought its potential buyers would like to be, or should want to be. Waters's photograph is not as sexually charged as Boyd's. Her expression is open, her smile innocent rather than provocative, and her attire suggests a glitzy night on the town rather than a clandestine assignation. Nevertheless, this photograph, like Boyd's, conveys a sensual allure distinctly free from the strictures of the culture of dissemblance and the ideals of race motherhood. In the end, however, neither kind of representation—that exemplified by the Walker Company ads nor that of these alluring images—conveyed black women as whole humans.

Racialized language permeates the text of this Golden Brown advertisement as it did those of the recording companies. However, rather than street-smart slang or nostalgic drawl, this language is distinctly political in tone and content. In emphasizing Ethel Waters's status as one of "Our Race Stars," Golden Brown claimed her as a representative black woman in the politicized language of the New Negro era. Golden Brown sought to emulate and best the Walker Company in every way. Not only did they sell very similar cosmetic products and utilize photographs of popular performers to advertise them but they also claimed for themselves the same role in the struggle for racial advancement. They, too, were in the beneficent business of beautifying the race. The text in the ad states, "The Golden Brown Beauty treatment, originated by Madame Mamie Hightower never fails, because she spent years of work to find the right beauty treatment for Our Race." In another advertisement, Golden Brown advised readers that "Pride in Our Race demands that we look Light, Bright, and Attractive," indicating that Golden Brown products would assist customers in achieving such an appearance. The text of every Golden Brown ad concluded with a version of the clarifying, politicized slogan, "We have no desire to be white, but we should have the clear, bright and attractive appearance that nature intended."[32]

Figure 3.10 Golden Brown Chemical Company Advertisement featuring Ethel Waters, *Chicago Defender*, 25 August 1923, 20. Reprinted by permission of ProQuest, LLC and The Chicago Defender Newspaper.

Furthermore, Golden Brown publicized itself as a black-owned business operated by a "Madame Mamie Hightower," an ostensible race mother contributing to African American economic independence. Much of the text of the ads was written in an intimate first person style purported to be the voice of this black woman entrepreneur. However, Mamie Hightower was most likely the wife of Zack Hightower, a black man who worked as a porter for the Memphis-based and white-owned wholesale drug company Hessig-Ellis, which owned the Golden Brown Company. Although Mrs. Hightower may have sometimes worked out of her home as a beautician serving the Memphis black community, she did not own a beauty salon, much less develop a line of original products or operate a cosmetic manufacturing firm. She probably had nothing to do with the invention and sale of the Golden Brown product line.[33] Promoting the purely fictional account of Madame Mamie Hightower's rise from Beale Street salon owner to nationally successful entrepreneur, Golden Brown traded upon Mme. C. J. Walker's well-known story—itself an idealized account tirelessly disseminated by the Walker Company—to increase its sales.

In this way, the sex-race marketplace operated in the frenetic, circular fashion of a whirlpool, cynically exploiting its own exploitative fictions, even exploiting the hope of self-determination itself. Here, the ideal New Negro race mother was reduced to a wholesale fictional commodity, exploited to the point of ridicule. Caught in such a whirlpool of myth, fantasy, stereotype and constructed images proffered for sale and delectation, representations of black women in the marketplace contorted the humanity of their living counterparts. Understood through the sex-race marketplace, black women were never simply performers or customers but always spectacles and objects serving not only the market of the migrants' desires but more truly the maintenance, despite modernization and industrialization, of the racial and sexual imbalance of power.

This fantastic, deceitful, chimera-filled cultural space was the birthplace of the New Negro woman. It was through black women's participation in the sex-race marketplace that they first learned to consider other kinds of existences, and it was to the marketplace they turned to acquire the goods to try to turn the mirage into reality.

CONSUMING HERSELF: FASHIONING THE NEW NEGRO WOMAN

Blues music and the blueswoman as an icon and commodified image figured prominently in both urban black nightlife and the sex-race marketplace that surrounded, mythologized, sold, and popularized that entertainment culture. The "blueswomen" of the sex-race marketplace were not only performers of blues music but also the cooks, social workers, maids, teachers, laundresses, and prostitutes they had been and might be again after the limelight dimmed. The blueswomen were the embattled, unabashed, newly urban black women whose disappointments and dreams were recorded on the race records. Through the proliferation and effects of the modern sex-race marketplace, all black women were blueswomen. Every black woman was a spectacle and a suspicious object for the surrounding culture. Black women watched and consumed the blueswomen as popular icons and, in turn, were themselves consumed by their fellows—men and women of all races desiring and envying and fantasizing about them, disapproving observers, racial spokesmen seeking to uplift or liberate them, cultural producers who utilized them as the raw materials of their art—as well as by slummers who entered Harlem or the South Side or walked down Beale Street to get a taste of blues culture and to see the sights, which included the Harlemites, the South Side Chicagoans—the fascinating black people who lived in these and other segregated urban enclaves.[34]

Much like the images of Katheryne Boyd and Ethel Waters used in the advertisements discussed earlier, publicity photographs of blueswomen, or performing women, displayed them as beautiful, desirable, dazzling women richly dressed in the most fashionable, even outlandishly gaudy, clothing, jewelry, and hairstyles. They were most often photographed in stage costume like the one Ethel Waters wore for her Paris performance—a sumptuous dress designed to flatter the figure, a hat or headdress worn like a crown, and sparkling jewels grandly displayed, all signifying their regal status among popular entertainers. Always, they were photographed to reveal and display a creation or ideal manufactured by and for someone else. In the photograph, the New Negro woman became a blueswoman, an image meant to appeal to an audience. Captured in the following photographs are various versions of the commodified New Negro woman. Each represents a particular construction of modern black womanhood, the figure of the black woman used to exemplify one fantasy or another.

An early publicity photograph shows an Ethel Waters different from the Parisian version, one elegantly and simply attired in a satin strapless gown, dangling earrings and sparkling ring (Figure 3.11). She wears no headdress but her head is encircled by a halo of light, a trick of the camera that emphasizes the long line of her neck, shoulder, and back and places the right side of her face in silhouette. Her short hair is brushed back from her forehead. Her expression is serious, perhaps reverent. Her eyes are focused slightly above and to the left of the camera, and she does not smile. Her hand resting on her breast, her posture and her stance facing the left rather than the camera, and the far-away look in her eyes all suggest regal or proud self-possession.

Figure 3.11 Ethel Waters photograph inscribed to piano player Mary Lou Williams, Mary Lou Williams Collection, Subseries 2D, Box 9, Folder 7, Institute of Jazz Studies, Dana Library, Rutgers University, Newark Campus, Newark, New Jersey. Reprinted by permission of the Institute of Jazz Studies.

Although recorded on film, she has eluded capture, and neither the camera nor the viewer possesses her.

A similar effect of self-possession is achieved in a different vein by Josephine Baker, the internationally recognizable diva of the Paris stage (Figure 3.12). Here the infamous performer is displayed in the nude. She wears large hoop earrings and a choker necklace of three rows of metallic

Figure 3.12 Josephine Baker, 1927, Photographs Collected by James Weldon Johnson and Carl Van Vechten, Box 1, Josephine Baker folder 1, JWJ Collection, Yale Collection of American Literature, Beinecke Rare Book and Manuscript Library, New Haven, Connecticut. © Condé Nast Archive/ Corbis. Reprinted with permission.

beads. A primary light comes from the photographer's left so that Baker's shadow is clearly outlined on the wall behind her and looms over the photograph in a majestic or haunting way. Baker stands on a platform covered with undulating, shiny fabric so that she seems to rise out of a sea. She covers her breasts with her hands. Her fingers are laced with ropes of pearls and a drape of the fabric. The pearls and fabric flow from her hands and fall the length of her body to her feet. In this way, the middle of her torso and her pubis are covered while her thighs and sides are revealed. Her expression is serious. Her mouth is closed softly, not sternly but with no hint of a smile. Her eyes look directly into the lens and thus directly into the eyes of the viewer, though she is positioned slightly above the camera. She could be a statue looking down upon smaller humans revering her. She could be Venus seducing mortal men. The shadow behind her heightens this effect of her superiority. Other lights shine upon her from several locations at once so that she is lit from below and behind as well as from her right side and from the top. The undersides of her arms glow with ethereal light, as do the top of her lacquered head and her right shoulder. Within this play of light and shadow, glimmering fabric and precious stones, Baker is revealed but not exposed. It seems she cannot be possessed. She indeed appears superior to her viewers.

Yet Josephine Baker is the woman whose nude, barefoot dance in a banana skirt is legendary as an example of European primitivism and exploitation of black female bodies in the service of cultural imperialism. Her self-possession in the photograph here is a trick of the light, a performance on her part and on the part of the photographer.

Blueswomen, or performing black women, like Ethel Waters and Josephine Baker, lived in and subsisted on this play of light and shadow. It was, quite literally, their bread and butter. Like the performances they document, these photographs were performances of seduction and temptation, commodified fantasies sold at market value. It was the blueswoman's job to manipulate the sex-race marketplace, to navigate its exploitative powers as long and as successfully as she could.

A nude photograph of professional musician and amateur vamp Nora Holt achieves a very different effect from that created by the nude of Josephine Baker (Figure 3.13).[35] Nora Holt was the first black woman to earn a master's degree in music, worked as the music critic for the *Chicago Defender*, and later founded the National Organization of Negro Musicians. She was known and respected by many New Negro luminaries, including Langston Hughes and James Weldon Johnson, and the ever-present white critic, novelist, and chronicler Carl Van Vechten. She was one of novelist Nella Larsen's friends. Holt was also widely known for her audacious antics, such as stripping and dancing in the nude at Harlem society parties. Van Vechten labeled her "the prize vamp, white or black, of the world."[36] Married five times and the heir of a significant fortune left her by her first husband, she often supplemented her income, and her fun, by performing in clubs and cabarets in the great cities of the world as well as by hiring herself out to perform at white society parties.

Figure 3.13 Nora Holt photographed by James Marquis Connely, Chicago 1930, Photographs Collected by James Weldon Johnson and Carl Van Vechten, Box 5, Nora Holt folder, JWJ Collection, Yale Collection of American Literature, Beinecke Rare Book and Manuscript Library, New Haven, Connecticut.

In the photograph, the light shines from the left directly above Holt's face so that her head and exposed breasts are the fully illuminated focus of the image, and the room seems otherwise dark. She reclines on a dark couch or chair with her shoulder blades resting against the arm of the furniture and her neck and shoulders bent backward over it. A white fur hangs over the back of the chair or couch to her side. Her head is turned toward the camera, and she looks directly into the lens. Her mouth is slightly open as if she were panting. Her knees are bent and her legs bent at the hip with her hands resting on her knees. The position of Holt's body thus suggests breathy, preening anticipation of sex. She wears quite a bit of makeup, especially eye shadow. Her eyebrows are drawn in near half circles over her eyes, and she wears lipstick shaped to her lip line in a bow. She has used cosmetics as a costume to heighten the effect of her performance and, perhaps, to highlight the distance between her "real" self and the version depicted in this photograph. Her hair is straightened and styled in curls pinned back from her face. She wears hoop earrings, one of which hangs down from her ear with the force of gravity, emphasizing the total, vulnerable suspension of her head and the arch of her back. Here, as in the other publicity photographs, the blueswoman is beautiful and glamorous, successful and wealthy, very sexy and desirable. But this is a different game of seduction. Holt is not unattainable but readily available, even offering herself. Perhaps this photograph is more "pornographic" than "artistic." Holt's image here promises satisfaction whereas Baker's and Waters's taunt and provoke. Like the photograph of Katheryne Boyd used in the Pluko advertisement, it suggests the blueswoman is ready for an illicit sexual assignation. The fur and lace pantalets insinuate Holt has recently stripped off her rich street attire or glamorous costume for the benefit of the viewer who, at least for the moment, owns her utterly. Holt surely enjoyed her manipulation of the marketplace's ingrained hyper-sexualization of black women. Fearlessly, she took that representation in her hands, molded and maximized it to augment her reputation as a vamp, her fun, and her income.

Depicted and adorned as "queens" and "stars," exotic icons and primitive fantasies in the sex-race marketplace, the blueswomen were all real people who had achieved a great deal of a certain kind of success. They, too, were migrants who had traveled unfamiliar and daunting urban landscapes. They, too, had looked to the marketplace in search of a fantasy to escape into, a dream to chase. Miraculously, they were one day fortunate enough to find themselves, their very own faces reflected there. But they must have known that woman in the reflection was not who they really were. The greatest power of the sex-race marketplace was its ability to wholly obscure that distinction between real, human black women and their glamorous, exotic, erotic representations.

To some extent, photographs, along with every other medium of recorded images, are incapable of capturing New Negro womanhood, or indeed any version of "real" humanity. Photographs are always constructions, performances on the part of the subject and creations on the part of the photographer. Just as blueswomen were performing when they struck alluring or comedic or overtly sexual poses before the camera, so were regular New Negro women performing—perhaps simply performing their best selves,

Figure 3.14 Group portrait of beauty contestants (SC-CN-97-0287), *The Interstate Tattler* Photograph Collection, Photographs and Prints Division, Schomburg Center for Research in Black Culture, The New York Public Library, Astor, Lenox, and Tilden Foundations, New York, New York. Reprinted with permission.

the selves they wanted to record and remember—when they stood before the camera and smiled. Likewise, when they dressed to present themselves to the public, adorned their bodies with fashionable clothing, wore shoes with the right heel, selected makeup of the right shade, plucked their eyebrows to shape them as Ethel Waters's were shaped, and styled their hair in the marcel waves many blueswomen wore, they were culling images and ideals from the sex-race marketplace and performing its glamour.

The young women in the last photograph here seem to be in their twenties (Figure 3.14). They are dressed in evening gowns, and there is a bandstand in the background, suggesting they are attending a dance or ball. They are contestants competing in a beauty competition sponsored by either Caspar Holstein, Harlem club-owner, gangster, and benefactor of the famed *Opportunity* literary contests, or the *Inter-State Tattler* newspaper, represented by its editor Bennie Butler standing on the left, or both.[37] Thus, the event occasioning the photo of these young women was undergirded by two of the most important promoters of the period whose combined funding, exposure, and commentary helped develop the notion of the New

Negro and to sell it. The influence of these worldly men lends the ambience a bit of risqué glitz, for they were not unassailably honorable escorts for naïve young ladies. Due to Holstein's and Butler's prominence, it was likely that the winner of this contest would become the object of a great deal of exposure and scrutiny in the sex-race marketplace. She would share the limelight that was the blueswoman's habitat.

The women in the front row hold flags in their laps that read "Howard" and "Lincoln," the names of prestigious African American universities. Each woman wears a banner across her chest. The glare of the light in the photograph renders most of the banners illegible, but three of them read "Miss New York," "Miss Howard," and "Miss Harlem." Apparently, the women were competing to decide which of them best represented young New Negro womanhood in beauty, form, and accomplishments. Thus, their local communities—their schools, their neighborhoods—had determined them to be exemplary New Negro women. Despite the elite university flags, however, these women do not seem uniformly bourgeois in their deportment, respectability, and style. Indeed, they are a rather eclectic, even mismatched, group. Their differences suggest a diversity of backgrounds in region, class, and education, and perhaps they have various reasons for their participation in this event. Many seem uncomfortable in their surroundings, arranged as they are to face the camera, preparing to have their images forever recorded in the "plain ink" so mistrusted by some of their fellow New Negroes. Perhaps the women pictured here are best understood as fellow aspirants, seeking to be awarded the imprimatur of selection, to achieve prominence and respect within their communities, to embody a version of modern, sophisticated, confident New Negro womanhood particular to each of them.

The women's attire certainly proclaims them as fashionable women showing off their best clothing. All of the women wear short-sleeved or sleeveless gowns that appear to be made of satin, silk, or lace cut with v-shaped or rounded necklines to gently emphasize their long necks and rounded busts. All wear pearl or bead necklaces to further decorate their torsos. Gone are the high collars and long sleeves that covered the bodies of the Reconstruction generation's Victorian ladies and the Walker Company's paragon. Under their skirts, they wear silken stockings. The gleam of "Miss New York's" can be seen because she has crossed her legs at the knee, a bold, forgetful, or simply ignorant violation of the rules of respectable, early twentieth-century deportment. She wears pointy-toed pumps with two-inch heels and a delicate strap fastened across the top of the foot. The pointy toes of similar slippers peek out from under the gowns of the other women, who have crossed their legs at the ankle or not at all, as bourgeois gentility demanded. Right down to the tips of their toes, then, these women perform their different relationships to social class and

New Negro bourgeois aspirations. As well, all were dressed in the latest fashions. Indeed, their gowns are remarkably similar.

As much as their clothing, if not more, their hair and makeup mark them as New Negro women. More distinctive than their similar gowns, their hairstyles seem individually tailored to suit each woman's face and figure. Each wears her hair in a straightened style, and several wear their hair bobbed, or cut short so that it hangs somewhere between the earlobes and chin. Many have marcel waves, while others have brushed or pinned their hair back from their faces. Only one of the women, second from the left in the front row, seems to have attended this event without wearing makeup. All of the rest wear at least powder, and four are obviously wearing lipstick, while the others may be wearing lighter shades. Three of these representative women are darker-skinned, and one of these, the third from the left on the front row, is wearing a cosmetic that is much too light for her skin tone. The second girl from the left on the back row, though she appears to have a medium brown skin tone, also looks as though she is wearing makeup too light for her. Each girl thus appears as if she is wearing a mask of white powder. Perhaps they sought to obey the sentiment driving Golden Brown's decree that New Negro women were to be "light, bright, and attractive" to represent the race well. Some of the women, the first, second, and third from the left in the back row in particular, have shaped their eyebrows into delicate lines like the ones worn by Ethel Waters.

These women do not go topless, nor do they sport spaghetti strapped or strapless dresses that bare the whole of their shoulders, chests, and backs to onlookers. They are not performers brazenly and intentionally selling themselves as commodities in the marketplace. Nevertheless, they have adorned themselves in moderate versions of the figure-revealing, skin-baring, cosmetic-enhanced fashions the blueswomen popularized and the sex-race marketplace sold and disseminated. They have heeded Madame C. J. Walker's call to beautify themselves on behalf of racial advancement, but they have progressed further than she intended. To a lesser extent than the icons of the sex-race marketplace, but just as earnestly, they are performing New Negro womanhood and testing their prowess in the arts of allure. Using the tools provided by the marketplace and drawing upon the fantasies available there, they have become as glamorous as they can be, perhaps as they dare to be.

Thus, the swirling whirlpool of the sex-race marketplace encircled the self-conceptions, bearing, and lived realities of the human New Negro women its fantastic images represented. New Negro women walked with the sex-race marketplace imprinted on their skin, both because they drew from it the styles and products that adorned their bodies and because onlookers observed and recognized them through the veil of the conceptions and fantasies the marketplace cast over them. In this way, the New Negro woman was created in and through the sex-race marketplace, out of the self-presentations and aspirations the migrants themselves provided as fodder but also out of the vagaries of an unequal society adapting to its new imperial circumstance and seeking means to retain ties to a familiar sociocultural order.

As well as to escape the economic ravages of the boll weevil, the clutches of terrorizing lynch mobs, and the wandering hands of assaulting men, African American migrants flooded the cities in order to enjoy a way of life wholly different from the one they had known, to conceive new versions of themselves and of their reality. The sex-race marketplace, perhaps to a greater extent than the increasingly hostile, inconstant market for wages, goods, and services, helped them create those new identities and realities. It was in the sex-race marketplace that the style, art, and conspicuousness of the new urban dwellers were sold as spectacle and entertainment and to which those same migrants turned to acquire the goods—clothes, beauty products, race records, deportment, style, and sense of well-being—that would showcase the success of their arduous journeys and make them New Negroes according to its prescriptions.

The interwar sex-race marketplace was powerful in its discursive reach, affecting the identities, subjectivities, and ideologies of each of its consumers, observers, and critics, shaping the ways in which they understood both themselves and what blackness meant in their world. The New Negroes drew upon the sex-race marketplace and participated in it as they created their new political and cultural identities. They were largely known through its representations, and they lived in its swirling midst.

The New Negroes understood the many means by which popular culture shapes ideas about race and sex and the range of identities and self-determinative possibilities available. As the previous chapters have explored, the New Negroes adopted a multitude of strategies to control their representations in the marketplace and thus to shape their subjectivities. And they did succeed in wresting more control over racial representations and participation in the construction of racial meanings than they had ever accessed before. However, their efforts moved in divergent, often competing directions even as the marketplace itself acted as a whirlpool, constantly circling, repeating itself, giving and taking, adapting and absorbing every effort, insidiously remaking modernity to reinforce long-standing racial regimes.

New Negro women helped to form the sex-race marketplace in its complex multiplicity, and their understandings of the modern fashions, entertainments, luxuries, and identities they sought were partially shaped by its influence. Nevertheless, they understood themselves to be caught in its rapids—misrepresented within the discourse shaping the racial and sexual politics of their early twentieth-century world. New Negro women's resistance to the marketplace confirms its existence and its power. Their words reflect their efforts to determine their fates and identities within and despite its vagaries.

CHAPTER 4

⌒⌣⌒

Solidarity, Sex, Happiness, and Oppression in the Words of New Negro Women

"Within her soul," award-winning social worker Elise McDougald declared of the New Negro woman, "she knows little of peace and happiness."[1] Although McDougald purported to speak for the great cross-section of African American women in her essay "The Task of Negro Womanhood," she only reliably represented those whom she praised and of whom she considered herself a part—the strivers who were integrating business, the trades, and industry and those who toiled on behalf of the race in teaching, nursing, and social work. These words thus intimated her own anxiety and dissatisfaction, her own unhappiness. Indeed, viewed from the perspective of this forlorn, revealing sentence, McDougald's entire essay bespeaks a certain amount of veiled pain. Her tone becomes decipherable as false optimism, strained hope.

With this remarkable essay, published in Alain Locke's landmark 1925 collection *The New Negro*, McDougald inserted a black woman's voice among those of the largely male New Negro literati who were establishing themselves as the arbiters not only of black artistic talent but also of the correct, race-serving representation of the modern African American subjectivity. McDougald's essay duly praised those New Negro women whose professional or industrial pursuits seemed to confirm the race's departure from the subservience and backwardness of past generations. Thus, despite the unfulfilled need for "peace and happiness," McDougald declared that "the New Negro woman is courageously standing erect, developing within herself the moral strength to rise above and conquer false attitudes. She is maintaining her natural beauty and charm and improving her mind and opportunity. She is measuring up to the needs of her family, community and race, and radiating a hope throughout the land."[2] McDougald's New Negro woman was the consummate race mother. Her poise undermined white supremacist assumptions about black character while her accomplishments served the greater racial good. With these concluding words, McDougald attempted to strike a ringing note of optimism and progress. But the finality of her pronouncement lingers. No peace. No happiness. Some doubt in McDougald's well-ordered but restive mind whispered that the New Negro woman's self-sacrifice and embodiment of race motherhood was not enough to secure her fulfillment, nor did it restore the humanity constantly undercut by the sex-race marketplace.

The daughter of one of the founders of the National Urban League and a divorcee, McDougald, like the women she described, was holding her back rigidly straight while laboring on, gritting her teeth, and shouldering her burden.[3] She was doing her bit for the race but doing only a little, maybe nothing, for herself. She endeavored to take comfort and find joy in the successes of the race as a whole, to dissolve herself into the greater good. She wrote that the "grotesque Aunt Jemimas of the street-car advertisements" and portrayals of "feminine viciousness or vulgarity" in the theater houses formed a "shadow" over New Negro women, especially those striving, as she was, to contribute to racial advancement.[4] McDougald recognized and resented the power and pervasiveness of the sex-race marketplace. Her essay, hinting as it does at a range of intra-racial ruptures around class, sexuality, and gender relations, bespeaks a New Negro woman's dissatisfaction with the racial and sexual status quo and also hints at a critique of the masculinist agenda for racial advancement as it failed to provide opportunity for women's fulfillment. Even as she endorsed race motherhood and chided those women she considered too backward or immoral to advance the race, McDougald suggested the need for a woman-centered intervention in the racial and sexual discourses of the New Negro era.

A NEW NEGRO WOMEN'S DISCOURSE

In the Southern and Northern towns, cities, and metropoles to which African American women had migrated, they all worked—mostly in domestic service. Most also joined clubs, churches, and neighborhood associations; many participated in various political organizations and workers' unions. They bought things. Some married; some raised children. They lived, and they died. If this significant first generation of modern African American women is thought of at all, they are understood in the aggregate. There is an attempt to know them through the ideologies of the organizations they joined, through the various modes of the struggle for racial advancement, through the numbers that have been gathered and tallied to show various trends, anomalies, and divisions among them. [5] Largely missing is an understanding of New Negro women's subjective experience, especially in the face of the overwhelming social and cultural transformations they initiated and witnessed and the remodeled forms of racial and sexual oppression with which they contended. [6]

Although they were generally quite circumspect, some New Negro women did express their reflections on the racial and sexual politics of the period and their own efforts to determine their identities and fates. Some of the boldest in revealing themselves were the women novelists of the New Negro Renaissance such as Jessie Fauset and Nella Larsen, who used fiction as a forum to voice sexual and racial issues and air social criticisms on behalf of their characters that they did not publicly speak on their own behalf. Through their fiction, New Negro women like Fauset and Larsen explored themes of sexual desire, personal fulfillment, identity, and the efficacy of New Negro racial advancement ideologies.[7] Other New Negro women addressed these topics in prose essays, correspondence, and interviews recording their memories of the period. Together, these texts reveal a New Negro women's discourse on early twentieth century sexual and racial politics and African American women's access to the opportunities for self-determination that purportedly abounded in the era. This woman-generated, relatively private discourse critiques the masculinism of the period and also asserts a New Negro woman's subjectivity distinct from those evident in the sex-race marketplace and race motherhood. While their words acknowledge and sometimes even endorse aspects of these discourses, New Negro women also asserted their own subjectivity, insisting they were more complex and fully human than either dominant discourse allowed.

This New Negro women's discourse was comprised of four overarching themes. Black women were concerned with racial solidarity and the obligation to serve as race mothers, sexual politics within the race and in their own relationships, the personal struggle for some version of fulfillment and the ability to determine their own identities and destinies, and the omnipresent, seemingly omnipotent force of racial oppression. New Negro women turned these questions over in their minds, examined them from different angles, sometimes attended to one more than others. When they thought about their lives, or sat down to evaluate their condition, or endeavored to dream a world that would explain the nature of their lived experience, these were the topics to which their minds turned because these were the quandaries that formed their choices and thus shaped their lives. African American women struggled with intra-racial issues of loyalty, unity, mutual uplift, and individual aspirations; the negotiation of the power differentials between men and women in private relationships and in society; the definition of true fulfillment and if and how it might be reached; and the nature of the oppression that circumscribed their opportunities, shaped their self-perceptions and public images, and affected all of their personal, political, and social relationships. This New Negro women's discourse defined racial oppression according to black women's particular experiences in the decades of the early twentieth century and provides black women's perspectives on their opportunities to achieve the self-determination that was the hallmark of the era's racial aspirations.

The remainder of this chapter consists of sections addressing, in turn, solidarity, sexual politics, the quest for fulfillment, and oppression. In recognition of the interdependence and constant intersection of these issues in New Negro women's lives, each successive section builds on the insights offered in the preceding one. Likewise, each section draws upon the same range of sources, including prose essays, published oral histories, correspondence, and fiction. It was in such semi-private texts as their correspondence and fiction that New Negro women revealed their criticisms of the period's race politics and asserted the complex humanity of their personal selves in defiance of the limiting discourses of the era.

THE OBLIGATIONS OF SOLIDARITY

According to the New Negro ethos, the ideal black woman was one who devoted herself to the betterment, modernization, and advancement of her people by exemplifying the ideal of race motherhood. In the course of their lives, New Negro women learned that bearing the responsibility of advancing the race did not necessarily engender a sense of fulfillment, but neither did shirking that responsibility result in a sense of personal liberation for individual women. As their migrations and personal choices changed their circumstances and their social roles shifted, they still felt a profound racial unity based on their common heritage that was daily reinforced by the totality of the oppression they faced. At the same time, they struggled to reconcile this sense of solidarity and the obligation of race motherhood with their quest for individual self-determination and personal fulfillment. This struggle, this retention of individual desire and therefore hesitation or even refusal to completely submit oneself to the demands of the larger racial good, and, what is more, the audacity to voice an incomplete satisfaction with one's assigned role, is a hallmark of New Negro womanhood. Although the imperative to contribute to racial advancement remained, a new intimation of the possibilities for personal satisfaction and fulfillment beyond this emerged as women discovered the transformative possibilities of modern, urban life.

A New Negro graduate of the Tuskegee Institute, one of the great African American training schools founded by members of the Reconstruction generation as an exemplar of the ideology of uplift, Frances Mary Albrier described the ongoing imperative of racial solidarity as almost a religious vocation, an epiphany that came after a period of confusion and despair. She said "a great many students," including her, struggled through a time of

> wandering around . . . especially those in the South. They see so much and they realize that there are so many fields. Oh, I can be of value to my race and my people if I take this or if I take that. They become kind of lost until they can find themselves—find what they can better do to create an ambition to help people, to help the race. In my day and time, that was instilled in us through all of the organizations, even through the churches.

Realizing that some people might perceive such a vocation as "quite a burden to carry with you," Albrier conceded that it "makes you very careful," very aware that your behavior, moral standing, and deportment, if less than perfect, "would hurt the *entire* race."[8] Her elders of the Reconstruction generation had taught Albrier nothing of the sense that a career or a life path should be an individual or personally fulfilling pursuit. Those who were educated were privileged for a purpose, and that purpose was always racial advancement.

Essayist Marita Bonner described the New Negro generation's confrontation with the question of solidarity through a metaphor of a cat's desires.

> Somehow you feel like a kitten in a sunny catnip field that sees sleek, plump brown field mice and yellow baby chicks sitting coyly, side by side, one under each leaf. A desire to dash three or four ways seizes you.
>
> That's youth.
>
> But you know that things learned need testing—acid testing—to see if they are really after all, an interwoven part of you. All your life you have heard of the debt you owe "Your People" because you have managed to have the things they have not largely had.
>
> So you find a spot where there are hordes of them—of course below the Line—to be your catnip field while you close your eyes to mice and chickens alike.[9]

Because of "the debt [she] owe[s] '[Her] People,'" this black woman feels compelled to move to the South, "below the [Mason-Dixon] Line," and devote herself to their welfare and advancement. In order to do this, she must "close [her] eyes to mice and chickens alike," or ignore her "desire to dash" after her own dreams and needs. Her "catnip field" must be the work of race motherhood; she must find any satisfactions she might have within its narrow parameters. Bonner represented this repression as maturity. The urge to dash after the temptations of plump mice and chickens was a youthful one. However, even in her mature acquiescence to her perceived obligations, she remained uncertain that this seemingly inevitable vocation should be her life's work. She is going through the motions of repaying her debt to the race while waiting for the result of the "acid testing" that will reveal whether this vocation that has been instilled in her is "really[,] after all, an interwoven part of [her]."

As Bonner implied, the compulsion to return "below the Line" and devote oneself to the group was a constraining, even a disappointing, outcome of the arduous effort to attain educational and social improvement. It left little room for self-determination. But escape was not easy. The effort to break out from this stifling experience was hampered by gender considerations. A woman, Bonner reminded her readers, could not whimsically board a train to New York from Washington, D.C. to explore the sights and sounds. "For you know that—being a woman—you cannot twice a month or twice a year, for that matter, break away to see or hear anything in a city that is supposed to see and hear too much. That's being a woman. A woman of any color."[10] Women were prevented by convention and hampered by the threat of danger from traveling freely. They hesitated to leave their posts alone to pursue their own capricious interests for fear of disappointing their communities' expectations of selflessness and steadfast endurance. Besides, as Bonner pointed out, cities were places in which the sights and sounds were often shady, unseemly, and indecent. A "lady," as race-mothering African American women were expected to be, could not afford to be exposed to "too much."

New Negro progressivism presupposed the superiority and natural hierarchy of more educated, professional, and genteel black people over the great majority of the race. Such an ideology left little room for individual aspirations and, at its worst, could work to instill arrogance and resentment among African Americans rather than to promote unity. At the same time, however, their letters indicate that average African Americans from across the South and of all walks of life relied upon that shared duty of racial solidarity when they needed advice and assistance while preparing to transform their lives.

While women who aspired to be ladies, as Bonner did, felt compelled to submit to more social restrictions than those who dismissed such conventions, the great majority of African American women sought the protection of advice and assistance before they traveled and the comfort of numbers as they transgressed geographic and cultural boundaries in their migrations. Their letters reflect their reliance on the ties of racial solidarity to secure this protection in the face of the dangers facing black women. As one woman wrote, "I think peple as a race ought to look out for one another as Christians friends . . . now if you ever help your race now is the time to help me to get my family away."[11] In return, these women correspondents offered evidence of their ability and intention to represent the race well through hard work and high moral character.

> Gentlemen: I read [the] Defender every week and see so much good youre doing for the southern people & would like to know if you do the same for me as I am thinking of coming to Chicago about the first of June. and wants a position. I have very fine references if needed. I am a widow of 28. No children, not a relative living and I can do first class work as house maid and dining room or care for invalid ladies. I am honest and neat and refined with a fairly good education. I would like a position where I could live on places because its very trying for a good girl to be out in a large city by self among strangers is why I would like a good home with good people. Trusting to hear from you.[12]

Single and childless, without family or influence, this woman wrote from New Orleans seeking aid from the crusading staff of the widely circulated *Chicago Defender*. Relying on the newspaper staff's reputation for fearless racial advocacy as well as her presumption of their gentlemanly concern for the plight of ladies in need, this domestic worker represented herself as an honorable woman in need of a race man's protection. She was after all "a good girl" afraid of the moral and physical dangers of the "large city" full of "strangers." Identifying herself as a "good girl" was a bit of deliberate manipulation. A widow woman of twenty-eight years surely did not really think of herself or assume others would think of her as a child. Furthermore, she represented herself in the most favorable possible terms— "honest and neat and refined with a fairly good education"—given her aspirations and needs. Perceiving that her society, including her black professional social betters, might assume her to be immoral or degenerate because of the discursive power of images like the ones circulated through the sex-race marketplace, this woman sought to establish her innocence and worth. She would not embarrass those recommending her for the position she wanted nor violate the "trusting" relationship she sought to build between them.

Such supplications often described the poor conditions in the South under which the writers "were compelled to live" and thus called upon the empathy of fellow black people who could readily imagine or remember their own suffering under similar circumstances. A woman from Biloxi, Mississippi with a crippled ankle wrote asking for information about work for herself and her family.

[N]ow if you all see where there is some [position] open for me that I may be able too
better my condission[,] anser at once and we will com as we are in a land of starvaten.
From a willen workin woman. I hope that you will healp me as I want to get out of this
land of sufring[.] I no there is som thing that I can do[.] here there is nothing for me to
do[.] I may be able to get in some furm where I dont have to stand on my feet all day[.]
I dont no just whah but I hope the Lord will find a place[.] now let me here from you all
at once[.][13]

Describing her Southern home as a "land of starvation" and "suffering," this
woman demanded that her urgent request be heeded "at once." As a "willing
working woman," she felt she and her family ought not to be forced to
endure the endless hard labor and inadequate remuneration the South offered. Her correspondent must perceive her to be an industrious worker
laboring under impossible conditions and so help her escape. In the eyes of
these Southerners, beset as they were with the most virulent, economically
exploitative forms of white supremacy and the constant threat of violent
reprisal for their efforts to improve themselves, the bonds of solidarity were
reciprocal and necessary to their well-being and even their survival.

This was true of the solidarity among migrants themselves as well. Once
in their new, unfamiliar environments, they relied on their neighbors,
church members, and friends as well as their social betters to facilitate their
transitions and to help them settle into the routines of everyday life as their
new circumstances began to feel like home. After Melnea Cass graduated
from Virginia's Rock Castle convent school for African American girls in
1914, she migrated to Boston on her own to live with her aunt and initially
used her aunt's contacts to find work in various shop jobs before settling on
domestic service. After her marriage to a soldier in 1917, she quit working
outside the home at her in-laws' insistence but followed her mother-in-law's
example to begin an active career in civic volunteer work among her friends
and neighbors. Cass's mother-in-law, Rosa Brown, was the wife of a railroad
man and a domestic worker who continued to work outside the home even
as she discouraged her daughter-in-law from doing so. Brown was also a
church member, a suffragette, an active member of the NAACP, and a clubwoman. Cass relied on Brown's monetary support while living with her
during World War I and continued to follow her advice and example when
she "went housekeeping" and began to raise her own family after her husband returned. Brown introduced Cass to her network of community
women. "There were many women," she remembered, "a lot of women
around, just ordinary mothers and people who had families that I admired,
who were out trying to help all of us young people to do things. We had a lot
of good friends, older women, some of them . . . women whom we looked
up to, who were leaders in the community, just simple leaders. . . .

They were just simply people who lived in the community, who'd try to help you and tell you things to do . . . just good neighbors, that's all."[14] These ordinary women and simple leaders organized clubs to care for their children while they went to work and to assist new migrants to find work and housing and to acclimate to life in the city.

Thousands of miles away on the opposite side of the country, Frances Albrier, who had migrated from Tuskegee, Alabama to Oakland, California in 1920, had a similar experience. Although trained as a nurse and a social worker, Albrier frequently endured periods when she was unable to find professional employment, so she worked in domestic service. While she did so, she "lived in" and "came home only on weekends." For a time, she "boarded the children with a friend of [hers] who took care of" them, and she also relied on more formal organizations to help provide child care. As a member of the Women's Art and Industrial Club, which was affiliated with the California Association of the National Association of Colored Women, Albrier helped raise resources to support the Fannie Wall Home, an orphanage that provided boarding and day care services for the children of black working women. Sometimes Albrier entrusted her own children to their care.[15] For Albrier and Cass, the sense of intra-racial responsibility and solidarity created a network of women on whom they could rely to support their efforts to provide daily sustenance and which they diligently worked to maintain and pass on to the next generation.

The experiences of Cass and Albrier show that, while class distinctions were solidifying, they did not necessarily dictate the kinds of activities African American women engaged in nor the values that guided their daily lives. Describing herself, her mother-in-law, and her neighborhood friends as "clubwomen" as well as domestic workers and church members, Cass was certainly not the unwilling recipient of moralistic charity from Victorian ladies who attempted to impose unfamiliar values upon her; neither, at least in her view, did she and her friends seek to issue social commandments to the women they assisted. While Albrier was an educated woman who took professional work when she could get it, she was also frequently a domestic worker and the beneficiary of necessary charity from her fellow working black women. In the New Negro era, as migration transformed communities and social networks, many clubwomen were themselves migrants or former beneficiaries of clubwomen's charity. They met black volunteer women when they needed their help and then associated themselves with their clubs and churches as means to find friends and community and to continue to help themselves. After they were established in their new lives, they proceeded to help others who needed a similar kind of assistance.[16]

Women like Marita Bonner understood the gravity of their race's need for their labor and skill, but the social and cultural bonds of solidarity sometimes chafed nevertheless. New Negroes sometimes chastised or even excluded those they purported to assist. Reflecting the belief that all black people depended on one another for the achievement of both individual and race-wide success and advancement, Elise McDougald criticized the majority of black women for retarding racial progress. In her analysis of black womanhood's "difficulties" and means of "solving them," McDougald divided black women into four categories: elite women who did not work, women working in the professions, women working in industry, and the great mass of women "struggling on in domestic service" and through casual, periodic cycles of labor.[17] Although she purported to evaluate each group equally, she implied a condemnation for this latter group as inefficient, unprogressive, and detrimental to the prospects of all working black women, especially those seeking to prove that black women deserved greater employment in the better-paying, progressive fields of industrial work and professional and clerical services.

McDougald characterized the field of domestic work as one into which those who were "unsuccessful drift[ed]" when they found they could not make their way in the professions or industry. As noted previously, Frances Mary Albrier was one such woman. Trained as a professional, Albrier resorted to domestic service when she could not get nursing work. McDougald blamed such women, as well as new urban migrant women, for the failure of domestic laborers as a group to reach high standards of industriousness and efficiency. "New standards of household management are forming," she observed, "and the problem of the Negro woman is to meet these new businesslike ideals. The constant influx of workers unfamiliar with household conditions in New York keeps the situation one of turmoil." Furthermore, "the number of day or casual workers is on the increase" because "[t]he Negro woman . . . is revolting against residential domestic service."[18] Although she recognized that black women sought day labor rather than live-in positions in order to better care for their families, McDougald still lamented the lack of professionalism in this largest field of black women's employment. She disregarded and devalued their preference not to remain available to their employers all day and all night six days out of seven.

In her view, not only were these women retarding racial progress through their failure to exhibit "businesslike ideals" but they were also shaming the race through their "sex irregularities." McDougald used this term and a series of loaded but inexplicit phrases to imply her disapproval for working-class black women's fornication, illegitimate childbearing, adultery, prostitution, and pleasure-seeking immorality. These "irregularities" among the "lower grades of Negro women," she argued, were unfairly assumed to apply to all black women. Because of this, "the Negro woman . . . has been singled out and advertised as having lower sex standards" than the white woman. While defending the upstanding majority from these libelous misperceptions, McDougald also attempted to apologize on behalf of the "lower grades" by explaining away their behavior in terms of oppression. "The Negro woman has been forced to submit to overpowering conditions. Pressure has been exerted upon her, both from without and within her group. Her emotional and sex life is a reflex of her economic station."[19] The dire need for continued advancement was evident to McDougald, and she remained a committed worker in that endeavor. However, her words also evidenced a scorn for the working-class women whose unprogressive domestic labor and immoral personal lives supposedly tainted the whole race of women. She afforded them no agency, no possible reason—besides degradation—for their choices and lifestyles. She blamed them, not the dehumanizing power of the sex-race marketplace disseminating images of black "feminine viciousness and vulgarity," for hypersexual stereotypes about all black women. And she was palpably ashamed of them. New Negro progressivism and the bonds of solidarity meant that she must willingly and dutifully work toward their advancement and consider her own fate tied to theirs. It did not mean, however, that she had to like it.

A professional herself and an advocate of black women in industry, McDougald praised these two groups for their progressivism. For her, the clerical workers, social workers, nurses, and teachers were exceptionally inspiring. She devoted the majority of her article "The Task of Negro Womanhood" to their praise. They were the intelligent, efficient, dedicated components in the African American engine of progress. "Young college women" who became social workers were "anxious to devote their education and lives toward helping the submerged classes"; while nurses "carr[ied] the gospel of hygiene to the rural sections and minister[ed] to the suffering not reached by organizations already in the communities"; and the heroic "Negro teacher [was] bending herself to the task of imparting [the] power to hold the spiritual and mental balance under hostile conditions." These self-less race mothers were inspired by the knowledge that "the hope of the race [was] in the New Negro student."[20] Placing premium value on education, progress, and efficiency, McDougald identified the true New Negro women as those working in industry and the professions— those blazing trails into fields unfamiliar to the majority of black women and who were modernizing the mission of racial advancement through those positions.

Except for the revealing sentence at the conclusion of her essay, McDougald wrote as though these endeavors were wholly fulfilling, as if missionary service in the trenches of race motherhood and domestic responsibility was and ought to have been the totality of black women's existence. Some black women who had survived those trenches, however, expressed dissatisfaction with the quality of life it afforded. Race motherhood and New Negro progressivism required selflessness of women, and, despite the deeply ingrained and oft-repeated expectations of their elders and peers, some black women admitted to giving way to their selfish reservations and disappointments.

The pay was so low for teaching jobs in black schools that black women were compelled to supplement their incomes by working as laundresses and agricultural workers on the side. In their letters, aspiring migrants testified to the unsatisfying, inglorious work of toiling for the race. "Kind Sir," one wrote to *Chicago Defender* editor Robert Abbott,

> There is a storm of our people toward the North and especially to your city. We have watched your want ad regularly and we are anxious for location with good families (white) where we can be cared for and do domestic work. We want to engage as cook, nurse and maid. We have had some educational advantages, as we have taught in rural schools for few years but our pay so poor we could not continue. We can furnish testimonial of our honesty and integrity and moral standing. Will you please assist us in securing places as we are anxious to come but want jobs before we leave. We want to do any kind of honest labor. Our chance here is so poor.[21]

Although they were educated professionals lucky enough to have found work in their field of expertise, these women were so underpaid that they were quite willing to work as domestic servants in the North rather than continue to mother the race through teaching in the South. Instead of working for solidarity, they sought to put solidarity to work for them.

New Negro Renaissance authors Jessie Fauset and Nella Larsen wrote about black women's dissatisfaction with solidarity and the stultifying vapidity engendered by a life dedicated exclusively to race motherhood work.[22] Although they knew and befriended many of the same people, including Langston Hughes and James Weldon Johnson, Fauset and Larsen were not friends and did not travel in the same social circles. While Larsen might be considered one of the "bohemian" New Negroes who thumbed their noses at the social conventions and regularly socialized interracially, Fauset was a proud member of the established eastern black elite who belonged to all the right clubs and cherished her respectability. The two women's differing relationships to prevailing concepts of decorum and racialized gender politics are illustrated through their differing reactions to Nora Holt. Both women attended the late-night party celebrating a concert given by Paul Robeson and Lawrence Brown where Holt "danced entirely nude" simply for the fun of making herself a spectacle. Carl Van Vechten reported that "Jessie Fauset almost expired at this" due to her shock and disapproval, while Nella Larsen soon became friends with the outlandish vamp.[23] Their differing sensibilities were expressed in their fiction, yet both Fauset and Larsen drew complex black female characters dissatisfied with the status quo and used their stories to critique contemporary racial and sexual discourses.

Fondly remembered by Renaissance authors like Langston Hughes as "the midwife" of the literary movement through her post at *The Crisis* and her mentorship, Jessie Fauset dedicated herself to racial advancement and was a staple member of Harlem's elite social world and literary communities. In her novel *Plum Bun*, however, Fauset perhaps explored themes she dared not directly address among her friends and colleagues as she drew a character, Angela Murray, who seeks freedom from the obligations of solidarity.[24] Educated and certified to teach in the Philadelphia public schools, Angela wishes instead to become a famous painter. The imperative to advance the race combined with the racism that excluded all but a very few black people from other professions had made of "school-teaching" a burden under which young black people's true inclinations and "natural tendencies" were hidden away and left to wither. Of her teaching position in the school in the colored district of Philadelphia, Angela reflected that "just as she had anticipated, [she] did not want the job after she received it. She had expected to loathe teaching little children and her expectation, it turned out, was perfectly well grounded." Although intelligent and capable, Angela simply has no inclination for the most readily available professional position open to black women. In response to the suggestion that African Americans simply must perform so well as to prove their fitness for other kinds of work, Angela exclaims, "I'm sick of this business of always being below or above a certain norm. Doesn't anyone think that we have a right to be happy simply, naturally?"[25] Angela wants to live her own life, not in service to the race and not for the sake of disproving prejudiced assumptions. While Fauset ultimately showed that the kind of freedom Angela seeks in the beginning of her story—freedom not only to pursue her own aspirations and find her own fulfillment but also freedom from all responsibility to others and to higher principles—is an unworthy goal, she does uphold Angela's distaste for always living according to others' unfair and presumptuous expectations.[26]

Although renowned for her authorship of Renaissance novels and short stories, Nella Larsen began her adulthood as a nurse. Upon her graduation from New York's Lincoln Hospital and Home Training School for Nurses in 1915, Larsen accepted a seemingly prestigious position as head of the nurse training school at Tuskegee Institute. Motivated by naïve adherence to the ideals of race motherhood, she attempted to acclimate herself to the schedule of relentless work and exploitation expected of her and her nursing students in the name of "teamwork." During the year that she worked at

Tuskegee, Larsen was grossly underpaid for working fourteen-hour days in which she not only supervised the training of student nurses but also administered the hospital itself and instructed all the Institute's women students in domestic hygiene and pediatric health. Larsen taught her nursing students at bedside rather than in regular classes, as their services were immediately in demand in the hospital as well as in home service positions for local white families under the supervision of white doctors, work that was much more akin to domestic labor than professional nursing. Indeed, Larsen's role on the campus as a member of the faculty was not really secure as her student nurses were considered more of a workforce whose underpaid labor benefited the Institute. In fact, the "certificates" her students received upon graduation did not even qualify them for state Registered Nurse status or to sit for the state certification examinations. Their hard work and training, however, did afford the Institute the $1.00 to $4.00 per day per student paid by their patients in the local community.[27] In this case, the "teamwork" famous race leaders Booker T. Washington and R. R. Moton demanded of the Tuskegee Institute population was actually submissive adherence to inferior conditions and exploitative policies that failed to benefit the nurses and nursing students working there. Summarily released from her position, without any advance notice or severance pay, less than a year after she began it, Larsen learned a lesson about the unequal benefits of solidarity that she would carry with her throughout her life. It was a lesson she would incorporate, through biting, satirical representation of Tuskegee and the characters to be found there, into her fiction.

Larsen's novel *Quicksand* opens when the main character, Helga Crane, is realizing that her faculty post at the Southern black school Naxos, a fictional institution modeled on Tuskegee, is so constraining as to depress her spirit and render her insecure.[28] In her classes, Helga "gave willingly and unsparingly of herself with no apparent return." Her school materials were a collection of "drab books and papers," her situation required a "strenuous rigidity of conduct," the school itself was really "a big knife with cruelly sharp edges ruthlessly cutting all to a pattern, the white man's pattern" of morality, efficiency, and proper servility. It was a place where "enthusiasm, spontaneity, if not actually suppressed, were at least openly regretted as unladylike or ungentlemanly qualities" thus making her feel oppressed by the "trivial hypocrisies and careless cruelties" that seemed to have become "a part of the Naxos policy of uplift." Although Helga, unlike Angela of Fauset's *Plum Bun*, had originally come to Naxos full of naïve enthusiasm for "doing good to [her] fellow men," her disappointment teaches her to despise the place and literally flee the miserable duty of race motherhood. [29]

Larsen's depiction of Naxos and of the effects of its relentless demand for "teamwork" in the name of racial advancement refutes Frances Mary

Albrier's glowing impartation of the lessons she learned at the real Tuskegee. Albrier might have disagreed with or even disapproved of Larsen's portrait of her alma mater and the necessity of solidarity. Or, as a graduate of the nursing program a few years before Larsen taught there, she might have silently borne similar grievances. On one hand, Albrier's guarded, didactic statements seem intended to obscure any personal difficulties or resentments she might have had. On the other hand, perhaps she did willingly give herself up to the mission of racial advancement the institution instilled in her. Although New Negro women continued to rely on the assistance and support racial solidarity provided when they found themselves in unfamiliar or threatening situations, the most audacious and outspoken of them began to express impatience, resentment, and dissatisfaction with the imperative to dedicate one's imagination, intelligence, energy, and aspirations—one's whole life—to the effort of racial advancement. The New Negro woman was determined to demand choices for herself. She migrated; she expressed herself; she relied on her own judgment; she sometimes even shirked her prescribed duties. As Bonner's essay and Fauset and Larsen's characters exemplify, these modern black women sought to slip the constraints of an old-school ideology to reformulate solidarity according to their own needs and vision. As they remade themselves, they remade racial identity too.

As the African American population urbanized and therefore found ready access to an unprecedented degree of independence in the formulation of personal aspirations, the satisfaction of particular desires, and the opportunity to affiliate with a multitude of established and brand-new organizations of all ideological stripes, racial solidarity became a question of individual affiliation. Would each black person choose to live among and consider herself a willing partaker of the race and its quest for advancement? An impossible and therefore irrelevant question for the Reconstruction generation whose racial identity was overwhelmingly dictated by the intensely repressive society in which they lived and their dire need for one another's help and protection, this choice was one New Negro women risked pondering. Although their answers varied, it was their determination to ask the question that marked their modernity. The resulting diversity of racial affinity and personal politics worked to modernize the race as a whole. Solidarity encompassed questions of class identity, sexual deportment, education, political ideology, and conformity—all of which were in flux as African Americans migrated and the Reconstruction generation gave way to the New Negroes. In the interwar era, solidarity thus became one of the discursive sites at which New Negro women created themselves and expressed the modern, complex diversity of their humanity.

THE SEXUAL POLITICS OF RACE

In boldly criticizing and defying the bonds of solidarity, women like Bonner, Fauset, and Larsen defied not only the racial expectations laid down by their elders but also the accepted gender conventions of contemporary New Negro culture. As their words show, New Negro women endeavored to define their sexual selves in the interstices between the one-dimensional identities their society imposed upon them. They were neither the lascivious sirens and bluesy vamps of racialized popular culture nor the paragons of saintly non-sexual motherhood of progressive ideals and New Negro propaganda. In fact, Nella Larsen found such idealized paragons so unfitting as models for real black women that she ridiculed them in her fiction. In *Quicksand*, Helga "grinned a little" as she reflected on the "ladyness" of the women's dormitory matron Miss MacGooden who had never married because "there were . . . things in the matrimonial state that were of necessity entirely too repulsive for a lady of delicate and sensitive nature to submit to."[30] If women were really to be so pure as to embody the paragon as she was portrayed, they could never become proper wives and mothers.

As New Negro progressivism and race motherhood exemplify, the mission to institute a viable, valiant patriarchy among African Americans was a foundational tenet of New Negro racial advancement. By and large, most black women of the period agreed that men should take the lead in family affairs and provide for the family's support and shelter. Men should also behave as gentlemen—protecting, defending, and escorting their female companions when required and restraining their own emotions and desires in deference to feminine "delicacy." [31] However, New Negro women balanced this expectation of men's patriarchal responsibility with a pragmatic acceptance of the overwhelming economic circumstances demanding their participation in the workforce and with a personal recognition of their own capabilities and needs. They knew themselves to be competent, resilient, sensible, sensual humans responsible for their own well-being and that of their dependents. New Negro women hoped to find, as Marita Bonner put it, "a husband you can look up to without looking down on yourself."[32] In their recorded memories and fiction, New Negro women confronted the shifting terrain of modern, racialized sexual politics and detailed the trouble and anguish they encountered as they sought to wend their way toward personal fulfillment and sexual self-determination. Although they may not all have completed the journey, along the way they did construct a deepened and expanded New Negro woman's subjectivity.

In most black women's experience, Bonner's vision of marriage turned out to be a difficult ideal to meet. The sexual politics of their lives were shaped not only by their own desires and those of their mates but also by

communal, social, and cultural ideals and expectations that sometimes conflicted and often militated against the fruition of personal aspirations. As
they battled to shape their own lives, women, especially young women,
were expected to yield to almost everyone else and to every precipitating
factor except their own prerogatives.

One of those women who became a teacher after graduating from
school "because that was the only thing that black women could do in the
South in those days" besides work as sharecroppers or in other people's
houses as domestic servants, Alice Dunnigan endured community censure
and interference that added to the acrimony of her marriage.[33] While Dunnigan was happy enough with her teaching job, she found that her husband, his family, and her community disapproved of her because of the
relative independence and ease her professional employment afforded her.
She recalled,

> I began teaching at Mt. Pisgah in 1924. It was 1925, the next year, that we [she and
> Walter Dickinson] were married. . . . He wanted me to give up teaching, but I was not
> willing to do that at the time. . . . I think the one thing that "bugged" him most was the
> people in the neighborhood, who kept needling him about his wife not working—not
> helping him with the crops. Apparently they didn't consider teaching school as working.
> Some of the people, who opposed his marrying me, kept telling him that "other people's
> wives had to work, why can't yours work?" They referred to me as a "parlor princess," or
> something like that. Some would say, "Oh, she doesn't want you. You're just a poor farm
> boy and she's a parlor princess. She just wants to sit in the parlor (meaning the
> schoolhouse) all day and do nothing."

Class distinctions, gender ideals, and communal expectations combined to
conflict with Dunnigan's own inclinations and to sour her new relationship
with her husband. Rather than the committed and beloved local instructor
and community leader progressives presumed New Negro teachers to be,
Dunnigan was considered an uppity intruder by her neighbors and even
her in-laws. In their view, to endeavor to play the lady was to snub them
and imply she was too good to participate in their means of livelihood.
Dunnigan had completed high school and worked her way through the
teaching program at Kentucky State College precisely because she wished
to avoid working in the fields or as a laundress and living in debt from season to season as her parents did. But in an effort to please her husband and
fit into her new community, she ended up doing just that. Her husband
"vowed that teaching or not, I must help him with the farm work as other
farmers' wives did. Trying to be compatible, I agreed to help." Dunnigan
also assisted the family by financing them out of her teaching salary. Even
so, like the great majority of black farm workers, they ended up "in the hole"

or in debt to the farm owner at the end of the year and had no records to prove otherwise.

> The family finance, or lack of it, brought very bad feelings between us. The unpleasantness continued to grow until finally he decided that we would move away from his family, at my request. So we moved to a little town, Hopkinsville, twenty-one miles or so from where we were living. When we got there, neither of us had a job. He didn't try to get one. . . . Somebody had to go to work, and it happened to be me. . . . The only work I could find was that of a nursemaid. I didn't like that, because I knew nothing about caring for babies. Finally I went into the home laundry business, just as my mother had done. Walter would sit on the porch and swing, while I tugged the bundles of dirty clothes home, washed and ironed them, and carried each family's clean laundry home in big baskets.

Not so concerned with his poverty, Dunnigan was acutely aware of her husband's failure to provide her his physical assistance and moral support. He was willing neither to allow her to work in the profession for which she had been trained nor to assist her as she performed the kind of work he considered appropriate. Instead, he was content to sit on the porch and watch her haul and sweat until she agreed to return to farm labor, which "is exactly what he wanted," and they moved to Pembroke, Kentucky.

Once they had arrived in Pembroke,

> he made a trade to work as a sharecropper. . . . Neither of us had any money, so he arranged for both of us to rise at five o'clock in the morning, and go up to what they called "the big house" (just like they did in slavery days), and do chores for food. To pay for our breakfast, he would milk the cows and I would cook the breakfast and wash the dishes. This held true for the other meals. Things continued to get worse and I couldn't stand that any longer. So I began looking for another school. I was finally called to teach at a school in Allensville the following fall. He still objected to my teaching. He told me that I ought to stay at home, as a farmer's wife should, and help with the crops. If I needed extra money, I could always earn it by washing clothes for some of these good white folks.

Walter seemed consistently jealous of his wife and wary lest her ability to find professional work should grant her undue independence from him. He preferred to see her employed in the service of white households and as dependent on their concessions as he was. As it happened, his attitude succeeded in driving her away. Dunnigan taught in Allensville for two or three years, until her teaching certificate expired and she had to return to school for a year to renew it. "While planning to go back to West Kentucky College, [Walter] told me that he didn't want me to teach, and if I insisted on going back to school, I could just go and stay. So I went! And I stayed! That is the last time I ever saw Walter Dickinson."[34]

Dunnigan's jubilation is likely a result of hindsight. At the time, she must have regretted the dissolution of her marriage very much, troublesome as it had been, for she had put so much time and effort into its maintenance. Balancing her professional status, her ambitions, and her personal needs against the expectations and preferences of the men in her life proved to be a lifelong problem for her, one she shared with many women of the New Negro generation, professionals or not.

When their marriages did go well, as Melnea Cass's did, it was often because New Negro women were willing and able to accommodate their husbands' prerogatives and so approximate the prized patriarchal ideal. Cass's husband, Marshall, "didn't really want [her] to work." She recalled,

> He used to see the women going by, friends of mine, with their children early in the morning, taking them somewhere, so they could go somewhere to work, and he'd be going to work and he'd say, "I hope you never have to do that." And he said, "While I'm living, you won't be able to do that. I wouldn't have it. Don't take my children anywhere. I want you to take care of them yourself." He was very definite about that. Take care of the children. So I always took care of my family, and cooked and sewed, and did all kinds of things in the house.[35]

Proud of her husband's determination to support her as his housewife, Cass was able to accede to her husband's demand because he earned enough money to support the family as well as to put by savings to pay off their mortgage and to support their children through college. This boon, combined with Cass's own preference to confine her work to her efforts on behalf of her family and her volunteerism, meant that Melnea and Marshall escaped the conflicts over money and economic prerogatives that plagued Alice Dunnigan and Walter Dickinson. Melnea Cass was able to control her fate through migration and the life she made for herself in the city apparently without sacrificing her sexual or personal fulfillment. It seems her marriage was one in which she could "look up to" her husband "without looking down on" herself. Cass might have characterized herself as a race mother. Or, she might have thought of her housewifery as work she performed for the benefit of her family alone, without any reference to the good of the race at large. In any case, it is clear that her marriage both exemplified the ideals of New Negro patriarchy and succeeded in providing for her happiness as well as her well-being.

Whether or not most New Negro women maintained "organized" families or found fulfillment in their personal relationships, as Cass did, they still sustained a belief in the efficacy of deferring to men's greater physical strength and protection. Reflecting on her relationships with men, Alice Dunnigan declared, "I take the position . . . that black women have for too long been forced into complete independence, having to play the supportive role for themselves and their children, and having been necessarily subjected to hard work as a means of supplementing the family income." She continued,

> Most black women might welcome the opportunity to have a reliable husband on whom they can depend for support, and to have a strong shoulder to lean on. I certainly would! And furthermore, I am one of those women who enjoys being treated like a lady. . . . I feel that I am being respected, if a man opens a door for me, or if he helps me in and out of a car, or if he lights my cigarette, or holds my arm while crossing an icy street or busy thoroughfare. This is the type of courtesy that I adore.[36]

This was a kind of support and compatibility Dunnigan never found in her private life.[37] New Negro women like Dunnigan sought mates who could accept their capabilities and recognize their autonomy while also allowing them to feel protected by equally capable, devoted partners. As Elizabeth Cardozo Barker stated, "The most liberated and fulfilled women I know are those who have good husbands and have successfully reared a family. That is a beloved woman."[38] Women like Barker, Dunnigan, and Cass focused on the success or failure of their personal efforts to secure the companionship they craved. But, as their stories make clear, the power relations of black men's and women's personal relationships were affected by a larger sociocultural politics of sexual and racial power, identity, and representation.

As authors, New Negro women commented on their complex participation in that politics and recognized the power dynamics of black women's efforts at sexual self-determination in the face of sustained discursive and material exploitation and oppression. New Negro women used fiction as a space to explore the unspeakable, that which they did not or could not incorporate into New Negro politics. They posited attitudes, actions, and emotions on behalf of their characters that they may not have dared to express for themselves. In the New Negro era, the black woman's novel became a means of violating moral and social taboos in order to voice the politics of black women's sexual self-determination.[39] In novels, black women expressed their whole, true selves through the dreams, desires, and struggles of their characters. This meant perilously removing the mask of dissemblance they habitually wore. It also meant writing against the grain of black women's representations in New Negro men's fiction.

Male New Negro authors such as Claude McKay and Langston Hughes succeeded, in part, by recreating the sex-race marketplace in their writing. Through characters such as Hughes's "Harriett" and "Tempy" and McKay's

"Rose" and "Felice," these authors portrayed black women according to the marketplace's needs and expectations for easily definable types and primitivism.[40] Celebrating the newly urban black folk, they focused on the black working class and developed their novels from the points of view of young black males. Hughes's Tempy, who is unyielding, humorless, and upstanding, serves as the exemplary race mother who maintains her household in perfect order, moralistically disdains her less scrupulous relatives, and selflessly devotes herself to her children, although without expressing much warmth toward anyone. On the other hand, Hughes's Harriett and McKay's Rose and Felice are all carefree prostitutes and blueswomen who function within the novels' themes to titillate readers with depictions of "Harlem's teasing browns, who give themselves so neatly to sluttery," as one reviewer exulted.[41] Devoting themselves to the black male protagonists, these female characters—the upstanding race mother and the happy-go-lucky prostitutes and blueswomen—also serve the masculinist project of asserting rightful black male leadership and patriarchy. Hughes and McKay celebrated such characters as Harriet and Felice and the freewheeling lifestyle they represent without ever addressing the multilevel dangers and injuries such socially marginal, illicit activities entailed for black women.[42]

In endeavoring to push beyond such facile, one-dimensional representations to address the vicissitudes of black women's human sexual expression, black women's fiction paralleled the blueswomen's lyrics and performances. But, in creating a whole cast of characters along with their pasts and destinies, black women novelists reserved greater autonomy to fully consider and explain black women's perspectives on the sex-race discourse that so affected their experiences and opportunities.[43] In their novels, New Negro women expressed their proscribed thoughts about sexual desire and individual aspiration and their profound discomfort with the imperative that they dedicate their lives and bodies to the newly redefined politics of racial advancement and the establishment of a New Negro patriarchy.

Through her character Angela's adventures while passing as a white woman in *Plum Bun*, novelist Jessie Fauset explored the machinations of the unevenly matched game of sexual politics that all women were compelled to play. Seeking a wealthy white husband who can grant her the "position, power, wealth" she thinks necessary to secure her freedom, Angela gambles her virginity and suffers defeat, both because her lover has the advantage of greater skill and less to lose and because her own desire for him overwhelms her wits.[44] In a thoroughly modern assertion of New Negro women's sexual self-determination, Fauset grants her main character the agency of individual sexual desire and the satisfaction of her lust. Furthermore, she does not then plunge her character into a fit of suicidal self-abnegation nor abandon her to some dreadful fate as a prostitute or other thoroughly degraded woman. Neither does she detail or celebrate the affair in a prurient way. Fauset avoids confining Angela in any one-dimensional space. Although Angela's hope for marriage to a white man is disappointed and her supreme self-confidence and optimism subdued, she goes on to regain her footing in the city's social scene and economy. "Angela's brief episode with Roger had left no trace on her moral nature; she was ashamed now of the affair with a healthy shame of its unworthiness; but beyond that she suffered from no morbidness."[45] Life goes on beyond the dreaded loss of virtue through extramarital, interracial sexual relations, and Fauset preserves for her character all the ambition and natural desire of a healthy, beautiful young woman.

Instead of condemning Angela, Fauset uses her affair with Roger Fielding to point out the imbalance between women's and men's social and sexual power and to posit marriage as the only satisfactory arbiter between them. Angela realizes "the apparently unbridgeable difference between the sexes; everything was for men, but even the slightest privilege was to be denied a woman unless the man chose to grant it."[46] Thus, what Fauset calls "the conventions"—the dictates of sexual morality forbidding extramarital sexual relations and exalting marriage—were more than "granite-like," arbitrary rules but standards of conduct that worked to protect women against men's exploitative power. Belatedly, Angela learns that "all the advice which older women pour into the ears of growing girls could be as true as it was trite."[47] Despite her fictional critique of sexual politics and the double standard, Fauset remained a believer in the efficacy of marriage as a protective, fulfilling space for women.

As Fauset seems to assert by maintaining Angela's professed whiteness throughout these scenes in particular, all women stumbled through the dangerous game in which women must "be careful not to withhold too much and yet give very little," but the stakes for black women were even higher.[48] Angela reasonably assumed that she would have no opportunity to fulfill her dreams of success and independence if she were known to be a black woman. African American women knew that they were "always already sexual" in the eyes of their society.[49] A rich, secure white man such as the one she wanted to catch would be unlikely to knowingly wed a "Negress." Indeed, it seems that Fauset maintains Angela's purported whiteness precisely to confront and contradict the fallacious and detrimental notion that black women were more sexual, more tempting and tempted, and therefore inherently less respectable than their white counterparts. Angela's lover does not consider her odd or unduly promiscuous. He never suspects her to be other than the attractive young white woman she presents for him. By maintaining Angela's whiteness in these scenes, Fauset both challenged

the conventions of ladyhood—the idea that a true lady was above such cor-
poreal considerations and bodily desire—and the stereotypes coating black
women's skin. The difficulties of securing sexual self-determination and the
perils of acting upon one's desires were all more acute for black women.
However, Fauset implied these perils without fully exploring them. Angela
has other discoveries to make. Nella Larsen, on the other hand, confronted
such questions directly and with equal determination in her fiction.

Larsen's *Quicksand* focuses on protagonist Helga Crane's keen awareness
of the quagmire of racial and sexual quandaries facing black women. Helga's
racialized sexuality, her shame and confusion as a result of its potency, and
the constant use the surrounding society attempts to make of it continually
drive her out of prospective homes. From Naxos, she flees to Chicago, from
there to Harlem, from Harlem to Copenhagen, Denmark, from Copenhagen back to Harlem, and finally to the "tiny Alabama town" that would
become her final resting place.[50] In each location, imposed racial and sexual
subjectivities combine to oust her from a position she initially thinks comfortable and preferable to her previous location. Although Helga is self-
centered, highly sensitive, and materialistic, Larsen presents her problems
as the result of social ills rather than personal angst. Helga's sensitivity causes
her to constantly feel the pinch of all the restraints and expectations pulling
at her. She is pained by situations and processes others simply accept as
their due or as the natural order. In Helga, Larsen has created the perfect
character through which to explore the difficulties black women faced,
many of which were so common and insidious as to seem unremarkable.

Masterfully weaving themes and symbols throughout her text, Larsen
provides an incisive comment on New Negro sexual politics and the pitfalls
of facile, romantic notions regarding the contract of marriage and the cycle
of reproduction. Over the course of the plot, Helga is involved with three
black men, James Vayle, Dr. Robert Anderson, and the Reverend Pleasant
Green. Each relationship reveals a different facet of the stacked deck against
black women in the game of sexual politics. James Vayle is Helga's fiancé
when the text opens at Naxos. She ultimately describes him as "snobbish,
smug, servile."[51] He is all of these but also grasping, possessive, and objecti-
fying when it comes to black women. Unexpectedly reunited with Vayle at a
party in Harlem, Helga is amused to find him angrily disapproving of interracial socializing. Embarrassed to have to articulate his reasons, Vayle indicates a white man dancing with a black woman and bursts out, "You know as
well as I do, Helga, that it's the colored girls these men come up here to see.
They wouldn't think of bringing their wives." He then "blushed furiously at
his own implication." Helga calmly responds by pointing out the white
man's wife dancing in the arms of a black man and deftly changes the subject. She has snidely bested him in this small argument. Larsen's implication,

however, is not that Vayle is wrong in his presumption that most white men consider black women ripe for sexual exploitation. After all, Helga has just returned from Copenhagen where she had the painful experience of being insultingly propositioned by a prominent Danish painter. Rather, Vayle evidences black men's presumption of ownership and control over black women's sexuality. Far from scrupulously principled himself, he has just boldly appraised Helga's appearance and implied a desire to have sex with her.[52] He is not so much indignant that white men covet black women for exploitative means as he is jealous of black women's attention and sexual favors. It is an issue of men's sexual ownership and control over women rather than one of racial solidarity and honor. Helga delights in disproving Vayle's assumption in this particular case, not to refute the fact of white men's oppressive power but to assert herself on behalf of black women's self-determination and thus challenge Vayle's oppressive presumption of proprietorship over black women's bodies.

Despite Helga's best efforts to outdo him, Vayle remains unperturbed and unfailingly arrogant. She expresses her reservations about marriage and her resolution not to have children, and Vayle argues with her, insisting that black middle-class sterility is "one of the things that's the matter with us" as a race. Voicing the tenets of race motherhood, he expects Helga and all educated, relatively privileged black women to offer their reproductive capacities for the benefit of racial advancement. Although Helga demurs, stating, "Well, I for one don't intend to contribute any to the cause," Vayle persists.[53] She is amazed to find that, despite their opposing views, Vayle is still determined to marry her. He plainly wants to possess her, to conquer her will and her body for the augmentation of his ego and the fulfillment of his own prerogatives.

Repelled by and "very sorry for James Vayle," Helga has few qualms about rejecting him. However, she is continually perturbed by her interactions with and reflections on Dr. Robert Anderson. It is not until the conclusion of her story that Helga realizes "how deeply, how passionately, she must have loved him" even from the time of their first interview at Naxos.[54] The most complex male character in the novel, Anderson presents Helga with her greatest challenge. He understands her completely, which renders her vulnerable. To him, she is the essence of a "lady," not a paragon of chastity and propriety but a truly graceful, perceptive, and delicate woman worthy of great respect. The grand mutual passion between Helga and Dr. Anderson, however, goes unconsummated. They both feel terribly uncomfortable with the degree of lust crackling between them. It is improper. Even setting aside Dr. Anderson's marriage to Helga's friend Anne in the middle of the plot, the passion between them threatens their status as respectable, sober, intelligent people whose existence refutes the ubiquitous contemporary images of black hypersexuality and bestiality circulated by the sex-race marketplace. For Helga, this dread of sexual impropriety is not wholly new. She has always been ashamed of the power of her sensuality. It is not something she controls but that, to a great extent, controls her and allows others, including Dr. Anderson, to manipulate her.

Anne understands the passion between her husband and Helga and summarizes it well:

> Anne had perceived that the decorous surface of her new husband's mind regarded Helga Crane with that intellectual and aesthetic appreciation which attractive and intelligent women would always draw from him, but that underneath that well-managed section, in a more lawless place where she herself never hoped or desired to enter, was another, a vagrant primitive groping toward something shocking and frightening to the cold asceticism of his reason. Anne knew also that though she herself was lovely—more beautiful than Helga—and interesting, with her he had not to struggle against that nameless and to him shameful impulse, that sheer delight, which ran through his nerves at mere proximity to Helga.[55]

Dr. Anderson's marriage to Anne is calmly affectionate and brings out the socially acceptable best in both of them. Dr. Anderson's relationship to Helga, however, would reveal within each of them the "jungle creature" that Helga unsuccessfully attempts to bury inside herself and that Dr. Anderson habitually disavows. Helga shamefully enjoys her furtive sojourns into her inner "jungle," but this is a guilty pleasure Dr. Anderson does not allow himself.

Too late for the salvation of her peace of mind, Helga realizes "that no matter what the intensity of his feelings or desires might be, he was not the sort of man who would for any reason give up one article of his own good opinion of himself. Not even for her. Not even though he knew that she had wanted so terribly something special from him." Within New Negro sexual politics, Helga threatens Anderson's "good opinion of himself" not simply because her presence tempts him to commit adultery but more significantly because she brings out the lawlessness in him. Without meaning to be, she is a "Jezebel" leading him outside the bounds of the rules, manners, and habits that identify him as a New Negro gentleman.[56] Rather than shirk the duties of respectability with her, he instead abandons her to her shame and profound disappointment. Larsen depicts the ideals and sexual politics of New Negro society as so strict as to compel its members to maintain their adherence to propriety even to the point of denying themselves their greatest chance for happiness. Although Anderson pronounces Helga a "lady" and loves her for her complexity, she is not lady enough to suit the ideal of New Negro womanhood, and she thus loses this crucial round in the game of racialized sexual politics.

Through her representations of New Negro gentlemen James Vayle and Dr. Anderson, Larsen offers a damning critique of both race motherhood and the ideal New Negro gentlemen who were to support and exemplify its tenets of patriarchy and respectability. She reveals both as wholly inimical to the revelation of New Negro women's humanity and sexual self-determination. Rather than to support, protect, and cherish black women, this discourse worked to flatten and deaden them within its ideals and to shame and ostracize those who defied it. Helga suffers because her complexity renders her one of the unprotected outsiders.

In her relationship with Dr. Anderson, Helga took the initiative in determining her sexual self. She went forward to meet him and to accomplish their "consummation" boldly, but she was rebuffed. The next time she played the game of sexual politics, she lost more miserably and more completely than she had ever dreamed she could. In a wild fit of self-deceiving folly in the immediate wake of the devastating conclusion of her relationship with Dr. Anderson, Helga succeeds in seducing into wedlock "the grandiloquent Reverend Mr. Pleasant Green, that rattish yellow man."[57] With this marriage, she hopes to make herself the upstanding, respectable race mother Dr. Anderson thinks her incapable of embodying. From Harlem she returns with Reverend Green to Alabama and endeavors to fit into the rhythm of life in the small, rural black community of his congregation. As she elaborates her protagonist's fate, for this is where Helga will end her life, Larsen brings into stark relief the self-negation required of women in traditional, patriarchal marriage, the terrors of childbirth, the bondage that is motherhood.

Racked with pain, chronic nausea, and constant faintness, Helga strives to resign herself to this new life and maintain the illusion of happiness she initially saw in it. Pregnant again, she has become the mother of three children in the space of twenty months and struggles to care for them, keep house, and perform her racial uplift duties as the minister's wife while her husband absents himself from home on errands to his adoring female congregants. Observing that the women of her community shoulder similar duties easily, efficiently, and apparently painlessly, Helga seeks the advice of her neighbor, Sary Jones, who "had had six children in about as many years." Sary replies, "Tain't nothin', nothin' at all, chile," and advises Helga that she "takes it too ha'd. Jes' remembah et's natu'al fo' a 'oman to hab chilluns an' don' fret so." Helga protests, "But I'm always so tired and half sick. That can't be natural." "Laws chile, we's all ti'ed," Sary replies. "An' Ah reckons we's all gwine a be ti'ed till kingdom come. Jes' make de bes' of et, honey. Jes' make de bes' yuh can." Sary further advises Helga to "jes' put yo' trus' in de Sabioah [Savior]."[58]

Feeling "shame that she should be less than content" and "humbled and oppressed by the sense of her own unworthiness and lack of sufficient faith,"

Helga attempts to follow this advice, to put aside her own feelings and stoically accomplish her chores. She resigns herself to going without "the great ordinary things of life, [such as] hunger, sleep, freedom from pain." For this effort, her community praises her, and she rises in their opinion from an "uppity, meddlin' No'the'nah" to a "mighty sweet lil' 'oman."[59] As Alice Dunnigan learned while her marriage crumbled around her, black women were expected to forget, or at least set aside, their own desires and needs for the sake of their marriage and children and in order to accommodate themselves to the standards of their communities. They were to live according to their husbands' prerogatives and in the circumstances he provided. Helga seems to learn this lesson well. However, Larsen considered these expectations and the resignation that made them seem palatable a great trick played on women to maintain an oppression so insidious that it seemed the natural course of events.

Having survived the difficult, days-long labor of birthing her fourth child and emerged from the coma-like lethargy that followed it, Helga reflects with new eyes upon her situation. The pain of this last birth had lifted her veil of resignation. "In that period of racking pain and calamitous fright Helga had learned what passion and credulity could do to one." Her own desire for sexual love and security combined with her willingness to believe in her husband's religion and in the "naturalness" of her continuous reproduction, illness, and disappointment had made Helga into a sickly, helpless mother of four trapped in a marriage to a man who repulsed her in a town that refused to accept her. Through Helga's awakening, Larsen showed how harrowing a woman's life could be if, like Helga, she was aware of the pain and suffering she was enduring rather than simply accepting it as the due course of events. Here, Helga's sensitivity is at work again. She keenly feels the discomforts others fail to perceive, ignore, or dismiss. She chafes at the legal ties that grant her husband access to and rights over her body, money, and very life; at the fierce bonds of motherly love that prevent her from deserting her children to escape Alabama, for "to leave them would be a tearing agony, a rending of the deepest fibers"; at strings of which other women, her neighbors, her friends in Chicago and Harlem, were wholly oblivious. Larsen showed that society bent the most mundane aspects of women's lives—their very life cycle—toward the maintenance of their subjugation, but that this was not generally perceived because women were taught to accept it without question. Having created in Helga a black female subjectivity perceptive to these aspects of sexual oppression, Larsen places them in stark, unavoidable relief.

Larsen's *Quicksand* thus becomes a definitive polemic on black women's near complete inability to determine their sexual destinies and the psychological and physical prices they paid for attempting to do so in the face of the power of patriarchy and the pervasiveness of sexual-racial oppression. She defied the New Negro patriarchal imperative and the ideal of race motherhood to emphatically recount black women's ongoing subordination and to show that the rise of a black patriarchy would represent little progress or freedom for them. Larsen spoke for all the New Negro women who endeavored, out of desire and necessity, to shape their own lives against the odds of a sexist-racist society and a masculinist New Negro racial advancement politics that simplistically valorized patriarchy and romanticized motherhood. Herself then married to physicist Elmer Imes, whom her biographer describes as "a man much like Dr. Anderson," Larsen did not use her novel to voice a wholesale rejection of matrimony.[60] Rather, she critiqued the racial obligations, gendered limitations, and intersecting sexual and racial discursive forces working against the formation and recognition of New Negro women's full, multifarious subjectivity.

The New Negro woman who emerges from Larsen's and Fauset's novels and from the interviews quoted earlier was sexually liberated and aware of her allure. She sought love, companionship, and partnership and found inadequate any relationship lacking respect or joy. In her quest to determine her own sexual destiny, she did not necessarily conform to race-serving expectations in reproduction or wifely subservience. Her versions of partnership and companionship, while diverse, were of her own making. And she found that if she, like Alice Dunnigan or Larsen's Helga, were caught in a disrespectful, abusive, or simply unhappy marriage that did not serve her needs, those bonds could chafe to the point of injury or even death. Thus she reserved for herself the right to be free of them. Despite ongoing adherence and reliance on racial solidarity, mostly willing, if sometimes reluctant, acceptance of the duties of racial advancement, and a desire to partner respectably in marriage, the New Negro woman would defy all of these, if need be, in order to preserve herself. Without fanfare or the creation of a politics out of this self-preservation, New Negro women quietly critiqued and resisted masculinist definitions of race loyalty and New Negro patriarchal conventions in order to assert the value of their own perspectives and seek their own fulfillment.

HAPPINESS AND SELF-DETERMINATION

New Negro women hoped that their efforts at self-determination would afford them greater opportunities to shape fulfilling, happy, loving lives. Overwhelmingly, they envisioned their happiness in heterosexual terms. Their novels and essays as well as their oral histories reflect such romantic visions. They would marry the right man, have a family of their own, be able to support that family well financially and emotionally, and not have to work too hard to do so. By and large, they agreed with Marita Bonner when she wrote,

> At least you know what you want life to give you. A career as fixed and as calmly brilliant as the North Star. The one real thing money buys. Time. Time to do things. A house that can be as delectably out of order and as easily put in order as the doll-house of "playing-house" days. And of course, a husband you can look up to without looking down on yourself.[61]

Bonner envisions a married life utterly without the hardships endured by Alice Dunnigan or Larsen's Helga Crane. This was a bourgeois, companionate married life likely unattainable for most New Negro women. The creation and maintenance of a successful black nuclear family, whether working- or middle-class, patriarchal or companionate, was not easy in the midst of migration and economic exploitation, particularly if it was to provide the wife and mother her primary source of fulfillment, as Bonner and Fauset seemed to imagine it should. Beyond the attainment of a happy married life, New Negro women's happiness depended on the availability of a discursive space in which the fullness of their humanity became recognizable and accepted. Race motherhood, defining black women's subjectivities through its masculinist priorities and emphasizing their gendered duties to the cause of a patriarchal vision of racial advancement, worked against such recognition and acceptance. Such a space did not exist within the sex-race marketplace, which always reduced New Negro women to their bodies or to the uses to which their color, sexuality, faces, and figures could be put in the maintenance of established racial and sexual tropes. Even as they helped to construct the marketplace with their consumption, productions, participation, and belief in its wares and myths, New Negro women were still flattened and swallowed within its swirling vagaries. Through their words, New Negro women constructed a discourse that recognized them and critiqued their discursive exclusions, yet they spoke almost exclusively to themselves. In the face of all that contended against their ability to shape their own destinies and subjectivities, many New Negro women regretfully and ominously concluded along with Elise McDougald that there was little happiness to be had.

Fauset and Larsen expounded on the question of happiness as one of the major themes in their fiction. Their protagonists, Angela and Helga, functioned for different reasons as social outsiders. The two novelists drew characters whose quest for lasting happiness and varying success point to the exigencies that were particular to black women's lives, but they posited opposing resolutions to the quandaries common to New Negro women's experiences. While Fauset sought to reconcile fulfillment with racial solidarity through marriage and adherence to the patriarchal ideals of the period, Larsen explored the risks of independent self-determination and ultimately showed her readers how unlikely black women were to find fulfillment, especially through patriarchy. For Fauset, marriage served as the only space that could offer recognition and acceptance of a New Negro woman's subjectivity. Larsen ultimately concluded that no such space could exist and suggested the happy New Negro woman was the one who accommodated herself to the necessity of doing without it.

In *Plum Bun*, Angela commits the racial and the woman's sin of individuality. She proceeds in her quest for her own happiness in defiance of the dictates of her society and regardless of the solidarity required for the struggle for racial advancement. She chooses not to sacrifice a "burnt-offering of individualism for some dimly glimpsed racial whole."[62] At almost any cost, Angela seeks "Freedom! That was the note which Angela heard oftenest in the melody of living which must be hers." For her, in the first half of her story, "freedom" meant whiteness. "Colour or rather the lack of it seemed to the child the one absolute prerequisite to the life of which she was always dreaming." She considered "being coloured in America . . . nothing short of a curse."[63] To escape this curse and achieve the freedom that would mean access to wealth, power, consequence, and respect, Angela moves away from her home in the black section of Philadelphia to pass for white in Greenwich Village, New York City. In passing as a white woman, Angela seeks the power to form that discursive space that would allow her to shape her own destiny.

As she pursues her love affair with Roger Fielding and her dream of becoming a sought-after painter, Angela repeatedly revises her notions of freedom and happiness. Through heartache, loneliness, and disappointment, Angela eventually finds her way back to blackness, to accepting and liking herself, and therefore to the key that will open the space of self-determination, according to Fauset's formulation. Her struggles teach her to value the racial solidarity and heterosexual love she previously dismissed as an encumbrance or a means to an end. Although she begins as an outsider, a black woman dissatisfied with her racial status and therefore at odds with everyone who knows her and too secretive with her new friends to gain real intimacy, Angela's ideas and goals evolve, and she is slowly enveloped into the community of Harlem and returned to her family. She comes to see Harlem as the liberating space she has been seeking, a place where she can be her best self without fear of restriction or rejection because of her color. Fauset depicts the New Negro communities of Harlem as large, varied, and sophisticated enough to grant Angela the freedom to choose and follow her own prerogatives. Angela sees Harlem at last as a city, a black enclave, of "signal opportunities."[64] There, teaching is no longer the only career open to her, and she need not dread marrying one of the local boys who seem more like younger brothers than romantic suitors.

Thus, through her discovery of Harlem and her subsequent return to blackness, Angela's dreams are fulfilled insofar as her quest for freedom is concerned. However, having learned to distinguish that freedom and her career success from a deeper spiritual satisfaction and joy, Angela does not feel happy. She pursues her painting studies in the great artistic center of Paris rather listlessly. As busy as she was in her studio and in her explorations of the city, "there was no chance for actual physical loneliness, yet Angela thought after a few weeks of persistent comradeship that she had never felt so lonely in her life."[65] Angela remains in this state—devoted to her work, accepting her disappointment—until her hero, Anthony Cross, appears on Christmas morning as a gift from fate.

Angela's love for Anthony represents her fruition as a woman. Through this culminating relationship, Fauset outlines her vision of New Negro women's self-determination and the only route to happiness the author considers plausible. In coming to her love for Anthony, Angela has learned to see marriage "as an end in itself; for women certainly; the only, the most desirable and natural end. From this state a gifted, an ambitious woman might reach forth and acquit herself well in any activity. But marriage must be there first, the foundation, the substratum." She knew she would find her happiness in "all the sweet offices of love; the delicate bondage that could knit together two persons absolutely *en rapport*" and that "at the cost of every ambition which she had ever known she would make him happy. After the manner of most men his work would probably be the greatest thing in the world to him. And he should be the greatest thing in the world to her. He should be her task, her 'job,' the fulfillment of her ambition."[66] Having found her "substratum" and finally come into the full flowering of her womanhood, Angela might still go on to become a great artist. Fauset suggests, however, that the fulfillment of this career goal matters much less than the deeper, absorbing happiness of adoring and being adored by a worthy man. Fauset evinces the notion that women's fulfillment is to be found in marriage to a worthy patriarch and devotion to his self-determination. Her conception of New Negro women's proper role is akin to Oscar Micheaux's in *Within Our Gates*. As Sylvia eventually "understood that . . . Dr. Vivian was right after all" and that her "thinking [had] been warped," so does Angela come to see her efforts to find independent self-determination as misguided and that her only role and source of happiness is as Anthony's "tender wife." Thus, for Fauset, the companionate marriage functions as the discursive space in which the New Negro woman is appreciated for her full self and finds fulfillment.

Larsen refuted the notion of marriage as the fulfillment of a woman's "true" or "natural" ambition and the only foundation for her happiness. Through Helga's disastrous marriage and ruinous motherhood by which "the children used her up," Larsen showed women who dreamed of finding their ultimate fulfillment solely through patriarchal coupling to have been deluded, even foolish, as Helga was when she married the Reverend Green. Over and again, Helga curses herself as "the damnedest kind of a fool" and demands to know "how could she, how could anyone, have been so deluded?"[67] For Helga, love is a joke, and the wrong marriage a swamp-like coffin in which a woman's body soon rots. Larsen insists her readers focus on themes and circumstances beyond the private and the individual. Helga's story and choices are particular to her, but the circumstances that shaped and constricted them are social and formed through sexual and racial discourses.

In *Quicksand*, Helga's idea of happiness is encapsulated in her concept of home. Helga finds herself trapped in her coffin of quicksand because she could not find a home that would support her fulfillment, a discursive space that would fully accept, comfort, and support her. By this she means a space, a social role, "a place for herself," "her proper setting" in which she can be her whole self, her simple human self, without having to conform to or deny others' concepts of and uses for her, a place of permanent "happiness and serenity."[68] Women were taught that marriage to the right man and the social role of wife was just such a space, but Helga finds this to be a false lesson. Throughout the novel, she runs from spaces imposing identities upon her, spaces shaped by patriarchal New Negro discourses and by the sex-race marketplace, and she never succeeds in determining a subjectivity for herself.

In the whole of the novel, the only person who seems an apt model for the type of woman a happy and comfortable Helga might be is Audrey Denney. Like Helga, an attractive and profoundly sensual woman who stands outside of social norms, Audrey is known to entertain both white and black male company. "She goes around with white people," Helga's friend Anne comments, scandalized and indignant. Helga refrains from replying but reflects within herself that "Anne's insinuations were too revolting."[69] She chafes at the assumption that Audrey is immoral or that her relationships are contemptible simply because her social circle is interracial. Beyond this objection, Helga is disturbed by Audrey's effect on her. She is as curious about Audrey as the men who encircle her cabaret table. Audrey took "quietly and without fuss the things which she wanted."[70] She seems to be the consummate self-determined New Negro woman. For this quiet, simple rebellion against social convention and New Negro ideals of ladyhood and solidarity, however, Audrey is nearly shunned by respectable New Negro women. Anne is annoyed to see that Audrey continues to be successful in securing the company of desirable men and declares, determinedly, that "she ought to be ostracized."[71]

This is a risk Helga remains steadfastly unwilling to take. Even at the moment when she anticipates consummating her passionate love for Robert Anderson, Helga hesitates for fear of social condemnation. "For Helga Crane wasn't, after all, a rebel from society, Negro society. It did mean something to her. She had no wish to stand alone."[72] In every situation, "all her efforts had been toward similarity to those about her."[73] More than anything, Helga craves acceptance, but her nature—her sensuality, her sensitivity and perceptiveness, her moody, artistic sensibility—render her a woman apart. If she is to accept herself and achieve the peaceful, comfortable inner security she needs to find happiness, Helga must also accept her singularity and the risk of standing alone. She must learn independence. It is something she simply cannot do. Instead, she seeks confirmation of her worth in the acceptance and good opinion of those surrounding her. This is how she ends up married to Pleasant Green. She conforms to the demands and ideals of race motherhood in an effort to prove her acceptability.

Helga's society was structured against women's independence and self-determination. It is not entirely the fault of her quirky personality that she finds it so very difficult to accept her weirdness and face the possibility of a life alone. How can Helga be considered wrong? According to New Negro prescriptions, a woman was supposed to find her happiness in marriage and motherhood. A sensuous, intelligent, beautiful woman should not stand alone or seek her own satisfactions. She ought to devote herself to others, to ideals, to New Negro patriarchy, to her people. Furthermore, the surrounding society, shaped by the sex-race marketplace and its flat depictions of black women as inhuman, worked to prevent the formation of black women's complex, fully human subjectivity. There was no space for Helga Crane to achieve the acceptance she craves and thus accept herself and find happiness.

Of all the New Negro women writing about race and womanhood, Nella Larsen may have been the boldest, the least acclimated to the expectations of early twentieth-century U.S. society and New Negro gender politics. She pushed her criticism of her society, its hypocrisies, and the punishments it habitually meted out to black women further than her peers, but she nevertheless represented them. Dunnigan's disappointing marriage; McDougald's lack of peace; Bonner's caveat that the husband who would bring happiness not require his wife to look down on herself; Fauset's soaring fantasy of fairytale love coming just in time for Christmas—to one degree or another, they all recognized the precariousness, the improbability, of a black woman's happiness. New Negro women's happiness could exist in discursive spaces offering full recognition of black women's complexity, diversity, capabilities, pain, joy—their simple humanity. While individual women, like Melnea Cass, could and did build such spaces in their private lives, the overwhelming, combined power of race motherhood and the sex-race marketplace worked against their formation, especially as hegemonic sites for the construction of black female subjectivity.

Even the novels Larsen and Fauset wrote, as incisive as they were on multiple levels, failed to create such a space as they were misread and often handily dismissed in their own time for a supposed undue preoccupation with respectable representations of the New Negro bourgeoisie. Whether they celebrated or denounced the novels, moreover, white and black critics overwhelmingly misunderstood their themes and characters, often largely because the novels focused on educated black women rather than the expected masculine black "folk" made popular through primitivism.[74] Ensnared between race motherhood and the sex-race marketplace, New Negro women recognized their own complex humanity, but they despaired of being understood as such within the popular culture and political perceptions of their day.

OPPRESSION

Sometimes, in the depths of their disapprobation and discontent, New Negro women thought they must be cursed. Fauset despaired in a letter to a friend, "Oh Langston, you think life is hard and complicated! It is, it is! But when one adds to that being a woman! Oh, God doesn't like us."[75] Their reflections on solidarity, sexual politics, and happiness point toward black women's keen understanding of the nature of the particular oppression plaguing them. It was not simply that black women were oppressed according to both their race and their sex. The oppression they endured was a fusion of racial and sexual, physical, material, and discursive dehumanizations, and it was relentlessly compounded by the demand that they shroud the particulars of their oppression in silence.

In her essay, "On Being Young—A Woman—and Colored," Marita Bonner reflected on the effects of white supremacy. "Every part of you becomes bitter," she wrote.

> You long to explode and hurt everything white; friendly, unfriendly. But you know that you cannot live with a chip on your shoulder even if you can manage a smile around your eyes—without getting steely and brittle and losing the softness that makes you a woman.
>
> For chips make you bend your body to balance them. And once you bend, you lose your poise, your balance, and the chip gets into you. The real you. You get hard.

. . . And many things in you can ossify . . .

And you know, being a woman, you have to go about it gently and quietly, to find out and to discover just what is wrong. Just what can be done.[76]

Above all else, New Negro women must not allow themselves to get "hard." A "hard" woman was not a real, feminine woman. New Negro women were thus required by decorum, gender ideals, and conventions to maintain their gentleness, even in the face of virulent racism. They were compelled to find a way not to feel what they felt. Furthermore, they must proceed "quietly" in their efforts to identify "just what is wrong" and "just what can be done." Any resistance or protest against their oppression must not be named as such and must not take the form of loud lamentation, mass demonstration, or widely disseminated propaganda. These actions, too, would undermine their femininity and "harden" them.

Bonner complained that "white friends who have never had to draw breath in a Jim-Crow train" commanded that she "not grow bitter." Such friends, she observed, "have never had petty putrid insult dragged over them—drawing blood—like pebbled sand on your body where the skin is tenderest. On your body where the skin is thinnest and tenderest." The thinnest and most tender skin is the genital skin. The repetition of this last image and its deeply personal nature suggest the intimate ravages of white supremacist terror—rape, molestation, sexual harassment—and a bodily, sexual aspect of black women's oppression. Bonner implies that sexism and racism intersect to compromise a black woman's intimate womanhood as well as her femininity. She is not only in danger of growing hard, of "ossifying," in her personality and emotions but also of being violated and bloodied.

The particulars of black women's oppression were difficult to define not only because they were complex but even more so because they were unspeakable. Solidarity and decorum, even simple politeness, demanded that black women maintain a silence regarding their oppression. Such silences buttressed the masculinist understandings of racism as an oppression predominantly affecting black men and of black women as rightfully subordinated to the role of helpmeets in the articulation of New Negro political ideologies and strategies.

According to Elise McDougald, "true sex equality [had] not been approximated" among African Americans any more than among white people in the interwar years. In black families, men's "baffled and suppressed desires to determine their economic life [were] manifested in overbearing domination at home." Even as she sought to define the problem of intraracial sexual inequality, McDougald found it necessary to qualify her censure of black men's excesses. Themselves oppressed by racism, black men were not fully to blame for their domination of black women. But were black men the only ones suffering the frustrations and hardship of economic and racial oppression? On whom were black women to unload their pain? McDougald refrained from addressing such questions. Instead, she urged "young Negro womanhood . . . to . . . grasp the proffered comradeship [of black men] with sincerity." Rather than identify the deleterious effects of black men's patriarchal aspirations and physical dominance as an integral aspect of the oppression they battled, McDougald further declared, New Negro women should adhere to the dictates of a masculinist solidarity. She approvingly observed that they directed their efforts and activism "chiefly toward the realization of the equality of the races, the sex struggle assuming the subordinate place."[77] Solidarity demanded that black women diminish their particular oppression and the injuries they suffered, especially at the hands of black men, for the greater racial good. The quest for racial advancement, defined as it was through masculinism, was to predominate over the battle of black women's particular "sex struggle."

In the New Negro era, black women's oppression was a padded prison relentlessly muffling the voices they raised in attempts to define themselves, a terrorism of misapprehension that often erupted in sudden violent attacks of lynching, rioting, and rape, a demand and denial that kept them hauling, sweating, and laboring according to the prerogatives of others. It was an oppression plainly stated in the Jim Crow exclusion and economic exploitation perpetrated by the dominant society, manifest in the street-car advertisements and theatrical images that so plagued Elise McDougald, evident in the fencing off of Marita Bonner's catnip field of youthful desires and dreams, and, most painfully, hidden in the sexual possession and familial duties to which, as Larsen observed, black men expected black women to cheerfully subject themselves. Theirs was an oppression black women partly shared with black men but that also insidiously stalked them through their sexual desires, their love, their maternal instincts, their very womanhood. It was an oppression that invaded and raided black women's intimate selves and purported to name them through its self-serving manipulation of the spoils.

Sometimes obliquely, sometimes through symbolism, sometimes through fiction, sometimes directly, a few black women dared to speak about that oppression in its multiple forms. In a number of ways, New Negro women stepped from behind the curtain of the culture of dissemblance to express themselves, to determine themselves, and to testify to their repression. Flowing beneath the surface of the sex-race marketplace and in contradistinction to the discourse of race motherhood and the emphatic New Negro demand for patriarchal power were the muted voices of black women's multivalent discussions of the necessities, emotions, and physical and discursive parameters shaping their worlds. As consummate New Negroes, they shared with black men the desire to achieve racial and individual self-determination. Their writings are full of the quest to create themselves according to their own aspirations and the efforts to find the means of achieving such liberating power. Their versions of self-determination, however, were marked as much by the necessity of defying restrictive ideals of proper femininity and proscriptions of women's prerogatives as by their generational rebellion against the mores of their elders and the belittling racial etiquette of Jim Crow white supremacy.

In the New Negro era, black women explicitly and implicitly challenged and sometimes even negated the restrictive definition of good and worthy womanhood handed down to them by their elders and imposed upon them by their male counterparts. While the majority of them may have remained silent, their thoughts and feelings on these issues going unrecorded, this did not mean that they toed the line of the gender prescriptions and sexual proscriptions set for them within New Negro discourses. They recognized prejudice and unfairness according to gender as well as the links between sexuality and racial identity and racism. They made small strides and offered quiet criticisms aimed at the accomplishment of their individual self-determination. One by one, they went to school; they married or divorced; they sought lucrative, satisfying work; they wrote poems, novels, and essays; and they migrated. They endeavored to transform themselves and their prospects and to define and choose their own identities by making the daring journey out of the old and into the new.

Astute New Negro women like McDougald, Bonner, Larsen, and Fauset understood that black women's subjectivities were not wholly or even mostly self-constructed and that they were being used to "prove" the subjectivities of others more discursively powerful and outspoken than they could be. Seeking to right this wrong in the name of self-determination, their discourse contested the masculinism evinced in New Negro racial advancement ideologies and the dehumanizing effects of the sex-race discourse that so distorted their identities and constrained their opportunities. Through that discourse they asserted the value and the goodness of their womanhood, but few heard or understood them. Despite the best efforts of these few, daringly outspoken women, their words formed a mere trickle against the tide of combined racism and sexism. The complicated intersections and creative constructions forming New Negro womanhood remained unacknowledged within New Negro conceptions of racial identity and visions of liberation. Thus, little chance existed that early twentieth-century popular culture or U.S. society at large would recognize them either.

Through their migrations, filmmaking, consumption, publications, performances, cultural and entrepreneurial productions, diverse political formulations, and integration of a range of professional and industrial fields, the New Negroes gained more power over the shape and operation of race in the interwar period than African Americans had possessed in any preceding era of U.S. history. They helped to construct a modern racial politics and intervened in racial discourses as they were reformulated in the interwar years. Their interventions and encroachments on racial power dynamics were all explored through ideals, identities, and ideas focusing on New Negro women. Then, too, the insidious, modern effort to maintain white supremacy through cooptation and commodification was also made manifest on black women's bodies and subjectivities. New Negro women symbolized the race's hopes for the future through their reproductive and mothering capacities, even as they also epitomized the otherness and exoticism of blackness as they were represented in the sex-race marketplace. With so much depending on their stability as mothers and reliability as symbols of otherness, and with modern racial advancement ideologies being formulated around black manhood and the achievement of patriarchy, black women's subjectivities were more deeply and more permanently subsumed by intersecting racial and sexual, interracial and intra-racial oppressions during the New Negro era. In this way, New Negro women's liberation or self-determination was rendered more tenuous than before. The race motherhood and sex-race marketplace discourses combined and prevailed, and the perspectives and particular circumstances of New Negro women remained obscured within them.

NOTES

INTRODUCTION

1. A native of Columbus, Georgia, where she began performing in minstrel shows in 1900 at the age of fourteen, Rainey is said to have never performed in New York City. Her music was nevertheless familiar and well-loved throughout the nation. She is known as the "Mother of the Blues" for her fusion of older, rural styles with more urban, classic blues. Rainey made her first recording with Paramount Records in 1923 and toured with her own band, Madame Gertrude Rainey and Her Georgia Smart Sets, from 1917 until about 1924. She was one of Bessie Smith's mentors, and insiders knew that she often engaged in lesbian relationships with her band members and others. This is one of the socially subversive practices she acknowledges through her "Prove It On Me Blues." See Kellner, *The Harlem Renaissance*, 293–294, and Albertson, *Bessie*.
2. Gertrude Rainey, "Prove It On Me Blues," Paramount Records 12668, June 1928.
3. E. Franklin Frazier, "Three Scourges of the Negro Family," *Opportunity* 4, no. 7 (July 1926): 210.
4. For more on the rationales of the new KKK, see MacLean, *Behind the Mask of Chivalry*.
5. The freedmen were the generation of African American adults made free by the initiatives they took during the upheavals of the Civil War, the Emancipation Proclamation, and finally the Thirteenth Amendment to the Constitution. "Reconstruction generation" is used here to identify the freedmen's children, those African Americans born, roughly, between 1865 and 1885, while the New Negroes were born between about 1885 and 1905. Generally, the members of the Reconstruction generation were the parents of the New Negroes. Anthony M. Platt in *E. Franklin Frazier, Reconsidered* also uses this generational periodization.
6. Deborah Gray White, *Too Heavy a Load*, 114–115.
7. For more on the racial consequences of urban progressivism, see Kevin Mumford, *Interzones*.
8. Mumford, *Interzones*, xviii. In addition, James R. Grossman calculates that 56,442 migrants over the age of ten years settled in Chicago between 1910 and 1920. See Grossman, *Land of Hope*, Appendix A.
9. Although the primary evidence suggests the New Negro ethos rose in Southern cities as it rose in Northern and Midwestern ones, the secondary information on African American popular culture and the developments in African American politics in Southern cities during the interwar years isonly just emerging.
10. See Mumford, *Interzones*, xviii. Emphasis added.
11. The use of the term "discourse" in this book signals an analytical reliance on Michel Foucault's theories of social relations, knowledge, and power and the use cultural historians and literary critics have made of them. See Michel Foucault, *The History of Sexuality, Volume I* and, particularly, Foucault, "Two Lectures, January 1976" in *Power/Knowledge*.

I adopt the term to describe the matrix of hegemonic understandings and popular assumptions through which meaning is made and assigned in a given society. While all social actors contribute to the formation of their society's discourses, power (based in economics, political influence, and respectability) determines the degree to which different members affect and shape social discourses. In the United States, for example, due to long-standing yet dynamic racial discourses, white people have maintained and exerted power over black people. White people have furthermore held the majority of the power over the meanings, use, application, value, and relevance of words and symbols relating to race, including black bodies. In this way, white people have dominated racial discourses, and it is through that discursive domination that racism is enacted and race continues to have meaning. In other societies—such as Brazil, for example—long-standing racial discourses also exist but may assign different meanings and values to similar words, symbols, and bodies. A human construction, discourse is historical, evolving over time and according to changes in culture, economy, and politics. Discourses intersect with and affect one another, and levels and hierarchies of discourse exist according to national, social, and political groups.

The term "subjectivity" as I use it here is related to discourse. A person's subjectivity, or socially acknowledged identity and representation, is determined through and in discourse. Particularly for oppressed peoples, subjectivity is distinct from individual identity, for a person's identification of herself and personal understandings of her meaning in society may be quite different from her society's hegemonic understanding of her, her character, and what she represents. In achieving more participation in the formation of racial discourses, the New Negroes were exercising more control over and changing their subjectivities.

12. Jayna Brown provides an excellent discussion of primitivism in the context of sexual-racial discourses and black female dancing bodies. See Brown, *Babylon Girls*, 157–162.

13. For an in-depth discussion of the intersecting racial and sexual politics of the segregated cabaret and its connections to primitivism and processes of exploitation, see Vogel, *The Scene of Harlem Cabaret*.

14. For more information on the impact of rising urban blues culture on sexuality and gender in African American politics, see White, *Too Heavy a Load*, 124–131; Douglas, *Terrible Honesty: Mongrel Manhattan in the 1920s*; Mumford, *Interzones*; and Lewis Erenberg, *Steppin' Out*.

15. Davarian Baldwin, Deborah Gray White, Kevin Mumford, Anthony M. Platt, and others who have published recently on African American politics in this period also utilize this periodization and concept of "New Negro." See Baldwin, *Chicago's New Negroes*; White, *Too Heavy a Load*; Mumford, *Interzones*; and Platt, *E. Franklin Frazier, Reconsidered*.

16. Paula Giddings points out how optimistic Ida B. Wells and her peers were in the years before the *Plessy vs. Ferguson* decision was handed down and consequently how ill-prepared they were for its consequences. Giddings also points to this generation's failure to recognize that race, instead of class, education, or deportment, was quickly becoming the primary arbiter of humanity and civic fitness as one reason for their deployment of the class-biased strategy of racial uplift. See Giddings, *Ida, A Sword Among Lions*, 97, 148–149.

17. For an in-depth intellectual history of African Americans' development and application of uplift and its class implications, see Gaines, *Uplifting the Race*. Paula Giddings, Deborah Gray White, Victoria Wolcott, and other historians of black women and intra-racial gender politics also address uplift and its gender and class politics in their work.

18. Du Bois, "Criteria for Negro Art"; Alain Locke, ed. *The New Negro*; George Schuyler, "The Negro-Art Hokum"; Langston Hughes, "The Negro Artist and the Racial Mountain."

19. For a detailed historical study of transformations in black manhood ideals and class identity in this period, see Martin Anthony Summers, *Manliness and Its Discontents*. And see Victoria Wolcott, *Remaking Respectability*, for an extended discussion of this

transformation of gender in African American politics as it proceeded in one model city. Although this is not her focus, Deborah Gray White also contends that a new masculinism infused black politics in the New Negro era. See White, *Too Heavy a Load*, 110–141.

On class as a tenet of advancement among New Negro organizations, see Holloway, *Confronting the Veil*, 10–11. Holloway points out that most of the well-known black organizations of the New Negro era, such as the African Blood Brotherhood, the Brotherhood of Sleeping Car Porters, the Universal Negro Improvement Association, and (I would add) the National Urban League, were race-based organizations concerned with black economic well-being that advanced ideologies based in class as much as in race.

20. Historian Michele Mitchell provides ample evidence that this intra-racial discourse focusing on pure homes and exalting mothers permeated the Reconstruction generation across lines of class and region as African Americans endeavored to martial dominant ideals of morality and decorum to the race's defense. See Mitchell, *Righteous Propagation*.

21. Terrell is quoted in D.W. Culp, ed., *Twentieth Century Negro Literature*, 173. See Deborah Gray White, *Too Heavy a Load*, chapters 1–3 for more detail on the activities and feminist ideology of the NACW.

22. See Anna Julia Cooper, "The Higher Education of Woman" in *A Voice from the South*; Deborah Gray White, *Too Heavy a Load*; and Evelyn Brooks Higginbotham, "Chapter 5: Feminist Theology," in *Righteous Discontent* for more on these activities among black clubwomen.

23. This rationale for the emergence of a new, concerted masculinism and the waning of black women's self-determinative, intra-racial power in the New Negro era is culled from several historical and cultural analyses of race, gender, and African American women's roles as symbols and agents in the reformation of racial discourses as well as my own research. I have combined the theories of Victoria Wolcott, Candice Jenkins, Jayna Brown, Melinda Chateauvert, and Deborah Gray White, who all posit an increased masculinism among the New Negroes, although their explanations of the source or reason for this increase vary. See Wolcott, *Remaking Respectability*; Jenkins, *Private Lives, Proper Relations*; Brown, *Babylon Girls*; Chateauvert, *Marching Together*; and White, *Too Heavy a Load*.

24. Anne Stavney's analysis of the "moral mother" icon so prominent in images gracing the pages and covers of leading New Negro publications supports my contention here. Static and flat, the moral mother was often depicted supporting black urban life on her shoulders or back, yet her supportive role also rendered her separate, even excluded, from that life and its modern transformations. These images, Stavney asserts, "effectively discount the option of black female identity existing in public, urban space," the space of the New Negro, the race's political engagement, strategizing for the future, and modernity. See Stavney, "Mothers of Tomorrow," especially 547.

25. Although I do not find a coherent politics advocating black women's individual self-determination and decrying interracial and intra-racial sexism among New Negro women, I do think such a feminist politics and discourse may have been "grounded," according to historian Nancy Cott's use of that term, in this era. Some New Negro women, such as Nella Larsen, Jessie Fauset, Zora Neale Hurston, Marita Bonner, Elise McDougald, and Bessie Smith, did articulate a developing consciousness around the particular oppression resulting from the intersection of race and sex in social discourses and in their own experiences. However, that consciousness did not cohere into a concerted New Negro feminist politics or praxis shared and activated by a group of New Negroes. Indeed, many of these women had never met and seem to have come to their feminist (or proto-feminist) consciousness independently. Nevertheless, the New Negro women's considerations and meditations on the intersection of sex and race, as well as the questions of racial unity and solidarity those considerations raised, formed the foundation for later black feminist thought.

Conversely, historian Ula Taylor identifies a "community feminism" within the Universal Negro Improvement Association and in Garveyite ideology, citing as self-determinative the women's commitment to the organization's racial mission, their belief in the benefits of patriarchy, and their fearless criticism of men's failure to provide patriarchal support. Yet Taylor fails to fully reconcile the women's subordination under men's control and their commitment to modern patriarchy with any understanding of women's particular liberation from or critique of sexism. Since the birth of the term in the 1910s, feminism has signified the advocacy of equality between the sexes and the denunciation of sexism, which is social and political hierarchy placing men above and dominant over women, rather than simply a form of women's self-determination by any means. It remains unclear, then, how the Garveyite women's strident insistence on patriarchal support and acceptance of their own gendered subordination might be termed feminist, especially in the modern, post-Victorian era. See Taylor, *The Veiled Garvey* and Cott, *The Grounding of Modern Feminism*.

26. It was black feminist literary scholarship that first addressed questions of gender and sexuality in the New Negro era—not only in the period's literature but also in its performers and performances. *Prove It On Me* extends feminist analyses of the intersections between race, sexuality, gender, and class found, especially, in the work of Hazel Carby, Claudia Tate, Ann DuCille, Saidiya Hartman, and Hortense Spillers. Likewise, the book has evolved in its various stages through emulation of the cultural historical methods used by Mary Renda in *Taking Haiti*, Anne McClintock in *Imperial Leather*, Ann Laura Stoler in *Carnal Knowledge and Imperial Power*, and Jayna Brown in *Babylon Girls*. These historians adapted the methods of literary criticism and literary and cultural theory to elucidate the historical, racialized, and gendered meanings of certain bodies, practices, and symbols and to illuminate their ongoing significance. *Prove It On Me* also stands upon the insights revealed through histories of black women and African American gender discourses written by scholars such as Paula Giddings, Tera Hunter, Deborah Gray White, Michele Mitchell, Barbara Ransby, Evelyn Brooks Higginbotham, Jennifer Morgan, and a rising multitude of others. Such historians have broken new ground in utilizing innovative methods to recover black women's voices and experiences and to reveal the deep, dynamic significance of intersections of race, sexuality, and gender in African American lives and political strategies as well as in the political, cultural, and social fabric of the United States.

CHAPTER 1

1. Evelyn Preer, "Movie Queen Tells Courier Readers of Her 'Film Thrills,'" *Pittsburgh Courier*, 11 June 1927.
2. Preer, "Movie Queen Tells Courier Readers of Her 'Film Thrills.'"
3. Evelyn Preer, "My Thrills in the Movies No. 2," *Pittsburgh Courier*, 18 June 1927.
4. Sister Francesca Thompson, "Evelyn Preer, 1896–1932."
5. Floyd J. Calvin, "Evelyn Preer Ranks First as Stage and Movie Star," *Pittsburgh Courier*, 16 April 1927. For Oscar Micheaux's claim, see "Evelyn Preer, Noted Actress, Dies in Los Angeles," *New York Age*, 26 November 1932.
6. For the history of Preer's work with Oscar Micheaux, see Thompson, "Evelyn Preer, 1896–1932"; Sister FrancescaThompson, "From Shadows 'n Shufflin' to Spotlights and Cinema: The Lafayette Players, 1915–1932"; and Charles Musser et al., "An Oscar Micheaux Filmography: From the Silents through His Transition to Sound, 1919–1931."
7. The first company of what would become several troupes of the Lafayette Players was founded by Anita Bush as the Anita Bush Stock Company in Harlem in 1915 and performed at the Lincoln Theater. It moved to the Lafayette Theater and took its name later that year. Thompson describes the Players' work as "serious" and "legitimate" drama

because it was not minstrelsy nor musical theater nor vaudeville—types of performance in which African American performers were "merely a source of ridicule and sport." See Thompson, "From Shadows 'n Shufflin' to Spotlights and Cinema," and Thompson, "The Lafayette Players:1915-1932."

8. Evelyn Preer's career is recounted in her obituaries and at length in Thompson's articles. See Thompson, "From Shadows 'n Shufflin' to Spotlights and Cinema"; Thompson, "Evelyn Preer, 1896–1932"; "Clarence Muse Pays Perfect Tribute to the Late Evelyn Preer on Behalf of a Grateful Theatrical Profession," *Pittsburgh Courier*, 10 December 1932; "Evelyn Preer, Noted Actress, Dies in Los Angeles," *New York Age*, 26 November 1932, 1; and Harry Levette, "Stage Mourns Evelyn Preer," *Chicago Defender*, 26 November 1932.

9. Floyd J. Calvin, "Evelyn Preer Ranks First as Stage and Movie Star," *Pittsburgh Courier*, 16 April 1927.

10. Advertisement for *Within Our Gates* at E. B. Dudley's Vaudette Theater, Detroit, *Chicago Defender*, 24 January 1920, 7.

11. For information on Micheaux's biography and race filmmakers of this period, see Jacqueline Stewart, *Migrating to the Movies*; Pearl Bowser and Louise Spence, *Writing Himself into History*; Pearl Bowser, Jane Gaines, and Charles Musser, eds. *Oscar Micheaux and His Circle*; and Bestor Cram and Pearl Bowser, dir. *Midnight Ramble*. For a comprehensive filmography of Micheaux's silent productions, see Charles Musser et. al. "An Oscar Micheaux Filmography" in *Oscar Micheaux and His Circle*.

12. Advertisement for *Within Our Gates* at Dooley's Atlas Theater, Chicago, *Chicago Defender*, 31 January 1920, 8.

13. "Summary: The African American Cinema I," in *The Origins of Film (1900-1926)*, DVD Liner Notes.

14. The events of the Red Summer are summarized in Nell Irvin Painter, *Standing at Armageddon*, 362–365.

15. Claude McKay, "If We Must Die," *Liberator* (July 1919): 21.

16. Manthia Diawara, "Black American Cinema: The New Realism," *Black American Cinema*, 3, 4.

17. Willis N. Huggins to the Editor, *Chicago Defender*, 17 January 1920.

18. "At the Movie Houses," clipping from GPJ Collection.

19. "Within Our Gates" review, clipping from GPJ Collection.

20. "Mischauex [*sic*] Stages Another Picture," clipping from GPJ Collection.

21. Associated Negro Press, "Race Problem Play Raises Fuss in Chicago," 20 January 1920, clipping from GPJ Collection.

22. Indeed, due to Micheaux's practice of continuously editing his films according to his own whims and to appease censors, as well as the fact that *Within Our Gates* was lost for many years and only restored to us through its Spanish version *La Negra*, we cannot be certain that the film we know today is the same film Micheaux released in 1919. However, *Within Our Gates* retained the integrity of its plot and its most controversial scenes depicting lynching, attempted rape, and the wanton expression of white supremacist brutality. The many published reviews and advertisements, indeed the disapproval of the censor boards themselves, confirm this. The current version of this seminal New Negro film is a congruent whole and fits descriptions of it found in reviews published in the period of its release. It seems that the current version of *Within Our Gates* is close to Micheaux's original, and contemporary film critics accept it as such. For information on the rediscovery of *Within Our Gates*, see "Summary: The African American Cinema I," in *The Origins of Film (1900–1926)*, DVD Liner Notes; Pearl Bowser, Jane Gaines, and Charles Musser, "Introduction: Oscar Micheaux and Race Movies of the Silent Period" in *Oscar Micheaux and His Circle*; Bowser and Spence, *Writing Himself into History*; and Jane Gaines, "Fire and Desire: Race, Melodrama, and Oscar Micheaux" in *Black American Cinema*.

23. Associated Negro Press, "Race Problem Play Raises Fuss in Chicago," 20 January 1920, clipping from GPJ Collection.

24. Telegram, Theodore A. Ray to Honorable Frank T. Monney, 19 March 1920, GPJ Collection. Hammond may have seen a different version of the film from the one now available, or he was simply mistaken in his assertion that *Within Our Gates* depicts scenes of slavery. On the other hand, it is tempting to speculate that Micheaux's incisive comment on racial oppression led viewers to liken contemporary black living conditions to the tribulations their forebears endured as slaves.

25. Information about the distribution of *Within Our Gates* is derived from correspondence and clippings in the GPJ Collection, Reel 8, and from Musser et al. "An Oscar Micheaux Filmography" in *Oscar Micheaux and His Circle*.

26. George P. Johnson to Oscar Micheaux, 13 August 1920, GPJ Collection.

27. George P. Johnson to Oscar Micheaux, 10 August 1920, GPJ Collection.

28. Oscar Micheaux to George P. Johnson, 14 August 1920, GPJ Collection.

29. "Mischauex [*sic*] Stages Another Picture," clipping in GPJ Collection.

30. Oscar Micheaux, dir., *Within Our Gates*.

31. This exchange between the two white women could be read as a microcosm of the split into regional factions of politically engaged women involved in the suffrage debate. Micheaux's meaning here cannot be fully deciphered, but he may be commenting on the lamentable ability of Southern white women to cow their purportedly more liberal Northern counterparts into submission to Jim Crow policies and the exclusion of black women, such as Sylvia, from participation in politics and social questions affecting the race. He may also be suggesting the insufficiency of woman's suffrage as a tenet of racial advancement strategy because black women would remain less powerful than white women and because white women's racism would be reflected in their votes and serve to increase the power of white supremacy. For more information on the racial politics of U.S. feminism and the suffrage movement, see Ellen Carol DuBois, *Feminism and Suffrage*, 162–202; Glenda Elizabeth Gilmore, *Gender and Jim Crow*; and Louise Michele Newman, *White Women's Rights*,—56–85.

32. Jane Gaines defines *Within Our Gates* as a "race melodrama" in the tradition of nineteenth-century melodramatic fiction about black people and race in her article "*Within Our Gates*: From Race Melodrama to Opportunity Narrative" in *Oscar Micheaux and His Circle*.

33. Critic Gerald Butters agrees that Sylvia's place at the center of the film provides Micheaux with "numerous opportunities to construct varying portrayals of African-American manhood." See Gerald R. Butters, Jr., *Black Manhood on the Silent Screen*, 151.

34. See Jacqueline Stewart, *Migrating to the Movies*; Butters, *Black Manhood on the Silent Screen*; and Bowser and Spence, *Writing Himself into History*.

35. Chad Williams, *Torchbearers of Democracy*, 7.

36. My analysis of the historical relationship between ideals of manhood, patriarchy, and citizenship is principally supported by the arguments of Gail Bederman, *Manliness and Civilization*, 14,20–21 and Nancy F. Cott, *Public Vows*, 81–93. Chad Williams analyzes World War I in particular as an arena in which black men tested and asserted modern notions of racialized manhood, and he also asserts that black soldiers returned from the war with a newfound determination to assert their manly citizenship within the United States. See Williams, *Torchbearers of Democracy*.

37. Critic Michele Wallace points out, however, that these deprecating stereotypical characters were more humanized in Micheaux's films, particularly *Within Our Gates*, than they were in mainstream Hollywood movies, especially *The Birth of a Nation*. Wallace argues that Micheaux uses stereotypes strategically to counter mainstream filmic representations of black life and character and specifically provides motivations and human depth to such stock figures as the black fool or stool pigeon, such as Old Ned and Efrem, and the black

criminal such as Larry Prichard. See Wallace, "Oscar Micheaux's *Within Our Gates*: The Possibility for Alternative Visions" in *Oscar Micheaux and His Circle*. In employing such stereotypes, moreover, and providing them with humanity and motivation, Micheaux seems to suggest that they are real, or fair representations of black realities, and thus uses them to critique intra-racial African American relations and practices, such as the sexual politics of heterosexual relationships.

38. Du Bois, "Returning Soldiers," *The Crisis* (May 1919), 13. Italics in original.

39. Anastasia Curwood concurs. "Although the descriptor 'New Negro' applied to men and women, the ideal New Negro was male and New Negro men prioritized the rights and responsibilities of manhood as central to the New Negro project," she writes. See Curwood, *Stormy Weather*, 54.

40. See Butters, *Black Manhood on the Silent Screen*, 159–161 and Gaines, "Fire and Desire," 52.

41. Bowser and Spence offer an interpretation identifying the new couple as "companions-in-struggle" and Sylvia as the bearer of "the gauntlet of social justice." See *Writing Himself into History*, 141–142.

42. There are as many different interpretations of these seemingly disjointed and frankly confusing final scenes as there are critiques of *Within Our Gates*. Stewart's analysis is particularly compelling in her reading of Sylvia as a tragic mulatta who is redeemed by her marriage and through whom the race is to maintain its patriotism and enter full citizenship. However, I find little basis for Stewart's conclusion that Sylvia's marriage will necessarily be a non-patriarchal, companionate one in which she will retain her career in teaching and activism. Indeed, Micheaux is much more likely to have joined his fellow New Negro men in extolling the benefits of traditional, patriarchal marriage. As Anastasia Curwood explains, "New Negro men fully expected New Negro women to play a supportive role as they sought to rehabilitate black manhood" through patriarchal marriage. Furthermore, Stewart does not fully account for Dr. Vivian's high-handed assessment of Sylvia's views as "warped" or the proclamation that he "was right after all." See Stewart, *Migrating to the Movies*, 226–236 and Curwood, *Stormy Weather*, 8.

43. The majority of the advertisements for *Within Our Gates* describe it as "The Greatest Preachment against Race Prejudice and the Glaring Injustices Practiced Upon Our People." See, for example, Advertisement for *Within Our Gates*, *Chicago Defender*, 24 January 1920, 5.

44. Associated Negro Press, "Race Problem Play Raises Fuss in Chicago," review of *Within Our Gates*, 20 January 1920, clipping from GPJ Collection.

45. Jane Gaines provides an extensive technical analysis of Micheaux's use of "cross-cutting" as a filmic narrative form throughout the rape sequence in *Within Our Gates*. She supports my contention that Micheaux used this technique "to give the attack on Sylvia an additional charge. . . . The scene is thus symbolically charged as a reenactment of the White patriarch's ravishment of Black womanhood, reminding viewers of all of the clandestine forced sexual acts that produced the mulatto population of the American South." She goes on to observe that "the parallelism of the rape and the lynching scenes assert the historical connection between the rape of the Black woman and the lynching of the Black man, the double reaction of the Reconstruction period to Whites' nightmare vision of Blacks voting and owning property." See Gaines, "Fire and Desire," 56, 60.

46. Mary Church Terrell, "Lynching from a Negro's Point of View," in *Black Women in White America: A Documentary History*, 207–208, 210.

47. "Within Our Gates" review, GPJ Collection.

48. "Within Our Gates" review, *Chicago Defender*, 24 January 1920.

49. See, for example, Walter White, "The Waco Horror," *The Crisis*, July 1916, supplement.

50. Ida B. Wells, *Southern Horrors: Lynch Law in All Its Phases*, 19, quoted in Patricia Schechter, *Ida B. Wells-Barnett and American Reform, 1880–1930*, 86. For more information on

Ida B. Wells's anti-lynching ideology, see Giddings, *Ida, A Sword Among Lions*; Schechter, *Ida B. Wells-Barnett and American Reform, 1880–1930*; Crystal Feimster, *Southern Horrors: Women and the Politics of Rape and Lynching*; Gail Bederman, "'The White Man's Civilization on Trial': Ida B. Wells, Representations of Lynching, and Northern Middle-Class Manhood" in *Manliness and Civilization*; and Wells's autobiography *Crusade for Justice*.

51. Seeking to refute this claim, the NACW came to advocate the uplift of black women in particular. They assumed that if black women were understood to be morally upright, if they more exactly embodied the ideal of Victorian ladyhood, they would both instill respect for all women in their sons and rightly attract the honorable attentions of black suitors.

52. Jacks is quoted in Maude T. Jenkins, "The History of the Black Woman's Club Movement in America," 61.

53. For more detail on the founding of the NACW, see White, Chapter 1, *Too Heavy a Load* and Paula Giddings, Chapters V and VI, *When and Where I Enter*.

54. Historian Stephanie J. Shaw has criticized this accepted interpretation of the NACW's founding. Noting the existence of two interstate black women's organizations when the NACW was founded in 1896 and the long-standing tradition of black women's "voluntary associations," Shaw argues that the National Association of Colored Women was merely "another logical step in the effort to maintain and/or improve important historical mechanisms for racial self-help." Furthermore, she asserts that it is "inappropriate to interpret the creation of the national coalition of African-American women's clubs as a response to the contemporary attacks on black female morality" because "those attacks rested on a historical tradition" of libelous understandings of black women's character. However, Shaw concedes that such attacks were "more public and more frequent" during the nadir era of the Reconstruction generation and that they "undoubtedly gave the organizers [of the NACW] an important 'cause' that could evoke an immediate response from the black community." Indeed, it seems that, in founding a national organization that would combine the memberships of their established clubs and organizations, black women determined to evolve their tactics and organize a new, united method of self-defense and mutual uplift. Why make any change if not in response to new circumstances and threats? The nadir era, which witnessed racial disfranchisement, the imposition of Jim Crow segregation, and the Supreme Court's establishment of the principle of "separate but equal" in public accommodations and civil services as well as a sharp increase in racialized lynchings, was a moment of emphatic expression of a newly brutal, vigorous racism,. The founding of the National Association of Colored Women was one of several new tactics African Americans developed to combat these heightened threats. See Stephanie J. Shaw, "Black Club Women and the Creation of the National Association of Colored Women," 19–20.

55. Mary Church Terrell, "Lynching from a Negro's Point of View," 210, 208, 209.

56. "Petition re. Lynching," James Weldon Johnson Scrapbooks, Box 2, Folder 1, James Weldon Johnson Collection in the Yale Collection of American Literature, Beinecke Rare Book and Manuscript Library, Yale University, New Haven, CT. (Hereafter JWJ Collection.)

57. The history of the NAACP's long, arduous, and ultimately unsuccessful battle to gain the passage of an anti-lynching bill that would allow the federal government to intervene, investigate, and prosecute mob violence when the states refused is documented in Zangrando, *The N.A.A.C.P. Crusade Against Lynching*. Zangrando convincingly argues that this battle, though lost, was the primary means by which the NAACP built its membership rolls among the masses and increased its prominence among legislators and philanthropists, thereby becoming the premier African American civil rights organization by the mid-twentieth century.

58. For a more detailed history of the Anti-Lynching Crusaders, see Feimster, "Ladies and Lynching."
59. "The Anti-Lynching Crusaders" pamphlet, James Weldon Johnson Papers, Series II, Box 26, Folder 6, JWJ Collection.

CHAPTER 2

1. Edith Sampson, "From the Diary of a Child Placing Agent," *Opportunity* 1, no.1 (January 1923): 11.
2. Sampson, "From the Diary of a Child Placing Agent," 11.
3. "Social Case Work and the Story of Annabelle," *Opportunity* 1, no. 4 (April 1923): 10.
4. This summary of the ideology and aims of African American social science and social work and its description as a black form of progressivism during the interwar period is culled from histories of race, gender, and progressive movements such as Mumford, *Interzones*; Kathy Peiss, *Cheap Amusements*; Mary E. Odem, *Delinquent Daughters*; Victoria Wolcott, *Remaking Respectability*; Christina Simmons, "African Americans and Sexual Victorianism in the Social Hygiene Movement, 1910–1940"; Nancy J. Weiss, *The National Urban League, 1910–1940*; and Jesse Thomas Moore, Jr., *A Search for Equality*.
5. Focusing on New Negro fiction and the art published in, and often gracing the covers of, seminal texts such as Alain Locke's *The New Negro*, *The Crisis*, and *Opportunity*, Anne Stavney identifies a recurring, static, and idealized representation of the New Negro woman as "moral mother" standing beyond and even excluded from the crucial, modern race work going on among black male thinkers in rising black urban centers such as Harlem. In such representations, "woman functioned as visual object and symbol, not as subject with voice and pen." "Iconized and idolized, she is without agency in contemporary racial and social protests, and without ground(s) in the modern urban landscape." See Stavney, "'Mothers of Tomorrow': The New Negro Renaissance and the Politics of Maternal Representation," 546, 549. The analysis in *Prove It On Me* shows how the "moral mother" functioned not only as a recurring representation in New Negro expression but also as a discourse of race motherhood that pervaded the period's constructions of racial identity, solidarity, and advancement.
6. For rich analyses of the gender politics of these organizations, see Chateauvert, *Marching Together,* and Taylor, *The Veiled Garvey*. Both books show that women as well as men advocated patriarchal ideals and supported women's subordination as avenues to safety, prosperity, and respectability for the race.
7. This emphasis on the role of New Negro professional women in forwarding the discourse of race motherhood is supported by Stephanie Shaw and Anne Stavney. Shaw argues that black women professionals attained their education and status specifically in order to contribute to this necessary work of racial advancement and that their families and communities instilled this priority in them from infancy. Shaw sees "an ethic of socially responsible individualism" at work in the professionalization of such women and celebrates this ethic as a path to success and safety from sexual and racial exploitation. As Stavney points out, however, while the New Negro professional woman served the greater racial good as "helpmeet and advocate," she was "championing those around her rather than promoting her own cause." And the safety she had attained "also kept her out of the geographical and discursive space claimed by urban black men. She was neither threatened nor threatening" to the racial and sexual status quo. See Shaw, *What a Woman Ought to Be and to Do,* 2, and Stavney, "Mothers of Tomorrow," 551.
8. Edward Franklin Frazier, "The Pathology of Race Prejudice," *Forum* 77, no. 6 (June 1927): 857, 856.
9. Frazier, "The Pathology of Race Prejudice," 859–860.

10. Frazier's analysis here echoes elements of Ida B. Wells's and Mary Church Terrell's Victorian anti-lynching arguments as discussed in the previous chapter, but he does not incorporate their Victorian black feminism. In referring to the masculine "Negro's home," Frazier does not go on to reclaim black women's subjectivities or to articulate black women's particular oppression as the clubwomen did a generation before. Indeed, the point of this section of the article is to defend black patriarchy and explain the inhumane irrationality of the practice of lynching black men for the often imagined crime of interracial sexual desire.

11. Frazier, "The Pathology of Race Prejudice," 861.

12. Ida B. Wells, *Southern Horrors*, 19, quoted in Schechter, *Ida B. Wells-Barnett and American Reform*, 86.

13. Frazier was fired from the Atlanta School of Social Work due to ongoing strife with a white woman co-worker who used her racial privilege to subvert Frazier's authority over her as head of the school. She was eventually able to convince the board that Frazier was mulishly unwilling to accommodate himself to Southern racial etiquette and therefore inappropriate for the position.

14. While he was working in Atlanta, Frazier endeavored to shield himself from undue criticism and injury by publishing his controversial scholarship under the name E. Franklin Frazier while working and living as Edward F. Frazier. This simple strategy apparently worked well until *Forum* published his article under his full name and the Atlanta press learned of it. For more on this episode, see Platt, *E. Franklin Frazier, Reconsidered*, 83–85; and Holloway, *Confronting the Veil*, 143–145.

15. Letter from Charles Johnson to Frazier, 29 June 1927 and Letter from Gustavus Steward to Frazier, 31 July 1927, quoted in Platt, *Frazier Reconsidered*, 84, 85.

16. Letter from Frazier to Nancy Cunard, 18 February 1932, quoted in Platt, *Frazier Reconsidered*, 82.

17. Indeed, Frazier originally wrote the article in 1924 and submitted it to numerous scholarly and popular publications over the course of three years, diligently seeking to publish it despite continuous rejections. Evidently, this was a topic on which he meant to be heard. On the other hand, it is clear from this timetable that he did not intend this article to serve as an insulting farewell to the South. See Platt, *Frazier Reconsidered*, 82–83; and Holloway, *Confronting the Veil*, 144.

18. Edward Franklin Frazier, "Training Colored Social Workers in the South," *Journal of Social Forces* 1, no. 4 (May 1923): 445–446.

19. Edward Franklin Frazier, "Social Equality and the Negro," *Opportunity* 3, no. 6 (March 1925): 165–168.

20. Frazier, "Social Equality and the Negro," 165.

21. Frazier, "Social Equality and the Negro," 166.

22. Frazier, "Social Equality and the Negro," 166–167.

23. Frazier, "Social Equality and the Negro," 167.

24. Frazier, "Social Equality and the Negro," 168.

25. Frazier, "Social Equality and the Negro," 166.

26. E. Franklin Frazier, "Three Scourges of the Negro Family," *Opportunity* 4, no. 7 (July 1926): 210.

27. E. Franklin Frazier, "Psychological Factors in Negro Health," *Journal of Social Forces* 3, no. 3 (March 1925): 488–490. The idea that this article might have been conceived in direct connection to "The Pathology of Race Prejudice" or that the two might have been written together is occasioned by a point made at the conclusion: "The writer has not gone into those psychological factors which we cannot discuss here; namely, the psychology of white people in relation to Negro health. This is of great consequence where we see a disposition on the part of whites to discount the value of Negro life, and to oppose efforts

to reduce infant mortality and increase his resistance to disease." These are among the points Frazier makes in his infamous article on white pathologies.

28. Frazier discussed family "disorganization" in several articles over the course of the 1920s. See, for example, "Three Scourges of the Negro Family," *Opportunity* 4, no. 7 (July 1926): 210–213, 234; "Is the Negro Family a Unique Sociological Unit?" *Opportunity* 5, no. 6 (June 1927): 165–166; and "The Negro Family," *Annals of the American Academy of Political and Social Science* 140: Special Issue on the American Negro (November 1928): 44–51.

29. Frazier, "Three Scourges of the Negro Family," 212.

30. Frazier, "Three Scourges of the Negro Family," 210. This was originally a paper presented at the National Urban League Conference in New York City on February 3, 1926.

31. Frazier, "Psychological Factors in Negro Health," 489.

32. Frazier, "Three Scourges of the Negro Family," 211.

33. Frazier, "Is the Negro Family a Unique Sociological Unit?" 166.

34. Frazier, "Three Scourges of the Negro Family," 211.

35. Frazier, "Three Scourges of the Negro Family," 211.

36. Frazier, "Three Scourges of the Negro Family," 212.

37. Frazier, "The Negro Family," 50–51.

38. At its zenith in 1927, *Opportunity* circulation reached a "sizeable" 11,000, while the powerful *Crisis* bested it, peaking at 95,000 in 1919 and declining to just under 30,000 by 1930. However, *Opportunity*'s dinners and contests for writers, artists, and essayists and their potential publishers were more popular and generally considered more successful, especially in advancing the winners' careers, and, when compared with Du Bois, Johnson was respected as the better, more impartial judge of literary merit. Johnson also recruited an impressive literary staff, including Countee Cullen and Gwendolyn Bennett. See Johnson and Johnson, *Propaganda and Aesthetics*, 35, 37, 48, 53–55.

39. Charles S. Johnson, "Editorial: We Begin a New Year," *Opportunity* 3, no. 1 (January 1925): 2.

40. Johnson's life and work are documented in Robbins, *Sidelines Activist: Charles S. Johnson and the Struggle for Civil Rights.*

41. Johnson, "Editorial: We Begin a New Year," 2.

42. Charles S. Johnson, "Editorial: Women's Brains," *Opportunity* 1, no. 4 (April 1923): 4.

43. Charles S. Johnson, "Editorial: Mortality of Negro Mothers," *Opportunity* 3, no. 4 (April 1925): 99.

44. Charles S. Johnson, "Editorial: Women Workers," *Opportunity* 3, no. 8 (August 1925).

45. Charles S. Johnson, "Editorial: Why Negro Babies Die," *Opportunity* 1, no. 7 (1923): 195–196.

46. Johnson, "Editorial: Women Workers."

47. Johnson, "Editorial: Mortality of Negro Mothers," 99.

48. Johnson, "Editorial: Women Workers." Here, Johnson expresses the general progressive attitude. Across racial lines, progressives endorsed the idea that working women's interests were best served by the awarding of a "family wage" to male workers, who were assumed to be heads of households. Progressive men and women espoused this view despite their knowledge that so many women workers were their own or their families' sole source of support. For more on support for the "family wage" among women working in the federal Women's and Children's Bureaus, see Cott, *The Grounding of Modern Feminism*, 192, 204–207.

49. Sadie Tanner Mossell, "Business Opportunities for Colored Women," *Opportunity* 1, no. 8 (August 1923): 250.

50. Cott confirms that women working as secretaries and other white collar support roles in business gained success by earning men's trust and through their "professional performance of the wifely adjunct role." Furthermore, their success would only mean that they advanced to the role of the power behind the throne of the dominant man in the office.

There was little possibility for women's individual advancement beyond supportive, secretarial work. See Cott, *The Grounding of Modern Feminism*, 190. Black women's performance of "the wifely adjunct role" in the offices of black-owned companies took on special significance given the imperative to form a black patriarchy as a means of combating racial oppression.

51. Eva D. Bowles, "Opportunities for the Educated Colored Woman," *Opportunity* 1, no. 3 (March 1923): 8.
52. Bowles, "Opportunities for the Educated Colored Woman," 9.
53. Bowles, "Opportunities for the Educated Colored Woman," 10.
54. Bowles elaborates on the varieties of social work in her article, but the many aspects of this profession were emphasized in other articles as well. Examples include Elise Johnson McDougald, "The Schools and the Vocational Life of Negroes," *Opportunity* 1:6 (June 1923): 8–11; Jane E. B. Harvey, "When Children Talk Health," *Opportunity* 3, no. 12 (December 1925): 374–375; Frederick L. Hoffman, "The Negro Health Problem," *Opportunity* 4:4 (April 1926): 119–121, 138; Franklin O. Nichols, "A New Opportunity for Schools," *Opportunity* 4, no. 9 (September 1926): 287–289; Louis I. Dublin, "The Health of the Negro," *Opportunity* 6, no. 4 (July 1928): 198–200, 216.
55. Helen Sayre, "Making Over Poor Workers," *Opportunity* 1, no. 2 (February 1923): 17.
56. Sayre, "Making Over Poor Workers," 18.
57. Sayre, "Making Over Poor Workers," 18.
58. Harvey, "When Children Talk Health," 374.
59. McDougald, "The Schools and the Vocational Life of Negroes," 8.
60. McDougald, "The Schools and the Vocational Life of Negroes," 9.
61. McDougald's pragmatism here reflects the general progressive line on working mothers. Social workers, labor reformers, and other women professionals working in the federal Women's and Children's Bureaus advocated the family wage for male workers, defended women's work outside the home purely on the basis of necessity and not for reasons of fulfillment or independence, and deplored the effects on their children of mothers' work outside the home. This was part of a pragmatic, strategic argument that sought to defend modern, working women from accusations that they were abandoning domestic duties out of selfish desires for "pin money" and personal fulfillment. See Cott, *The Grounding of Modern Feminism*, 179–211. For African Americans, these arguments held special significance because of the insecurity of black male workers' employment prospects, the necessity of black women's labor outside the home, and the perceived absence of principled, stabilizing black male leadership in African American homes and communities.
62. Elise Johnson McDougald, "The Task of Negro Womanhood," 382.
63. For more on the Brotherhood and the UNIA, see Chateauvert, *Marching Together*; Taylor, *The Veiled Garvey*; and Michele Mitchell, "What a Pure, Healthy, Unified Race Can Accomplish: Collective Reproduction and the Sexual Politics of Black Nationalism," *Righteous Propagation*.

CHAPTER 3

1. See Ethel Waters and Charles Samuels, *His Eye Is on the Sparrow* and Bruce Kellner, ed., "Waters, Ethel" in *The Harlem Renaissance*, 378–379.
2. Ann Douglas, *Terrible Honesty*.
3. Kevin Mumford, Jayna Brown, and Mary Renda discuss primitivism as a foundation of the racial and sexual discourses of the 1920s. Mumford and Brown particularly apply this understanding to their explorations of black women's subjectivities. See Mumford, *Interzones*; Brown, *Babylon Girls*; and Renda, *Taking Haiti*. Brown provides a compelling analysis of the differing ways that white and black performing women drew upon racial discourses in shaping their public images and performances in this period and

how those differences ultimately worked to privilege white women both materially and subjectively.

4. For more on the economic motivations of the migration, see James R. Grossman, *Land of Hope*. For a treatment of black women's specific experiences and motivations, see Darlene Clark Hine, "Black Migration to the Urban Midwest: The Gender Dimension, 1915–1945" in *The Great Migration in Historical Perspective*.

5. This information on increased black consumption as a result of the great migration is detailed in Robert E. Weems, Jr., *Desegregating the Dollar*, 14.

6. Edwards's publication *The Southern Urban Negro as a Consumer* (1932) is quoted and summarized in Weems, *Desegregating the Dollar*, 22–23. Paul K. Edwards was a white economist who worked at Fisk University with sociologist Charles S. Johnson, former editor of *Opportunity*.

7. The rise of the modern cultural industries and the primary role of advertising in that industry, especially as one central means of disseminating racialized, sexualized cultural cues, are explored in Simone Weil Davis, *Living Up to the Ads*; Sut Jhally, *The Codes of Advertising*; Carolyn Kitch, *The Girl on the Magazine Cover*; M. M. Manring, *Slave in a Box*; Roland Marchand, *Advertising the American Dream*; Kathy Peiss, *Hope in a Jar*; and McClintock, *Imperial Leather*.

8. This formulation of the existence and operation of the sex-race marketplace owes a great deal to Stallybrass and White's analysis of the pre-industrial European town market as a locus of cross-class cultural exchange and commodification of the "low-Other." See Peter Stallybrass and Allon White, *The Politics and Poetics of Transgression*, especially pages 27–28 and 38. I am also building upon the work of Renda in *Taking Haiti*, McClintock in *Imperial Leather*, Peiss in both *Cheap Amusements* and *Hope in a Jar*, and Manring in *Slave in a Box*.

9. For a discussion of these explicitly minstrel images and their roles in twentieth-century advertising, see Manring, *Slave in a Box*.

10. Du Bois, "Editing *The Crisis*," xxix.

11. The culture of dissemblance was a well-established political strategy by which black women of all classes sought to obscure their sexual selves in order to embody chaste morality and respectability and, through church and club activities, exhorted all black women to do the same. This culture of dissemblance was the best weapon oppressed women had developed to counteract the damaging stereotypes that not only humiliated them but also made them easy targets for rape and other forms of sexualized racist terror. However, this strategy for self-preservation was one of constraint rather than liberation. It rendered public sexual expression and desire taboo in New Negro discourse and muted, even silenced, autonomous women's voices around sexuality and desire. See Hine, "Rape and the Inner Lives of Black Women in the Middle West: Preliminary Thoughts on the Culture of Dissemblance."

12. Pamphlet in Mme. C. J. Walker Collection, Box 11, Folder 1, Indiana Historical Society, Indianapolis, Indiana (hereafter, Walker Coll.).

13. Walker Co. Advertisement, *Chicago Defender*, 30 August 1919, 7.

14. Letter from Mrs. B. F. Walker to Mr. F. B. Ransom, 4 April 1918, Walker Coll., Box 11, Folder 3. Mrs. B. F. Walker apparently had no familial relation to Mme. Walker.

15. Walker Co. Advertisement, *Chicago Defender*, 9 August 1919, 4.

16. Indeed, Mme. Walker had been at first a beneficiary and then a benefactor of the club-women's charity and social work while living in Chicago, before she became a beautician. See A'Lelia Bundles, *On Her Own Ground* and Letter from E. A. DeVere to F. B. Ransom, 21 May 1918, Walker Coll., Box 11, Folder 3.

17. Walker required her sales agents to become members of the Agents of the Madam C. J. Walker Mfg. Company Union. The primary purpose seems to have been to prevent

untrained beauticians from using the Walker products or using them in the wrong way. The agents in each town were then organized into a local Madam Walker Club, which were not labor unions but clubs in the tradition of the NACW, conducting civic and fund-raising work (Walker Coll. Box 7, Folder 3 and *1924 Year Book and Almanac, Published by the Madam C. J. Walker Mfg. Co.*, Box 13, Folder 24).

18. "Instructions to Agents," Walker Coll., Box 7, Folder 5.

19. "Short History of Madam Walker" in *1924 Year Book and Almanac, Published by the Madam C. J. Walker Mfg. Co.* in Walker Coll., Box 13, Folder 24.

20. After Madame Walker's death, her daughter, A'Lelia Walker, inherited the business and nominally took over her mother's position, but Madame Walker's primary aid, F. B. Ransom, retained his post and became the actual head of the company. Thus, the operation and policies of the company continued through the 1920s with little alteration. See Bundles, *On Her Own Ground* and Walker Coll., "Introduction to the Collection."

21. The company followed this advertisement strategy throughout the late 1910s and 1920s. In the mid-1930s and 1940s, it began to recruit models and distribute a beauty magazine in addition to placing more sophisticated advertisements in the press.

22. My analysis of images—both advertisements and photographs—is accomplished according to my own mixture of methodological practice and historical interpretation. It is also informed and underpinned by theory and information found in Jessica Evans and Stuart Hall, eds. *Visual Culture*; Gillian Rose, *Visual Methodologies*; and Deborah Willis, "Towards a New Identity: Reading the Photographs of the New Negro."

23. For discussion of editor Robert Abbott's recruitment of porters as distributors and the *Chicago Defender*'s support for their labor struggles, see Grossman, *Land of Hope*, 78.

24. Clara Smith was not related to Bessie Smith, although the two were sometime collaborators and friends in the early 1920s before the drunken fist fight that ended their friendship in 1925. See "Smith, Clara" in Kellner, ed. *The Harlem Renaissance*, 330–331.

25. Columbia Records Advertisement, *Chicago Defender*, 28 August, 1926, 8.

26. Columbia Records Advertisement, *Chicago Defender*, 18 September 1926, 6.

27. Paramount Advertisement, *Chicago Defender*, 31 July 1926, 7.

28. Columbia Records Advertisement, *Chicago Defender*, 21 June 1924, 5.

29. Bessie Smith, "Hateful Blues," Columbia 14023-D, October 1926; reissued on *Empty Bed Blues*, Columbia CG 30450, 1972. For more on Bessie Smith's life and career, see Chris Albertson, *Bessie*; Kellner, ed. "Smith, Bessie" in *The Harlem Renaissance*, 328–329; and Michelle R. Scott, *Blues Empress in Black Chattanooga*.

30. The financial records of the Walker Company are available in the Walker Collection, "Table, Product Sales," Box 10, Folder 2.

31. The histories of the Walker, Poro, and Golden Brown Companies, as well as others, are usefully summarized in Peiss, *Hope in a Jar*.

32. Golden Brown Chemical Company Advertisement, *Chicago Defender*, 22 September 1923, 22/A10.

33. Peiss documents this remarkable "ruse" in *Hope in a Jar*, 117–118.

34. This understanding of the effects of the sex-race marketplace and the consumption of black women is underpinned by the Stallybrass and White discussion of the relationship between "bourgeois observer" and "plebeian fair-goer" in the context of the spectacular medieval European fair or marketplace. See Stallybrass and White, *The Politics and Poetics of Transgression*, 42. It is also derived from Mumford's arguments regarding race, sexuality, and slumming in the "interzone." See Mumford, *Interzones*.

35. George Hutchinson discusses Holt at some length throughout his definitive biography of Nella Larsen. For more information on her, see Hutchinson, *In Search of Nella Larsen*; Kellner, *The Harlem Renaissance*; and Langston Hughes and Milton Meltzer, *Black Magic*, 178, 182.

36. Van Vechten is quoted in Hutchinson, *In Search of Nella Larsen*, 188.

37. Caspar Holstein was a well-known Harlem figure of West Indian descent who financed several events and contests of the New Negro era, including the *Opportunity* contests that brought Langston Hughes and Zora Neale Hurston to notoriety. As a club-owner, numbers-runner, and purveyor of illicit liquor, he necessarily often operated on the wrong side of the law. See David Levering Lewis, *When Harlem Was in Vogue,* and Kellner, ed. "Holstein, Caspar" in *The Harlem Renaissance*, 171–172. Published in New York, Butler's *Inter-State Tattler* newspaper provided coverage of New Negro celebrities and society events and gossip about prominent and little-known black people living, working, and playing along the eastern seaboard and throughout the Midwest. Butler stands on the left in the photograph. See Kellner, ed. "Inter-State Tattler" in *The Harlem Renaissance*, 185–186.

CHAPTER 4

1. McDougald, "The Task of Negro Womanhood," 382.

2. McDougald, "The Task of Negro Womanhood," 382.

3. McDougald's life is summarized in a number of publications and also for the small collection of her papers at the Schomburg Center. See "McDougald [Ayer], [Gertrude] Elise Johnson" in Kellner, ed. *The Harlem Renaissance*, 229–230, and Gertrude Elise Ayer Papers, Sc MG 277, Schomburg Center for Research in Black Culture, New York Public Library, New York, NY.

4. McDougald, "The Task of Negro Womanhood," 370.

5. Tera Hunter's seminal work on working-class African American women in Reconstruction-era Atlanta has gone a long way toward correcting this gap in the historiography, especially in her use of theory to read against the grain of recorded white perspectives and observations and her inclusion of chapters on black vernacular dance. See *To 'Joy My Freedom*. Historians such as Michele Mitchell and Anastasia Curwood have followed Hunter's example to recover and analyze black women's private lives and personal perspectives as well as intra-racial gender politics. See Mitchell, *Righteous Propagation,* and Curwood, *Stormy Weather*. Here, I attempt to build on these insights to further illuminate black women's subjective experiences in the New Negro era by using black women's own words to recover their feelings, the processes they initiated to remake their identities, and their changing ideologies relative to race, sexuality, and gender.

6. As I argue for the necessity of considering subjective experiences, especially around sexuality and desire, as crucial aspects of African American identity that have direct bearing on the course of racial advancement and African American history, my thought is aided by the work of Claudia Tate and, again, Darlene Clark Hine. Tate's work supports my implicit contention that seemingly individual, personal concerns like pain, desire, and the search for love and beauty—as well as sexuality and gender—have as much to do with the formation of black identities as race. Tate establishes this as she asserts the need to de-center the struggle for racial equality in black-authored fiction as a prerequisite for inclusion in the African American literary canon. As Tate complicates black subjectivity by de-centering black political struggle, however, I seek to complicate our understanding of racial politics by accounting for the role of sexuality and desire in black identity formation and the development of black ideologies of struggle. Tate is right to insist that accepted black subjectivity in literature has not been as complicated as it should be (or that when black subjectivity was more complicated than critics expected, the novel was excluded from the canon). I want to show that black women's experiences and identities were indeed complicated and to analyze why and how black women's images did not reflect that complexity as they were constructed in the discourse of the New Negro era. See Claudia Tate, *Psychoanalysis and Black Novels*.

In her essay on the "culture of dissemblance," also mentioned in Chapter 3, Hine has addressed the reticence of black women leaders of the Reconstruction generation, such as Pauline Hopkins and Mary Church Terrell, regarding discussion of their personal lives and sexuality. She proposes that these women developed a "culture of dissemblance," shrouding their private lives and sexual experiences in secrecy in order to protect themselves from offensive and exploitative associations with immorality and degeneracy. To my mind, Hine thus suggests that black women allowed themselves no acknowledgment of lust or sexual fulfillment as aspects of their public personas because to do so would have been personally and politically dangerous. Such a defensive mechanism results in both stigmatization of women who do acknowledge the need for sexual expression and an inability to incorporate a positive, self-generated sexuality into feminist racial advancement politics. Ultimately, I argue, this "culture of dissemblance" contributes to the inability of black women to claim their sexuality, desire, and sexual expression, and to incorporate these aspects of black identity into New Negro politics. See Darlene Clark Hine, "Rape and the Inner Lives of Black Women in the Middle West: Preliminary Thoughts on the Culture of Dissemblance," 912–920.

7. Critic Anne Stavney's analysis of New Negro engagement with the image of the "moral mother" and New Negro women authors' rejection of such one-dimensional representations and constricting ideals of New Negro womanhood supports my contention that New Negro women novelists wrote, in part, to intervene in interwar sexual and racial discourses and to provide alternate black female subjectivities. While arguing that all New Negro women fiction writers contributed to this intervention in intra-racial gender politics, Stavney focuses on Nella Larsen and her novel *Passing* (1929). See Stavney, "Mothers of Tomorrow," especially 552–558.

8. Malca Chall, "Interview with Frances Mary Albrier, Determined Advocate for Racial Equality," in *The Black Women Oral History Project*, 217–218. Emphasis in original.

9. Marita Bonner, "On Being Young—A Woman—and Colored," *Frye Street & Environs*, 3.

10. Bonner, "On Being Young," 5.

11. Letter from Augusta, GA, 12 May 1917, in Emmett J. Scott, "Letters of Negro Migrants of 1916–1918," *Journal of Negro History* 4, no. 3 (July 1919): 335. All the names and signatures of the authors of these letters have been deleted from the published article. I have retained the original spelling, grammar, and syntax, except where changes are necessary to clarify meaning.

12. Letter from New Orleans, LA, 7 May 1917, Scott, "Letters of Negro Migrants," 317.

13. Letter from Biloxi, MS, 27 April 1917, Scott, "Letters of Negro Migrants."

14. Tani Lahi Mottl, "Interview with Melnea A. Cass, February 1, 1977" in *The Black Women Oral History Project*, 307.

15. Chall, "Interview with Frances Mary Albrier," 267, 440.

16. This pattern is also evident in Madam C. J. Walker's life story. When she arrived in Chicago in the early 1900s, she initially relied on the charity of the local black women's clubs and church organizations of which she later became a member. See Bundles, *On Her Own Ground*.

17. McDougald, "The Task of Negro Womanhood," 370.

18. McDougald, "The Task of Negro Womanhood," 378–379.

19. McDougald, "The Task of Negro Womanhood,"379.

20. McDougald, "The Task of Negro Womanhood,"373, 374, 376.

21. Letter of unknown origin in "Letters of Negro Migrants," 318–319.

22. For information on their lives, see biographies and literary criticism of Jessie Fauset and Nella Larsen such as Cheryl Wall, *Women of the Harlem Renaissance*; Hutchinson, *In Search of Nella Larsen*; Carolyn W. Sylvander, *Jessie Redmon Fauset, Black American Writer*; and others.

23. Carl Van Vechten to Fania Marinoff, 6 May 1925, quoted in Hutchinson, *In Search of Nella Larsen*, 187. Van Vechten was a great friend of Nella Larsen, but Jessie Fauset confided to Langston Hughes that she never liked him. She commented, for example, "I'm not sure I can say truthfully that I like Mr. Van Vechten (this is very *entre nous*) but he is certainly an open sesame just now to a small group of us for pleasant moments." Fauset to Hughes, Friday [no date], Jessie R. Fauset Letters to Langston Hughes, Langston Hughes Papers, Series I, Box 61, Folder 1166, JWJ Collection.

24. Jessie Redmon Fauset, *Plum Bun: A Novel Without a Moral*. To a greater extent than in her other works, in this novel Fauset emphatically addresses the questions of race, gender, identity, and sexuality relevant to this book. Although I have consulted the original edition, I use the later edition with an Introduction by Deborah McDowell as my source in this book.

25. Fauset, *Plum Bun*, 48, 54.

26. Critic Cheryl Wall asserts that Angela "prizes the idea of freedom without having any sense of its meaning" because she passes for white in order to achieve her liberation. See Wall, *Women of the Harlem Renaissance*, 76. I disagree with Wall. I argue that Angela's ideas of freedom have evolved with the times and circumstances. She seeks not to escape the bondage of actual slavery as her parents did but the bondage of racial hierarchy and its circumscription of her subjectivity and material opportunities. Her mistake is not her notion or search for freedom but her means.

27. Hutchinson, *In Search of Nella Larsen*, 92–98.

28. Nella Larsen, *Quicksand*. Of all of her works, this is the novel in which Larsen levels her most starkly explicit gendered racial critique of Western society and New Negro discourses. Although I have consulted the original edition, I use the later edition combining the novels *Quicksand* and *Passing* as my source in this book.

29. Larsen, *Quicksand*, 1, 4, 5.

30. Larsen, *Quicksand*, 12.

31. Michele Mitchell provides an excellent analysis of the gender ideologies and ideals among the two generations of African Americans living during Reconstruction and the New Negro era. She has shown that African American racial advancement was presumed to depend on adherence to patriarchal family organization to a greater extent than historians have previously documented. See Mitchell, *Righteous Propagation*.

32. Bonner, "On Being Young," 3. This attitude exemplifies the "companionate marriage" ideal popular as an alternative to strict patriarchy in the interwar period. Nancy Cott discusses companionate marriage in her history of modern sexual politics. Proponents of the companionate marriage defended women's right to seek fulfillment and independence through work outside the home while maintaining the family life they thought it "natural" for every woman to want. This ideology depended on women's ability to find and marry a progressive, supportive, "cooperative husband" whose ego could withstand his wife's success outside of the home, her independence, and the requirement that he occasionally, though by no means habitually, help with the housework and child-rearing duties. In practice, the modern marriage often slipped between its "companionate" ideal and the typical, patriarchal marriage that functioned according to the common-law, popular conception of the marriage contract, which stipulated a wife's duty to perform domestic labor for her husband and his absolute authority over her while he owed her his material support. See Cott, *The Grounding of Modern Feminism*, 192–200.

33. Marcia Greenlee, "Interview with Alice Dunnigan, April 8, 1977" in *The Black Women Oral History Project*, 75.

34. Greenlee, "Interview with Alice Dunnigan," 84–86.

35. Mottl, "Interview with Melnea Cass," 314.

36. Greenlee, "Interview with Alice Dunnigan," 102.

37. Dunnigan's second marriage also ended in divorce due to general "incompatibility" in interests and outlook. Dunnigan also complained that her second husband was unable to support her and their son financially and that he resented her eventual success as a journalist and newspaper correspondent for the Associated Negro Press. See Greenlee, "Interview with Alice Dunnigan," 87, 89.

38. Greenlee, "Interview with Elizabeth Cardozo Barker," 122.

39. The historical significance of the black women's novel changed with this generation of authors. In *Reconstructing Womanhood*, critic Hazel Carby establishes that the black woman's novel was intended as a political act formulating ideology for the racial advancement activism of the Reconstruction generation. See *Reconstructing Womanhood*, especially page 95. I argue that the black woman's novel continued to function politically in the New Negro era, but its politics had shifted. Rather than an ideological focal point from which African Americans were to find their motivation and moral prescription for the work of racial advancement, the New Negro woman's novel became a space for the demonstration and critique of African American sexual politics. This new function for the black woman's novel emerged in tandem with the general thrust of the literary New Negro Renaissance in that the complete dedication of their lives and art to racial advancement politics was one of the expectations from which the New Negroes revolted. Langston Hughes's article "The Negro Artist and the Racial Mountain" is the best expression of this revolt. I find foundation for this assertion not only in the novels I analyze at length here but also in the work of Zora Neale Hurston and the other works by Larsen and Fauset.

40. Hughes's *Not Without Laughter* (1930) and McKay's *Home to Harlem* (1928) were critically acclaimed novels published in the New Negro era. For other prescient analyses of the relationship between Renaissance novels such as these and racial-sexual discourses, see Mumford, *Interzones*, 143, 179; and Vogel, *The Scene of Harlem Cabaret*.

41. James W. Ivy, "*Home to Harlem*: A Slice of Life," *The Messenger* (May–June 1928), reprinted in Theodore G. Vincent, ed., *Voices of a Black Nation*, 357.

42. Critic Shane Vogel asserts that Hughes and McKay were unfairly associated with primitivism because they belonged to a group of artists who "rejected the narratives and logics of normative racial uplift and sexual respectability" that editors such as Du Bois prized and were therefore not credited for their nuanced use of the cabaret space and "everynight" practices of regular African Americans "to critique both the racial and sexual normativity of uplift elites and the racial and sexual subjection of white spectatorial practices" and to posit instead "subjects that undertake the complex negotiations and contradictions of sexual and racial self-definition in American modernity." Vogel includes Nella Larsen in this group, which he calls the "cabaret school" within the New Negro Renaissance. I agree with this assessment of these three authors as critics of the social and class imperatives of New Negro progressivism and solidarity. Indeed, this is likely the reason that Larsen considered Hughes in particular a friend and comrade. However, Vogel readily concedes that "male writers were too frequently complicit in circumscribing and policing black women's sexual subjectivity" and that they frequently used "primitivist language and imagery" in their fiction and poetry. While Vogel rightly identifies McKay and Hughes as critics of "heteropatriarchy," he does not posit their works as critical of masculinism or sexism. Larsen and Fauset, while ultimately occupying opposing sides of the New Negro solidarity and progressivism debates, posed similar questions about intra-racial gender politics, male privilege, and African American women's subjectivity that Hughes and McKay all but ignore. As a result, perhaps despite their intentions, these male Renaissance authors' portrayals of black women characters align directly with the flat, primitivist portrayals of black women proffered within the sex-race marketplace. See Vogel, *The Scene of Harlem Cabaret*, 3–35, 79.

43. Ann DuCille describes this parallel between New Negro women novelists and blueswomen in her article "Blues Notes on Black Sexuality," 418–444.

44. Fauset, *Plum Bun*, 111.
45. Fauset, *Plum Bun*, 245.
46. Fauset, *Plum Bun*, 229.
47. Fauset, *Plum Bun*, 228.
48. Fauset, *Plum Bun*, 145.
49. Critic Ann DuCille uses this artful phrase to capture the matrix of stereotypes and fantasies encircling black women's bodies in Western society, a matrix which might be called the sex-race marketplace. See DuCille, "Blues Notes on Black Sexuality."
50. Larsen, *Quicksand*, 118.
51. Larsen, *Quicksand*, 129.
52. Larsen, *Quicksand*, 102–103.
53. Larsen, *Quicksand*, 103.
54. Larsen, *Quicksand*, 128.
55. Larsen, *Quicksand*, 94–95.
56. Larsen, *Quicksand*, 59, 108, 112.
57. Larsen, *Quicksand*, 118.
58. Larsen, *Quicksand*, 125. Helga's first pregnancy resulted in twin boys.
59. Larsen, *Quicksand*, 119, 126.
60. Hutchinson, *In Search of Nella Larsen*, 238.
61. Bonner, "On Being Young," 3.
62. Fauset, *Plum Bun*, 117.
63. Fauset, *Plum Bun*, 13, 53. Fauset consistently uses the British spellings of "color" and "colored." Probably the British spellings seemed to her to add a bit of glamour to the words—and to the identity.
64. Fauset, *Plum Bun*, 261.
65. Fauset, *Plum Bun*, 375.
66. Fauset, *Plum Bun*, 274, 293. Here Fauset evinces agreement with a strain of progressive interwar women's politics and gender ideologies that assumed that every woman wanted to find fulfillment through a heterosexual relationship and reproduction and that not wanting this was unnatural or even perverted. When push came to shove, the advocates of this position ultimately recommended the choice of family over career, assuming that a woman who wanted to could restart her career after the children were a little less needy or her husband a little more secure in his job, and so on. For them, motherhood and wife-hood should and did ultimately predominate over career considerations or fulfillment outside of the home. See Cott, *The Grounding of Modern Feminism*, 198–200.
67. Larsen, *Quicksand*, 123, 133, 130.
68. Larsen, *Quicksand*, 118, 67, 116.
69. Larsen, *Quicksand*, 60–61.
70. Larsen, *Quicksand*, 120.
71. Larsen, *Quicksand*, 60.
72. Larsen, *Quicksand*, 107.
73. Larsen, *Quicksand*, 72.
74. For examples, see reviews such as "White Negroes," Review of *Plum Bun*, *New York Times*, 3 March 1929; or T. S. Matthews, "What Gods! What Gongs!" Review of *Quicksand*, *Home to Harlem*, *Ol' Man Adam an' His Chillun*, and *Black Majesty*, *New Republic*, 30 May 1928. Hutchinson's comment about the reception of *Quicksand* might be applied to both novels, or indeed to all of these novelists' works. He wrote that the book "suffered the fate of many books ahead of their time: people tried to fit it into patterns to which they were accustomed and, not always satisfied with the fit, found the novel wanting." Hutchinson, *In Search of Nella Larsen*, 283. On the other hand, critics could also enjoy and recommend the novels without understanding them as Du Bois did in favoring *Quicksand* (and Jessie Fauset's

earlier work *There Is Confusion*) over McKay's *Home to Harlem* because it positively represented "the new, honest, young, fighting Negro woman" and seemed to counter what he
saw as McKay's "filth." W. E. B. Du Bois, "Two Novels," *Crisis* 35 (June 1928): 202.

75. Jessie Redmon Fauset to Langston Hughes, 23 April [no year—possibly 1925 or 1926],
Jessie R. Fauset Letters to Langston Hughes, Langston Hughes Papers, Series I, Box 61,
Folder 1166, JWJ Collection.

76. Bonner, "To Be Young," 6.

77. McDougald, "The Task of Negro Womanhood," 380, 381.

BIBLIOGRAPHY

ARCHIVAL COLLECTIONS
Indianapolis, Indiana
Indiana Historical Society
    The Madam C. J. Walker Collection

Los Angeles, California
University of California at Los Angeles, Young Research Library
    The George P. Johnson Negro Film Collection

Newark, New Jersey
Rutgers University, Institute of Jazz Studies, Dana Library
    George T. Simon Collection
    Mary Lou Williams Collection
    Photograph Archive

New Haven, Connecticut
Yale University, Beinecke Rare Book and Manuscript Library
    The James Weldon Johnson Collection in the Yale Collection of American Literature
        Carl Van Vechten Correspondence
        Dorothy Peterson Collection
        James Weldon Johnson Papers (Correspondence)
        Langston Hughes Papers

New York, New York
The Frank Driggs Collection (in private hands)
The New York Public Library, Schomburg Center for Research in Black Culture
    Casper Holstein Portrait Collection
    Gertrude Elise Ayer Papers
    Helen Armstead-Johnson Miscellaneous Theater Collections
    The Inter-State Tattler Photograph Collection
    Portraits—Women—Unidentified Collection

Records of the National Association of Colored Women's Clubs, 1895–1992 [microfilm]. Edited by Lillian Serece Williams and Randolph Boehm. Bethesda, MD: University Publications of America, 1993.

The Claude A. Barnett Papers, Part Two: The Associated Negro Press Organizational Files, 1920–1966 [microfilm]. Edited by August Meier and Elliott Rudwick. Frederick, MD: University Publications of America, 1985.

PERIODICALS AND NEWSPAPERS

Opportunity
The Birth Control Review
The Chicago Defender
The Competitor
The Crisis
The Messenger
The National Association Notes/ National Notes
The New York Amsterdam News
The New York Age
The Pittsburgh Courier

SELECTED PRIMARY PUBLICATIONS AND ORAL HISTORIES

Alexander, Sadie T. M. "Negro Women in Our Economic Life." *Opportunity* 18, no. 7 (July 1930): 201–203.

Anderson, Walter. "The Speakeasy as a National Institution." *Current History*, July 1932, 417–422.

Bethune, Mary McLeod. "The Problems of the City Dweller." *Opportunity* 3, no. 2 (February 1925): 54–55.

Bonner, Marita. "On Being Young—a Woman—and Colored." *The Crisis*, December 1925. Reprinted in *Frye Street & Environs: The Collected Works of Marita Bonner*, ed. Joyce Flynn and Joyce Occomy Stricklin, 3–8. Boston: Beacon Press, 1987.

Bowles, Eva D. "Opportunities for the Educated Colored Woman." *Opportunity* 1, no. 3 (March 1923): 8.

Calverton, V. F. "The Negro Writer." *New York Herald*, 26 May 1929.

Calvin, Floyd J. "Evelyn Preer Ranks First as Stage and Movie Star." *Pittsburgh Courier*, 16 April 1927, Section 2, p. 1.

———. "'Race Theater Has Reached Lowest Ebb,' Says Floyd J. Calvin." *Pittsburgh Courier*, 16 April 1927, Section 2, p. 2.

Chall, Malca. "Interview with Frances Mary Albrier, Determined Advocate for Racial Equality." In *The Black Women Oral History Project*, ed. Ruth Edmonds Hill, Vol. 1, 169–535. Westport, CT: Meckler, 1991.

Cooper, Anna Julia. *A Voice from the South by a Black Woman of the South*. Xenia, OH: Aldine Printing House, 1892. Reprint, with an introduction by Mary Helen Washington, New York: Oxford University Press, 1988.

Culp, D. W., ed. *Twentieth Century Negro Literature, or a Cyclopedia of Thought on the Vital Topics Relating to the American Negro*. Atlanta: J. L. Nichols, 1902. Reprint, New York: Arno Press, 1969.

Du Bois, W. E. B. "Returning Soldiers." *The Crisis*, May 1919. Reprinted in *Let Nobody Turn Us Around: Voices of Resistance, Reform and Renewal, An African American Anthology*, ed. Manning Marable and Leith Mullings. New York: Rowman & Littlefield, 2000, 2003.

———. "Criteria for Negro Art." *The Crisis*, October 1926.

———. "Editing *The Crisis*." *The Crisis*, March 1951. Reprinted in *The Crisis Reader: Stories, Poetry, and Essays from the NAACP's Crisis Magazine*, ed. Sondra Kathryn Wilson. New York: Random House, 1999.

Fauset, Jessie Redmon. *There Is Confusion*. New York: Boni and Liveright, 1924. Reprint, New York: AMS Press, 1974.

———. *Plum Bun, a Novel without a Moral*. New York: Frederick A. Stokes, 1929. Reprint, Boston: Beacon Press, 1990 with an Introduction by Deborah McDowell.

———. *Plum Bun, A Novel without a Moral*. First Edition. New York: Frederick A. Stokes, 1929.

Frazier, Edward Franklin. "Training Colored Social Workers in the South." *Journal of Social Forces* 1, no. 4 (May 1923): 445–446.

———. "Social Equality and the Negro." *Opportunity* 3, no. 6 (June 1925): 165–168.

———. "The Pathology of Race Prejudice." *Forum* 77, no. 6 (1927): 856–862.

Frazier, E. Franklin. "Racial Self-Expression." In *Ebony and Topaz, a Collectanea*, ed. Charles S. Johnson,119–121. New York, 1927. Reprint, Freeport, New York: Books for Libraries Press, 1971.

———. "Psychological Factors in Negro Health." *Journal of Social Forces* 3, no. 3 (March 1925): 488–490.

———. "Three Scourges of the Negro Family." *Opportunity* 4, no. 7 (July 1926): 210–213, 234.

———. "Is the Negro Family a Unique Sociological Unit?" *Opportunity* 5, no. 6 (June 1927): 165–166.

———. "The Negro Family." *Annals of the American Academy of Political and Social Science* 140, Special Issue on the American Negro (November 1928): 44–51.

Gray, Lillian B. "Can We as Girls of the Community Raise the Standard of Our Boys?" *National Association Notes*, April–May 1917, 7–8.

Greenlee, Marcia. "Interview with Alice Dunnigan, April 8, 1977." In *The Black Women Oral History Project*, ed. Ruth Edmonds Hill, Vol. 3, 67–109. Westport, CT: Meckler, 1991.

———. "Interview with Elizabeth Barker, December 8, 1976." In *The Black Women Oral History Project*, ed. Ruth Edmonds Hill, Vol. 2, 87–133. Westport, CT: Meckler, 1991.

Harvey, Jane E. B. "When Children Talk Health." *Opportunity* 3, no. 12 (December 1925): 374–375.

Hill, Ruth Edmonds. "Interview with Etta Moten Barnett, February 11, 1985." In *The Black Women Oral History Project*, ed. Ruth Edmonds Hill, Vol. 2, 135–234. Westport, CT: Meckler, 1991.

Hughes, Langston. "The Negro Artist and the Racial Mountain." *The Nation*, 23 June 1926, 692–694.

———. "Says Race Leaders, Including Preachers, Flock to Harlem Cabarets." *Pittsburgh Courier*, 16 April 1927, Section 1, p. 8.

———. *Not Without Laughter*, 1930. Reprint, New York: Collier Books, 1969, with an Introduction by Arna Bontemps.

Johnson, Charles S. "Editorial: Women's Brains." *Opportunity* 1, no. 4 (April 1923): 4.

———. "Editorial: Why Negro Babies Die." *Opportunity* 1, no. 7 (1923): 195–196.

———. "Editorial: We Begin a New Year." *Opportunity* 3, no. 1(January 1925): 2.

———. "Editorial: Mortality of Negro Mothers." *Opportunity* 3, no. 4 (April 1925): 99.

———. "Editorial: Women Workers." *Opportunity* 3, no. 8 (August 1925).

Johnson, Guy B. "The Negro Migration and Its Consequences." *Journal of Social Forces* 2 (1924): 404–408.

Larsen, Nella. *Quicksand*. New York: Alfred A. Knopf, 1928. Reprint, New Brunswick: Rutgers University Press, 1986, 2004, as *Quicksand and Passing*, ed. and with an introduction by Deborah E. McDowell.

———. *Quicksand*. First edition. The Negro in Unusual Fiction Series. New York: Alfred A. Knopf, 1928.

———. *Passing*. First edition. New York: Alfred A. Knopf, 1929.

Locke, Alain, ed. *The New Negro: Voices of the Harlem Renaissance*. New York: Albert & Charles Boni, 1925. Reprint, Simon & Schuster, 1992, with an introduction by Arnold Rampersad.

McDougald, Elise Johnson. "The Task of Negro Womanhood." In *The New Negro: Voices of the Harlem Renaissance*, ed. Alain Locke, 369–382. New York: Albert & Charles Boni, 1925. Reprint, New York: Simon & Schuster, 1992, with an introduction by Arnold Rampersad.

———. "The Schools and the Vocational Life of Negroes." *Opportunity* 1, no. 6 (June 1923): 8–11.

McKay, Claude. "If We Must Die." *Liberator* (July 1919): 21.

———. *Home to Harlem.* New York: Harper & Brothers, 1928. Reprint, Boston: Northeastern University Press, 1987, with a foreword by Wayne F. Cooper.

Micheaux, Oscar, dir. *Within Our Gates.* Chicago: Oscar Micheaux Book & Film Co., 1919. Reprint, Library of Congress Smithsonian Video, 1993 as "The Origins of Film: The African American Cinema I."

Mossell, Sadie Tanner. "Business Opportunities for Colored Women." *Opportunity* 1, no. 8 (June 1923): 250.

Mottl, Tahi Lani. "Interview with Melnea A. Cass, February 1, 1977." In *The Black Women Oral History Project,* ed. Ruth Edmonds Hill, Vol. 2, 269–415. Westport, CT: Meckler, 1991.

Preer, Evelyn. "Movie Queen Tells Courier Readers of Her 'Film Thrills.'" *Pittsburgh Courier,* 11 June 1927, Section 2, p. 1.

———. "My Thrills in the Movies No. 2." *Pittsburgh Courier,* 18 June 1927, Section 2, p. 2.

———. "My Thrills in the Movies No. 3." *Pittsburgh Courier,* 25 June 1927, Section 2, p. 2.

Sayre, Helen. "Making Over Poor Workers." *Opportunity* 1, no. 2 (February 1923): 17.

Schuyler, George S. "The Negro-Art Hokum." *The Nation,* 16 June 1926, 662–663.

Scott, Emmett J. "Letters of Negro Migrants of 1916–1918." *Journal of Negro History* 4, no. 3 (July 1919): 290–340.

———. "Additional Letters of Negro Migrants of 1916–1918." *Journal of Negro History* 4, no. 4 (October 1919): 412–465.

Smith, Madeleine R. "The Inter-Racial Forum." *Opportunity* 1, no. 6 (June 1923): 31–32.

Terrell, Mary Church. "Lynching from a Negro's Point of View." *North American Review,* 178, no. 571(June 1904); reprinted in *Black Women in White America: A Documentary History,* ed. Gerda Lerner. New York: Vintage Books, 1972, 1992, 207–208, 210.

SECONDARY PUBLICATIONS

"Summary: The African American Cinema I." In *The Origins of Film (1900–1926), DVD Liner Notes.* Washington, DC: Library of Congress, 1993.

Albertson, Chris. *Bessie.* New York: Stein and Day, 1972. Reprint, Revised and expanded ed. New Haven: Yale University Press, 2003.

Alexander, Eleanor. *Lyrics of Sunshine and Shadow: The Tragic Courtship and Marriage of Paul Laurence Dunbar and Alice Ruth Moore.* New York: New York University Press, 2001.

Anderson, Jervis. *This Was Harlem: A Cultural Portrait, 1900–1950.* New York: Farrar, Straus and Giroux, 1981.

Baldwin, Davarian L. *Chicago's New Negroes: Modernity, the Great Migration and Black Urban Life.* Chapel Hill: University of North Carolina Press, 2007.

Bederman, Gail. *Manliness and Civilization: A Cultural History of Gender and Race in the United States, 1880–1917.* Chicago: University of Chicago Press, 1995.

Bogle, Donald. *Toms, Coons, Mulattoes, Mammies, & Bucks: An Interpretative History of Blacks in American Films.* New expanded ed. New York: Continuum, 1989.

Bowser, Pearl, Jane Gaines, and Charles Musser. "Introduction: Oscar Micheaux and Race Movies of the Silent Period." In *Oscar Micheaux and His Circle: African-American Film-making and Race Cinema of the Silent Era,* ed. Pearl Bowser, Jane Gaines, and Charles Musser, xvii–xxx. Bloomington: Indiana University Press, 2001.

Bowser, Pearl, and Louise Spence. *Writing Himself into History: Oscar Micheaux, His Silent Films, and His Audiences.* New Brunswick: Rutgers University Press, 2000.

Boyd, Valerie. *Wrapped in Rainbows: The Life of Zora Neale Hurston.* New York: Scribner, 2003.

Brandt, Allan M. *No Magic Bullet: A Social History of Venereal Disease in the United States since 1880.* New York: Oxford University Press, 1987.

Brooks, Daphne A. *Bodies in Dissent: Spectacular Performances of Race and Freedom, 1850–1910*. Durham: Duke University Press, 2006.

Brown, Jayna. *Babylon Girls: Black Women Performers and the Shaping of the Modern*. Durham, NC: Duke University Press, 2008.

Brown, Mary Jane. *Eradicating This Evil: Women in the American Anti-Lynching Movement, 1892–1940*. New York: Garland, 2000.

Buck-Morss, Susan. "The Flaneur, the Sandwichman, and the Whore: The Politics of Loitering." *New German Critique*, no. 39 (1986): 99–140.

Bundles, A'Lelia. *On Her Own Ground: The Life and Times of Madam C. J. Walker*. New York: Washington Square Press, 2001.

Butters, Gerald R., Jr. *Black Manhood on the Silent Screen*. Lawrence: University Press of Kansas, 2002.

Carby, Hazel V. *Reconstructing Womanhood: The Emergence of the Afro-American Woman Novelist*. New York: Oxford University Press, 1987.

———. *Race Men*. Cambridge: Harvard University Press, 1998.

———. *Cultures in Babylon: Black Britain and African America*. New York: Verso, 1999.

Chapman, Erin D. "Myth of Matriarchy." In *The New Encyclopedia of Southern Culture*, ed. Nancy Bercaw, Charles Reagan Wilson, and Ted Ownby, Vol. 13: *Gender*, 178–183. Chapel Hill: University of North Carolina Press, 2009.

Chateauvert, Melinda. *Marching Together: Women of the Brotherhood of Sleeping Car Porters*. Chicago: University of Illinois Press, 1998.

Chauncey, George. *Gay New York: Gender, Urban Culture, and the Making of the Gay Male World 1890–1940*. New York: Basic Books, 1994.

Clark-Lewis, Elizabeth. *Living In, Living Out: African American Domestics and the Great Migration*. New York: Kodansha America, 1996.

Collins, Patricia Hill. *Black Feminist Thought: Knowledge, Consciousness, and the Politics of Empowerment*. Revised 10th anniversary ed. New York: Routledge, 2000.

Cott, Nancy F. *The Grounding of Modern Feminism*. New Haven: Yale University Press, 1987.

———. *Public Vows: A History of Marriage and the Nation*. Cambridge: Harvard University Press, 2000.

Cram, Bestor, and Pearl Bowser, dirs. *Midnight Ramble: The Story of the Black Film Industry*. Northern Lights Productions, 1994.

Curwood, Anastasia C. *Stormy Weather: Middle-Class African American Marriages between the Two World Wars*. Chapel Hill: University of North Carolina Press, 2010.

Davis, Angela Y. *Blues Legacies and Black Feminism: Gertrude "Ma" Rainey, Bessie Smith, and Billie Holiday*. New York: Vintage Books, 1998.

Davis, Simone Weil. *Living Up to the Ads: Gender Fictions of the 1920s*. Durham: Duke University Press, 2000.

D'Emilio, John, and Estelle B. Freedman. *Intimate Matters: A History of Sexuality in America*. New York: Harper and Row, 1988.

Dent, Gina, ed. *Black Popular Culture, a Project by Michele Wallace*. New York: Bay Press, 1983. Reprint, New York: New Press, 1998.

Diawara, Manthia, ed. *Black American Cinema*. New York: Routledge, 1993.

Douglas, Ann. *Terrible Honesty: Mongrel Manhattan in the 1920s*. New York: Farrar, Straus and Giroux, 1995.

DuBois, Ellen Carol. *Feminism and Suffrage: The Emergence of an Independent Women's Movement in America, 1848–1869*. Ithaca, NY: Cornell University Press, 1978.

Ducille, Ann. "Blues Notes on Black Sexuality: Sex and the Texts of Jessie Fauset and Nella Larsen." *Journal of the History of Sexuality* 3 (1993): 418–444.

Due, Tananarive. *The Black Rose*. New York: Ballantine Books, 2000.

Edwards, Brent Hayes. *The Practice of Diaspora: Literature, Translation, and the Rise of Black Internationalism*. Cambridge: Harvard University Press, 2003.

Erenberg, Lewis A. *Steppin' Out: New York Nightlife and the Transformation of American Culture, 1890–1930*. Chicago: Chicago University Press, 1981.

Evans, Jessica, and Stuart Hall, eds. *Visual Culture: The Reader*. London: Sage, 1999. Reprint, 2003.

Faderman, Lillian. *Odd Girls and Twilight Lovers: A History of Lesbian Life in Twentieth-Century America*. New York: Columbia University Press, 1991. Reprint, New York: Penguin Books, 1992.

Feimster, Crystal N. *Southern Horrors: Women and the Politics of Rape and Lynching*. Cambridge: Harvard University Press, 2009.

Ferrell, Claudine. *Nightmare and Dream: Anti-Lynching in Congress, 1917–1922*. New York: Garland, 1986.

Fields, Mamie Garvin, and Karen Fields. *Lemon Swamp and Other Places, a Carolina Memoir*. New York: Free Press, 1983.

Foucault, Michel. *The History of Sexuality, Volume I: An Introduction*. New York: Random House, 1978. Reprint, Vintage Books, 1990.

———. "Two Lectures, January 1976." In *Power/Knowledge: Selected Interviews and Other Writings, 1972–1977*, ed. Colin Gordon, 78108. New York: Pantheon Books, 1980.

Gaines, Jane. "Fire and Desire: Race, Melodrama, and Oscar Micheaux." In *Black American Cinema*, ed. Manthia Diawara, 49–70. New York: Routledge, 1993.

———. "*Within Our Gates*: From Race Melodrama to Opportunity Narrative." In *Oscar Micheaux and His Circle: African-American Filmmaking and Race Cinema of the Silent Era*, ed. Pearl Bowser, Jane Gaines, and Charles Musser, 67–80. Bloomington: Indiana University Press, 2001.

Gaines, Kevin K. "Assimilationist Minstrelsy as Racial Uplift Ideology: James D. Corrothers's Literary Quest for Black Leadership." *American Quarterly* 45, no. 3 (September 1993): 341–369.

———. *Uplifting the Race: Black Leadership, Politics, and Culture in the Twentieth Century*. Chapel Hill: University of North Carolina Press, 1996.

Garber, Eric. "A Spectacle in Color: The Lesbian and Gay Subculture of Jazz Age Harlem." In *Hidden from History: Reclaiming the Gay and Lesbian Past*, ed. Martin Bauml Duberman, Martha Vicinus, and George Chauncey, 318–331. New York: NAL Books, 1989.

Giddings, Paula. *When and Where I Enter: The Impact of Black Women on Race and Sex in America*. New York: Bantam Books, 1984.

———. *Ida, a Sword Among Lions: Ida B. Wells and the Campaign against Lynching*. New York: Harper Collins, 2008.

Gilmore, Glenda Elizabeth. *Gender and Jim Crow: Women and the Politics of White Supremacy in North Carolina, 1896–1920*. Chapel Hill: University of North Carolina Press, 1996.

Green, Adam. *Selling the Race: Culture, Community, and Black Chicago, 1940–1955*. Chicago: University of Chicago Press, 2007.

Griffin, Farrah Jasmine. *If You Can't Be Free, Be a Mystery: In Search of Billie Holliday*. New York: Ballantine Books, 2001.

Grossman, James R. *Land of Hope: Chicago, Black Southerners, and the Great Migration*. Chicago: University of Chicago Press, 1989.

Hall, Jacquelyn Dowd. *Revolt against Chivalry: Jessie Daniel Ames and the Women's Campaign against Lynching*. New York: Columbia University Press, 1979.

Harrsion, Daphne Duval. *Black Pearls: Blues Queens of the 1920s*. New Brunswick, NJ: Rutgers University Press, 2000.

Hartman, Saidiya V. *Scenes of Subjection: Terror, Slavery, and Self-Making in Nineteenth-Century America*. New York: Oxford University Press, 1997.

Hicks, Cheryl D. *Talk with You Like a Woman: African American Women, Justice, and Reform in New York, 1890–1935*. Chapel Hill: University of North Carolina Press, 2010.

Higginbotham, Evelyn Brooks. *Righteous Discontent: The Women's Movement in the Black Baptist Church, 1880–1920*. Cambridge: Harvard University Press, 1993.

———. "Clubwomen and Electoral Politics in the 1920s." In *African American Women and the Vote, 1837–1965*, ed. Ann D. Gordon et al. Amherst: University of Massachusetts Press, 1997.

———. "Rethinking Black Vernacular Culture: Black Religion and Race Records in the 1920s and 1930s." In *The House That Race Built: Black Americans, U.S. Terrain*, ed. Wahneema Lubiano. New York: Pantheon Books, 1997.

Hine, Darlene Clark. "Black Migration to the Urban Midwest: The Gender Dimension, 1915–1945." In *The Great Migration in Historical Perspective: New Dimensions of Race, Class, and Gender*, ed. Joe William Trotter, Jr., 127–146. Bloomington: Indiana University Press, 1991.

———. "Rape and the Inner Lives of Black Women in the Middle West: Preliminary Thoughts on the Culture of Dissemblance." *Signs* 14, no. 4 (Summer 1989): 912–920.

Holloway, Jonathan Scott. *Confronting the Veil: Abram Harris, Jr., E. Franklin Frazier, and Ralph Bunche, 1919–1941*. Chapel Hill: University of North Carolina Press, 2002.

hooks, bell. "Selling Hot Pussy: Representations of Black Female Sexuality in the Cultural Marketplace." In *Black Looks: Race and Representation*. Boston: South End Press, 1992.

Hughes, Langston, and Milton Meltzer. *Black Magic: A Pictorial History of Black Entertainers in America*. New York: Bonanza Books, 1967.

Hunter, Tera W. *To 'Joy My Freedom: Southern Black Women's Lives and Labors after the Civil War*. Cambridge: Harvard University Press, 1997.

Hutchinson, George. *In Search of Nella Larsen: A Biography of the Color Line*. Cambridge: Harvard University Press, 2006.

Jenkins, Candice M. *Private Lives, Proper Relations: Regulating Black Intimacy*. Minneapolis: University of Minnesota Press, 2007.

Jhally, Sut. *The Codes of Advertising: Fetishism and the Political Economy of Meaning in the Consumer Society*. New York: Routledge, 1990.

Johnson, Abby Arthur, and Ronald Maberry Johnson. *Propaganda and Aesthetics: The Literary Politics of Afro-American Magazines in the Twentieth Century*. Amherst: University of Massachusetts Press, 1979.

Kelley, Robin D. G. *Race Rebels: Culture, Politics, and the Black Working Class*. New York: Free Press, 1996.

Kellner, Bruce, ed. *The Harlem Renaissance: A Historical Dictionary for the Era*. Wesport, CT: Greenwood Press, 1984.

Kitch, Carolyn. *The Girl on the Magazine Cover: The Origins of Visual Stereotypes in American Mass Media*. Chapel Hill: University of North Carolina Press, 2001.

Krasner, David. *Resistance, Parody and Double Consciousness in African American Theatre, 1895–1910*. New York: St. Martin's Press, 1997.

———. *A Beautiful Pageant: African American Theatre, Drama and Performance in the Harlem Renaissance, 1910–1927*. New York: Palgrave Macmillan, 2002.

Lerner, Gerda, ed. *Black Women in White America: A Documentary History*. New York: Vintage Books, 1972, 1992.

Lewis, David Levering. *When Harlem Was in Vogue*. New York: Alfred A. Knopf, 1979. Reprint, New York: Penguin Books, 1997.

———. *W.E.B. Du Bois: Biography of a Race, 1868–1919*. New York: Henry Holt, 1993.

———. *W.E.B. Du Bois: The Fight for Equality and the American Century, 1919–1963*. New York: Henry Holt, 2000.

MacLean, Nancy. *Behind the Mask of Chivalry: The Making of the Second Ku Klux Klan*. New York: Oxford University Press, 1994.

Manring, M. M. *Slave in a Box: The Strange Career of Jim Crow.* Charlottesville: University Press of Virginia, 1998.

Marchand, Roland. *Advertising the American Dream: Making Way for Modernity, 1920–1940.* Berkeley: University of California Press, 1986.

Markovitz, Jonathan. *Legacies of Lynching: Racial Violence and Memory.* Minneapolis: University of Minnesota Press, 2004.

McClintock, Anne. *Imperial Leather: Race, Gender and Sexuality in the Colonial Contest.* New York: Routledge, 1995.

Mitchell, Michele. *Righteous Propagation: African Americans and the Politics of Racial Destiny after Reconstruction.* Chapel Hill: University of North Carolina Press, 2004.

Moore, Jesse Thomas, Jr. *A Search for Equality: The National Urban League, 1910–1961.* University Park: Pennsylvania State University Press, 1981.

Morton, Patricia. *Disfigured Images: The Historical Assault on Afro-American Women.* New York: Praeger, 1991.

Mumford, Kevin J. *Interzones: Black/White Sex Districts in Chicago and New York in the Early Twentieth Century.* New York: Columbia University Press, 1997.

Musser, Charles, Corey K. Creekmur, Pearl Bowser, J. Ronald Green, Charlene Regester, and Louise Spence. "An Oscar Micheaux Filmography: From the Silents through His Transition to Sound, 1919–1931." In *Oscar Micheaux and His Circle: African-American Filmmaking and Race Cinema of the Silent Era,* ed. Pearl Bowser, Jane Gaines, and Charles Musser, 228–277. Bloomington: Indiana University Press, 2001.

Newman, Louise Michele. *White Women's Rights: The Racial Origins of Feminism in the United States.* New York: Oxford University Press, 1999.

Odem, Mary E. *Delinquent Daughters: Protecting and Policing Adolescent Female Sexuality in the United States, 1885–1920.* Chapel Hill: University of North Carolina Press, 1995.

O'Kelly, Charlotte G. "Black Newspapers and the Black Protest Movement: Their Historical Relationship, 1827–1945." *Phylon* 43, no. 1 (Spring 1982): 1–14.

Painter, Nell Irvin. *Standing at Armageddon: The United States, 1877–1919.* New York: W. W. Norton, 1987.

Peiss, Kathy. *Cheap Amusements: Working Women and Leisure in Turn-of-the-Century New York.* Philadelphia: Temple University Press, 1986.

———. *Hope in a Jar: The Making of America's Beauty Culture.* New York: Henry Holt, 1998.

Platt, Anthony M. *E. Franklin Frazier, Reconsidered.* New Brunswick: Rutgers University Press, 1991.

Powell, Richard J. *Black Art and Culture in the 20th Century.* London: Thames and Hudson, 1997.

Regester, Charlene. "The African-American Press and Race Movies, 1909–1929." In *Oscar Micheaux and His Circle: African-American Filmmaking and Race Cinema of the Silent Era,* ed. Pearl Bowser, Jane Gaines, and Charles Musser, 34–49. Bloomington: Indiana University Press, 2001.

Renda, Mary A. *Taking Haiti: Military Occupation and the Culture of U.S. Imperialism, 1915–1940.* Chapel Hill: University of North Carolina Press, 2001.

Robbins, Richard. *Sidelines Activist: Charles S. Johnson and the Struggle for Civil Rights.* Jackson: University Press of Mississippi, 1996.

Roberts, Dorothy. *Killing the Black Body: Race, Reproduction, and the Meaning of Liberty.* New York: Random House, 1997.

Rooks, Noliwe. *Ladies Pages: African American Women's Magazines and the Culture That Made Them.* New Brunswick: Rutgers University Press, 2004.

Rose, Gillian. *Visual Methodologies: An Introduction to the Interpretation of Visual Materials.* London: Sage, 2003.

Sampson, Henry T. "Chapter 4: Micheaux Film Corporation: Oscar Micheaux." In *Blacks in Black and White: A Source Book on Black Films*. Metuchen, NJ: Scarecrow Press, 1995.

Savage, Barbara Dianne. *Broadcasting Freedom: Radio, War, and the Politics of Race, 1938–1948*. Chapel Hill: University of North Carolina Press, 1999.

Schechter, Patricia A. *Ida B. Wells-Barnett and American Reform, 1880–1930*. Chapel Hill: University of North Carolina Press, 2001.

Scott, Daryl Michael. *Contempt & Pity: Social Policy and the Image of the Damaged Black Psyche, 1880–1996*. Chapel Hill: University of North Carolina Press, 1997.

Scott, James C. *Weapons of the Weak: Everyday Forms of Peasant Resistance*. New Haven: Yale University Press, 1985.

———. *Domination and the Arts of Resistance: Hidden Transcripts*. New Haven: Yale University Press, 1990.

Scott, Joan W. "The Evidence of Experience." *Critical Inquiry* 17, no. 4 (Summer 1991): 773–797.

Scott, Michelle R. *Blues Empress in Black Chattanooga: Bessie Smith and the Emerging Urban South*. Urbana: University of Illinois Press, 2008.

Shaw, Stephanie J. *What a Woman Ought to Be and to Do: Black Professional Women Workers During the Jim Crow Era*. Chicago: Chicago University Press, 1996.

———. "Black Club Women and the Creation of the National Association of Colored Women." *Journal of Women's History* 3, no. 2 (Fall 1991): 11–25.

Simmons, Christina. "African Americans and Sexual Victorianism in the Social Hygiene Movement, 1910–1940." *Journal of the History of Sexuality* 4, no. 1 (1993): 51–75.

Sotiropoulos, Karen. *Staging Race: Black Performers in Turn of the Century America*. Cambridge: Harvard University Press, 2006.

Stallybrass, Peter, and Allon White. *The Politics and Poetics of Transgression*. Ithaca, NY: Cornell University Press, 1986.

Stavney, Anne. "'Mothers of Tomorrow': The New Negro Renaissance and the Politics of Maternal Representation." *African American Review* 32, no. 4 (1998): 533–561.

Stein, Judith. *The World of Marcus Garvey: Race and Class in Modern Society*. Baton Rouge: Louisiana State University Press, 1986.

Stewart, Jacqueline Najuma. *Migrating to the Movies: Cinema and Black Urban Modernity*. Berkeley: University of California Press, 2005.

Stoler, Ann Laura. *Carnal Knowledge and Imperial Power: Race and the Intimate in Colonial Rule*. Berkeley: University of California Press, 2002.

Summers, Martin. *Manliness and Its Discontents: The Black Middle Class and the Transformation of Masculinity, 1900–1930*. Chapel Hill: University of North Carolina Press, 2004.

Sylvander, Carolyn W. *Jessie Redmon Fauset, Black American Writer*. Troy, NY: Whitston, 1981.

Tate, Claudia. *Psychoanalysis and Black Novels: Desire and the Protocols of Race*. New York: Oxford University Press, 1998.

Taylor, Ula Yvette. *The Veiled Garvey: The Life & Times of Amy Jacques Garvey*. Chapel Hill: University of North Carolina Press, 2002.

Terborg-Penn, Rosalynn. "African American Women's Networks in the Anti-Lynching Crusade." In *Gender, Class, Race, and Reform in the Progressive Era*, ed. Noralee Frankel and Nancy S. Dye, 148–161. Lexington: University Press of Kentucky, 1991.

Thompson, Sister Francesca. "Evelyn Preer, 1896–1932." In *Black Women in America: An Historical Encyclopedia*, ed. Darlene Clark Hine, 938–939. Brooklyn, NY: Carlson, 1993.

———. "From Shadows 'N Shufflin' to Spotlights and Cinema: The Lafayette Players, 1915–1932." In *Oscar Micheaux and His Circle: African-American Filmmaking and Race Cinema of the Silent Era*, ed. Pearl Bowser, Jane Gaines, and Charles Musser, 19–33. Bloomington: Indiana University Press, 2001.

Vincent, Theodore G., ed. *Voices of a Black Nation: Political Journalism in the Harlem Renaissance.* San Francisco: Ramparts Press, 1973.

Vogel, Shane. *The Scene of Harlem Cabaret: Race, Sexuality, Performance.* Chicago: University of Chicago Press, 2009.

Wall, Cheryl. *Women of the Harlem Renaissance.* Bloomington: Indiana University Press, 1995.

Wallace, Michele. "Oscar Micheaux's *Within Our Gates*: The Possibilities for Alternative Visions." In *Oscar Micheaux and His Circle: African-American Filmmaking and Race Cinema of the Silent Era,* ed. Pearl Bowser, Jane Gaines, and Charles Musser, 53–66. Bloomington: Indiana University Press, 2001.

Waters, Ethel, and Charles Samuels. *His Eye Is on the Sparrow: An Autobiography of Ethel Waters.* New York: Doubleday, 1950. Reprint, New York: Da Capo Press, 1992.

Weems, Robert E., Jr. *Desegregating the Dollar: African American Consumerism in the Twentieth Century.* New York: New York University Press, 1998.

Weiss, Nancy J. *The National Urban League, 1910–1940.* New York: Oxford University Press, 1974.

Wells-Barnett, Ida B. *Crusade for Justice: The Autobiography of Ida B. Wells.* Chicago: University of Chicago Press, 1970.

White, Deborah Gray. *Too Heavy a Load: Black Women in Defense of Themselves, 1894–1994.* New York: W. W. Norton, 1999.

Williams, Chad. *Torchbearers of Democracy: African American Soldiers in the World War I Era.* Chapel Hill: University of North Carolina Press, 2010.

Willis, Deborah. *Picturing Us: African American Identity in Photography.* New York: New Press, 1994.

Willis, Deborah, and Carla Williams. *The Black Female Body: A Photographic History.* Philadelphia: Temple University Press, 2002.

Wolcott, Victoria W. *Remaking Respectability: African American Women in Interwar Detroit.* Chapel Hill: University of North Carolina Press, 2001.

Zangrando, Robert L. *The N.A.A.C.P. Crusade against Lynching, 1909–1950.* Philadelphia: Temple University Press, 1980.

THESES

Brown, Nikki L. M. "'Your Patriotism Is of the Highest Quality': African American Women and World War I." Ph.D. dissertation, Yale University, 2002.

Feimster, Crystal. "'Ladies and Lynching': The Gendered Discourse of Mob Violence in the New South, 1880–1930." Ph.D. dissertation, Princeton University, 2000.

Jenkins, Maude T. "The History of the Black Woman's Club Movement in America." Ph.D. dissertation, Columbia University/Teacher's College, 1984.

Summers, Martin Anthony. "Nationalism, Race Consciousness and the Constructions of Black Middle-Class Masculinity during the New Negro Era, 1915–1930." Ph.D. dissertation, Rutgers University, 1997.

Thompson, Sister Mary Francesca. "The Lafayette Players: 1915–1932." Ph.D. dissertation, University of Michigan, 1972.

Willis, Deborah. "Towards a New Identity: Reading the Photographs of the New Negro." Ph.D. dissertation, George Mason University, 2002.

INDEX

3/29/12